DR. OETKER

GERMAN
COOKING
TODAY

THE ORIGINAL

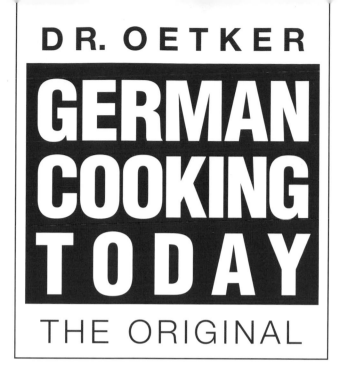

DR. OETKER

GERMAN COOKING TODAY

THE ORIGINAL

Dr. Oetker Verlag

Foreword

German Cooking Today, the recognized standard work that has had a fixed place in many German households for generations, is now available in a new English edition after detailed revision.

With many descriptive recipe photos, step-by-step photographs and of course the precise, detailed instructions of these recipes, the book is exceptionally clear and user-friendly. In all, this will ensure that even the inexperienced cook will be certain of success in making the dishes.

As well as many new recipes that arise from people's ever-changing eating habits, you will of course still find such popular German classics as Beef olives, Sauerbraten and Stuffed peppers in German Cooking Today.

All the recipes have been thoroughly tested and cooked in Dr. Oetker's test kitchen.

We wish you great pleasure with this book, every success in cooking the recipes and much enjoyment serving and eating the dishes.

CONTENTS

CONTENTS

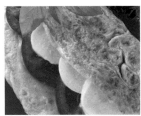

General information about this book

Read recipe through completely before you start cooking, or even better before buying the ingredients. The various stages of the recipe and the method will often appear much clearer if you have read it through first.

Please look at the indications of quantities and spoon measurements on the inside covers of the book because they will be very useful when following a recipe.

Preparation time:
Preparation time refers to the time it takes to carry out the actual work preparing and making the dish.
It does not include cooling down, marinating or soaking and waiting times.

Oven cooking times and oven temperatures:
The oven temperatures and oven cooking times indicated in the recipes are approximate values which can be reduced or increased depending on the individual heating performance of the oven, which varies, for instance, according to the material and design of the top and bottom heating elements. Therefore, please follow the manufacturer's instructions when using the oven and check whether the food is done towards the end of the cooking time indicated in the recipe. When roasting meat, the use of a meat thermometer is recommended.

Serving sizes and nutritional values:
The quantities of most of the recipes are for 4 servings. Where the number of servings or pieces is different, this is stated in the recipes. The nutritional values given in the recipes refer to this serving size and are only valid for the quantities indicated; where there is a range of serving sizes, the calculation is based on the average size. The following abbreviations are used: P = protein, F = fat, C = carbohydrate

Relevant information:
At the beginning of most sections you will find an extensive guide including general information and useful tips relating to the subject of the section. In addition, at the end of the book there is a general advice section about storing and processing food, cooking processes, cooking equipment, herbs and seasonings, and a list of cooking techniques.

Important note:
For dishes prepared with raw eggs that are also eaten raw, only use eggs that you know to be fresh. Store prepared food in the refrigerator and consume within 24 hours.

Soups

Soups are normally served as the first course of a menu, serving to stimulate the appetite and as a preparation for the dishes that follow.

The basis of a good soup is a strong, tasty stock. Stocks are made from bones, fish, beef, veal, poultry, game and vegetables. To round off the flavour, soup vegetables, a bouquet garni and/or a studded onion may be added.

Soup vegetables

These consist of equally-sized pieces of leeks, celeriac, carrots and sometimes Hamburg parsley or a sprig of flat or curly-leaved parsley. These are also sold prepacked. The actual ingredients and weight used may vary according to the season. The standard amount is about 200–300/7–10 oz, which is enough for 1–2 litres/1¾-3½ pints (4½-9 cups) of stock, but in some cases the selection may weigh up to 500 g/18 oz.

Bouquet garni for soup

This is a soup flavouring consisting of soup vegetables and herbs, for instance 1–2 sprigs thyme, 1 sprig lovage, 1–2 bay leaves and 1 sprig parsley. The bouquet garni ingredients are cleaned, washed and tied together with kitchen string, so that the bunch can easily be removed at the end of the cooking time.

Onion studded with bay leaf and cloves

The inedible outer skin of the onion is pulled off, then a diagonal cut about 2 cm/¾ in deep is made and 1 bay leaf is pushed into the slit. Then some cloves are pushed into the onion, sharp end first.

Making stock (broth)

1. Prepare the ingredients and put in a saucepan. (For a vegetable stock, the vegetables, cut into coarse dice, are sometimes first browned in hot cooking oil before the water is added. The browning process forms cooking products that give the stock a stronger flavour.)
2. Fill the pan with cold water to cover the ingredients and bring to the boil.
3. With a ladle, skim off the foam of coagulated protein and cloudy particles.
4. Add the soup vegetables only after skimming.
5. Reduce the heat and leave the ingredients to simmer uncovered over a low heat for at least 60 minutes.
6. Pour the finished stock through a fine sieve (perhaps a sieve lined with a cooking cloth) and use as directed in the recipe. If desired the half-cooked vegetables and meat or fish may be finely chopped and returned to the stock.

Tips

- If the ingredients are put in cold water, their flavour is more strongly extracted so that the flavour of the stock becomes fuller and stronger.
- If the ingredients (particularly meat) are put directly into boiling water, the pores close up immediately, that is, less meat juice escapes into the stock and the meat remains juicier. This method is employed if the meat is intended for further use.
- Do not add salt to stock until is being used in a soup, because pre-salted stock tastes even saltier when it has been kept.

- Do not cook any dough, rice or dumplings in clear stock since they will make the stock cloudy. Such garnishes should be cooked separately.
- A more concentrated stock can be made by increasing the amount of meat added, browning the ingredients before adding the water, or by reducing the stock.

Removing fat from the stock

If the hot stock is to be used immediately, you can
- skim off the specks of fat with a large, flat spoon, or
- draw absorbent kitchen paper over the surface of the stock, so that the paper lifts off the layer of fat.

If more time is available, let the stock cool down. The fat floating on the surface solidifies when it becomes cold and can then be easily lifted off with a large, flat spoon.

Freezing stock

Clear stock can be frozen, ideally in separate servings, (perhaps in ice cube trays), so that it is quickly available when required.

Instant products

If time is short, a commercial instant product such as bouillon powder or stock cubes may be used. The quantity to be used is given in the instructions on the packet. Another possibility is concentrated liquid stock, but this is quite expensive.

Cream soups

These are based on a stock thickened with a binding medium such as flour, starch, crème fraîche, vegetable purée, egg yolk or an egg yolk-cream mixture. Cream soups thickened with egg yolk, on its own or mixed, must not be brought to the boil after the yolk mixture has been added or the yolk will curdle.

Garnishes for soup

Suitable garnishes for soup include chopped herbs, diced tomato made from peeled tomatoes with the pips

removed, small crisp noodles, diced ham, whisked egg, cooked pasta or rice, steamed vegetables, fried diced bread (croutons, page 29), toasted almonds, semolina dumplings (page 29), meatballs (page 28), pancake strips, filled pasta (page 302), cooked egg garnish, (page 28), or steamed, finely shredded vegetables (julienne). Pasta, rice or dumplings should never be cooked in stock since they will make it cloudy. These garnishes should be cooked separately in salted water and only added to the stock shortly before serving. Pasta and rice should be only barely cooked, since they continue to cook in the hot stock or soup.

Thick soups

Thick soups contain a large quantity of meat or dumplings, making them more of a meal in themselves. It is a good idea to cook a larger quantity than is needed immediately and freeze what is left.

Chicken stock (photograph, bottom)

Classic (6 servings)

Preparation time: about 2 hours

**2 litres/3½ pints (9 cups)
water
1 bunch soup vegetables
1 onion
1 prepared boiling
chicken, 1–1.5 kg/
2¼–3¼ lb, with giblets
salt
200 g/7 oz cooked
asparagus pieces
(canned or bottled)
125 g/4½ oz (¾ cup)
cooked long grain rice
2 tablespoons chopped
parsley**

Per serving:
P: 32 g, F: 15 g, C: 6 g,
kJ: 1203, kcal: 287

1 Bring the water to the boil in a large saucepan.

2 Meanwhile prepare the soup vegetables. Peel the celeriac and cut out any bad parts. Peel the carrots and cut off the green leaves and tips. Wash the celeriac and carrots and let them drain. Remove the outer leaves of the leeks, cut off the root end and dark green leaves. Cut in half lengthways, wash thoroughly and leave to drain. Cut the prepared ingredients into small pieces. Peel the onion.

3 Wash the chicken and giblets if available under cold running water. Put them in the cooking water. Add 1 teaspoon of salt, bring everything to the boil and skim.

4 Add the soup vegetables and onion to the pan. Simmer uncovered over low heat for about 1½ hours.

5 Then pour the stock through a sieve, skim off any fat and season the stock with salt to taste.

6 Take the meat off the bones, remove the skin and cut the meat into small pieces. Add the meat, asparagus pieces and rice to the stock and heat them through.

7 Sprinkle the soup with parsley and serve.

Tip: You can also serve the chicken soup with cooked egg garnish (right of photograph, recipe page 28), semolina dumplings (left of photograph, recipe page 29), or meatballs (top of photograph, recipe page 28) as garnishes.
If you prepare the chicken soup up to and including point 5 on the day before it is to be eaten and leave it to cool, the fat will have solidified by the next day and you can simply remove it with a spoon.
Chicken soup without garnishes can be frozen.
Instead of canned or bottled asparagus you can also use cooked frozen asparagus.
125 g/4½ oz (¾ cup) cooked rice corresponds to about 50 g/2 oz (¼ cup) of uncooked rice.

Goulash soup
Classic

Preparation time:
about 80 minutes

**300 g/10 oz braising beef,
  e.g. shoulder**
**40 g/1½ oz margarine or
  3 tablespoons cooking
  oil, e.g. sunflower oil**
**1 litre/1¾ pints (4½ cups)
  meat stock**
200 g/7 oz onions
1 clove garlic
**1 yellow and 1 green
  pepper, each weighing
  200 g/7 oz**
200 g/7 oz tomatoes
**2 slightly rounded table-
  spoons tomato purée**
salt
freshly ground pepper
strong paprika powder
**½ teaspoon ground
  caraway**
dried marjoram
**a few dashes of Tabasco
  sauce**

Per serving:
P: 18 g, F: 15 g, C: 9 g,
kJ: 1011, kcal: 241

1 Rinse the beef under cold running water, pat dry and cut into cubes of 1.5–2 cm/½–¾ in. Melt the margarine or heat the oil in a pan. Brown the cubes of meat thoroughly on all sides in the margarine or oil. Add the meat stock and bring to the boil. Cover and cook over medium heat for about 40 minutes.

2 Meanwhile, peel the onions and cut into slices. Peel the cloves of garlic and dice finely. Cut the peppers in half. Remove the stalks and seeds as well as the white pith inside. Wash the peppers and cut into pieces.

3 Wash the tomatoes, leave to drain and make cross-shaped inci-sions in the ends. Scald briefly in boiling water and dip into cold water. Peel the tomatoes, remove the stalks and cut the toma-toes into quarters.

4 Add the prepared vegetables and tomato purée to the soup. Season the soup with salt, pepper, paprika powder, caraway and marjoram. Bring back to the boil, cover and cook for another 15 minutes or so.

5 Season the soup with salt, pepper, paprika and Tabasco sauce to taste.

Tip: Goulash soup is suitable for freezing. Instead of fresh tomatoes you can also use a can of peeled tomatoes (drained weight 250 g/9 oz).
You can also use ready-cubed meat.

Accompaniment: Nourishing country bread, rye bread or seeded grain rolls.

Fine fish soup
For guests

1 Cut off the stalks just above the bulbous stem of the fennel. Remove any brown parts and leaves and cut off the roots. Wash the fennel bulbs. Peel the carrots, cut off the ends and green leaves. Remove the outer leaves of the leeks and cut off the root ends and dark green leaves. Cut the leeks in half lengthways and wash thoroughly. Pat the vegetables dry.

2 Cut all the vegetables into thin strips (photograph 1). Peel the onion and chop finely. Peel the cloves of garlic and chop finely.

3 Rinse the fish fillets under cold running water, pat dry and remove any bones that remain. Cut into cubes of about 2.5 cm/1 in (photograph 2).

4 Heat the oil in a pan. Add the chopped onion, garlic and sliced vegetables. Braise lightly while stirring continuously. Add the fish or vegetable stock and bring to the boil. Now add the cubed fish fillets and cook uncovered for about 8 minutes over a low heat.

5 Rinse the shrimps or prawns under cold running water. Season the soup with salt, pepper and cayenne pepper. Add the shrimps or prawns to the soup (photograph 3) and cook for another 2 minutes.

Tip: Serve the soup with bread (e.g. French bread) as a light meal for 4 or as a first course for 6 people.
Sprinkle a tablespoon of chopped dill, basil or parsley on the soup before serving.
If desired, rinse some of the fennel leaves in cold water, pat dry, chop finely and sprinkle over the soup before serving.

Preparation time:
about 45 minutes

150 g/5 oz fennel
150 g/5 oz carrots
75 g/2½ oz leeks
1 small onion
2 cloves garlic
500 g/18 oz fish fillets,
e.g. cod or rose fish
4 teaspoons cooking oil,
e.g. olive oil or
sunflower oil
1 litre/1¾ pints (4½ cups)
fish stock or vegetable
stock
100 g/3½ oz shrimps or
prawns
salt
freshly ground pepper
some cayenne pepper

Per serving:
P: 29 g, F: 8 g, C: 4 g,
kJ: 878, kcal: 210

French onion soup
Classic

Preparation time:
about 45 minutes

about 600 g/20 oz onions
50 g/2 oz (4 tablespoons)
  butter or margarine
850 ml/30 fl oz (4 cups)
  vegetable stock
150 ml/5 fl oz ($^5/_8$ cup)
  white wine
salt
ground white pepper
30 g/1 oz (2 tablespoons)
  butter
8 slices baguette
50 g/2 oz ($^1/_2$ cup) grated
  Parmesan

Per serving:
P: 9 g, F: 21 g, C: 22 g,
kJ: 1428, kcal: 341

1 Peel the onions, cut in half and slice finely. Melt the butter or margarine in a pan. Add the sliced onions and braise lightly over medium heat while stirring continuously.

2 Add the vegetable stock, bring to the boil, cover and cook for about 10 to 15 minutes until soft. Add the white wine to the soup and season with salt and pepper.

3 Pre-heat the oven grill. Melt the butter in a large pan, add the baguette slices and fry on both sides until golden.

4 Pour the onion soup into large, heat-resistant soup bowls, place two baguette slices in each and sprinkle with Parmesan. Put the bowls in the oven under the pre-heated grill until the cheese has browned lightly.

5 Serve the onion soup immediately.

Tip: Serve as a light meal.
If served as a starter, the quantities given will make enough soup for 6 people, but in this case use 45 g/1½ oz (3 tablespoons) butter, 12 baguette slices and 45 g/1½ oz ($^3/_8$ cup) Parmesan.
If you do not have heat-resistant soup bowls, you can prepare the baguette slices separately. To do this arrange the baguette slices on a baking sheet lined with greaseproof paper and sprinkle them with Parmesan. Put in the oven pre-heated to 220 °C/425 °F, Gas mark 7 (in normal oven; with fan-oven: about 200 °C/400 °F, Gas mark 6) and brown the baguette slices lightly for about 5 minutes. Put the baguette slices on the soup before serving.

Cream of trout soup

Quick

Preparation time:
about 20 minutes

375 g/13 oz smoked trout
    fillets
50 g/2 oz (4 tablespoons)
    butter
35 g/1¼ oz (5 tablespoons)
    plain (all-purpose) flour
750 ml/1¼ pints (3½ cups)
    vegetable or fish stock
250 ml/8 fl oz (1 cup)
    whipping cream
4 tablespoons white wine
2-3 teaspoons
    Worcestershire sauce
salt, pepper, lemon juice
2 tablespoons chopped
    parsley

Per serving:
P: 23 g, F: 34 g, C: 10 g,
kJ: 1888, kcal: 451

1   Cut the trout fillets into pieces and remove any bones that
    remain.

2   Melt the butter in a pan. Stir in the flour and cook while still stir-
    ring until the mixture has turned light yellow. Pour in the hot
    stock and stir vigorously using a whisk, making sure that there
    are no lumps. Bring the mixture to the boil and cook uncovered
    over a low heat for about 3 minutes, stirring occasionally.

3   Now add the cream, white wine and Worcestershire sauce. Sea-
    son the soup with salt, pepper and a little lemon juice and bring
    to the boil again. Add the fish pieces and heat briefly in the soup.

4   Sprinkle the soup with parsley.

Pea soup with little sausages

For children

Preparation time:
about 80 minutes

250 g/9 oz dried peas
1.5 litres/2¾ pints
    (7 cups) water
250 g/9 oz streaky bacon
    (in one piece)
1 bunch soup vegetables
250 g/9 oz floury boiling
    potatoes
3 rounded teaspoons
    bouillon powder
1 teaspoon dried marjoram
1 onion

1   Put the peas in a sieve, rinse in cold water and put in a large
    saucepan with the water. Bring to the boil and add the bacon.
    Cover and cook for about 40 minutes over medium heat.

2   Meanwhile, prepare the soup vegetables. Peel the celeriac and
    cut out any bad parts. Peel the carrots and cut off the green
    leaves and tips. Wash the celeriac and carrots and let them
    drain. Remove the outer leaves of the leeks, cut off the root ends
    and dark green leaves. Cut in half lengthways, wash thoroughly
    and leave to drain. Wash the potatoes, then peel and rinse them.
    Slice or dice all the vegetables.

3   Add the bouillon powder, soup vegetables, potatoes and marjo-
    ram to the soup. Bring to the boil again, cover and cook for
    another 20 minutes. Peel and chop the onion. Melt the butter in
    a pan, add the chopped onion and brown lightly while stirring.

4   Remove the bacon from the soup, chop and return to the soup together with the fried chopped onion. Season with salt, pepper and bouillon powder.

5   Slice the Vienna sausages, add to the soup and heat them through. Sprinkle with chopped chives and serve.

15 g/½ oz (1 tablespoon) butter, salt, pepper
4 Vienna sausages
3-4 teaspoons chopped chives

Per serving:
P: 39 g, F: 31 g, C: 39 g,
kJ: 2479, kcal: 592

Cream of asparagus soup
Vegetarian

1   Wash the asparagus and peel carefully starting from the top and going downward, making sure that all the skin is removed but without damaging the tips. Cut off the lower ends and remove any woody parts. Reserve the peelings and ends. Rinse the asparagus and cut into pieces 3 cm/1¼ in long.

2   Fill a saucepan with 1 litre/1¾ pints (4½ cups) water. Add 1 level teaspoon salt and 20 g/¾ oz (1½ tablespoons) butter. Add the asparagus ends and peelings, bring to the boil, cover and cook for about 15 minutes over medium heat.

3   Strain this stock through a sieve, reserve the cooking liquid and bring back to the boil. Add the pieces of asparagus and bring to the boil. Cover and cook the asparagus for 10 12 minutes until cooked al dente.

4   Put the asparagus pieces in a sieve to drain and again reserve the cooking juices. Add milk to make up the quantity to 1 litre/1¾ pints (4½ cups).

5   Melt the remaining butter in a saucepan. Stir in the flour and continue stirring until the mixture turns light yellow. Add the measured amount of liquid to the mixture and stir vigorously with a whisk, making sure that there are no lumps. Bring the soup to the boil and cook uncovered for about 5 minutes over low heat, stirring occasionally.

6   Season the soup with salt, sugar, pepper and nutmeg. Stir the egg yolk into the cream and slowly add to the soup, stirring carefully to obtain a smooth, even mixture. Do not let the soup boil again. Add the asparagus pieces to the soup and heat them through. Sprinkle with parsley and serve.

Preparation time:
about 45 minutes

500 g/18 oz white asparagus
1 litre/1¾ pints (4½ cups) water
salt
sugar
60 g/2 oz (4 tablespoons) butter
about 300 ml/10 fl oz (1¼ cups) milk
30 g/1 oz (4 tablespoons) plain (all-purpose) flour
freshly ground white pepper
grated nutmeg
2 egg yolks of medium eggs
2 tablespoons whipping cream
3-4 teaspoons chopped parsley

Per serving:
P: 7 g, F: 21 g, C: 12 g,
kJ: 1117, kcal: 267

Fish stock
Good for preparing in advance

Preparation time:
about 75 minutes

1 bunch soup vegetables
1 kg/2¼ lb fish trimmings,
    e.g. small pieces of cod
1 onion
4 teaspoons cooking oil,
    e.g. sunflower or olive
    oil
2 litres/3½ pints (9 cups)
    water
salt
1 small bay leaf
1 clove
5 peppercorns
freshly ground pepper
1 small packet (0.2 g)
    saffron (optional)

Per serving:
P: 2 g, F: 5 g, C: 1 g,
kJ: 233, kcal: 56

1   Prepare the soup vegetables. Peel the celeriac and cut out any bad parts. Peel the carrots and cut off the green leaves and tips. Wash the celeriac and carrots and let them drain. Remove the outer leaves of the leeks, cut off the root ends and dark green leaves. Cut in half lengthways, wash thoroughly and leave to drain. Finely chop all the vegetables you have just prepared.

2   Rinse the fish trimmings under cold running water. Peel the onion and cut in quarters.

3   Heat the oil in a large pan. Add the soup vegetables and brown lightly, stirring all the time. Now add the water, 2 teaspoons salt and the fish trimmings. Add the onion quarters, bay leaves, clove and peppercorns to the stock. Bring the mixture to the boil and simmer uncovered over medium heat for about 40 minutes (the water should only bubble very lightly).

4   Strain the fish soup through a sieve and season to taste with salt and pepper, and with saffron if desired.

Tip: To make fish concentrate, reduce the soup by half by boiling it down. This fish soup can be used as a basis for other fish soups or sauces, for instance to make fine fish soup (page 15) or cream of trout soup (page 18). Fish soup is suitable for freezing.

Beef stock
Classic-takes a little while

1 Rinse the beef under cold running water and place in a large saucepan filled with 2 litres/3½ pints (9 cups) water, seasoned with 2 teaspoons salt. Bring to the boil and cook uncovered for about 60 minutes over medium heat, skimming the scum with a skimming ladle.

2 Meanwhile, prepare the soup vegetables for the stock. Peel the celeriac and cut out any bad parts. Peel the carrots and cut off the green leaves and tips. Wash the celeriac and carrots and let them drain. Remove the outer leaves of the leeks, cut off the root ends and dark green leaves. Cut in half lengthways, wash thoroughly and leave to drain. Peel the onions. Make a cut in one onion and insert the bay leaf, then stud with the cloves (photograph 1).

3 Add the soup vegetables, onions and peppercorns (photograph 2), bring the mixture to the boil again and simmer uncovered for another 1½ to 2 hours (the liquid should be bubbling gently throughout).

4 Remove the meat and strain the soup through a fine sieve or colander lined with a cooking cloth (photograph 3). Season the stock with salt.

Tip: Beef soup can be used as the basis of many dishes in which meat stock is used.
Beef soup may be served as clear soup with asparagus tips, soup vermicelli or cooked egg garnish (page 28), sprinkled with chopped parsley.
Beef soup is suitable for freezing.

Preparation time: about 3½ hours

750 g/1½ lb stewing beef, e.g. shoulder or shin
2 litres/3½ pints (9 cups) water
salt
1 bunch soup vegetables
2 onions
1 bay leaf
3 cloves
5 peppercorns

Per serving
P: 3 g, F: 1 g, C: 1 g,
kJ: 96, kcal: 23

21

Thuringian vegetable soup

Good value

Preparation time: about 75
minutes excluding defrosting time

**500 g/18 oz fresh or
  frozen chicken
  trimmings (pieces of
  back, necks, wings)**
1 bunch soup vegetables
**1.25 litre/2¼ pints
  (5½ cups) water**
salt
1 bay leaf
3 grains allspice
250 g/9 oz carrots
200 g/7 oz kohlrabi
**150 g/5 oz mangetout
  peas**
150 g/5 oz green beans
1 bunch chervil
**200 ml/7 fl oz (⅞ cup)
  whipping cream**
freshly ground pepper

Per serving:
P: 7 g, F: 17 g, C: 11 g,
kJ: 960, kcal: 229

1 Rinse fresh chicken trimmings under cold water or defrost
   frozen chicken trimmings according to the instructions on the
   packet. Prepare the soup vegetables. Peel the celeriac and cut
   out any bad parts. Peel the carrots and cut off the green leaves
   and tips. Wash the celeriac and carrots and let them drain.
   Remove the outer leaves of the leeks, cut off the root ends and
   dark green leaves. Cut in half lengthways, wash thoroughly and
   leave to drain. Coarsely chop all the vegetables you have just
   prepared (photograph 1).

2 Put the soup vegetables in a pan with the water, 1 teaspoon salt,
   the bay leaf and the allspice. Bring to the boil, skim off the scum
   (photograph 2), cover and cook for about 40 minutes over
   medium heat.

3 Meanwhile, peel the carrots, cut off the green leaves and the tips.
   Peel the kohlrabi. Wash the carrots and kohlrabi and leave to drain.
   Cut them into cubes or small slices. Top and tail the mangetout
   peas, wash them and cut the larger ones in half if necessary. Top
   and tail the green beans and remove any strings there may be.
   Wash them and cut or break them into small pieces.

4 When the stock is cooked, strain through a sieve and reserve
   1 litre/1¾ pints (4½ cups) of the liquid. Bring the liquid to the boil
   and add the vegetables one after the other. First add the beans,
   then after about 5 minutes add the carrots and kohlrabi. After a
   further 5 minutes, add the sugar peas. Cover and cook for a further 5-10 minutes.

5 Rinse the chervil, pat dry, pluck the leaves from the stems and
   chop finely. Stir the cream into the soup (photograph 3) and season with salt and pepper. Sprinkle with chervil before serving.

   Tip: Serve with small semolina dumplings (page 29) or meatballs (page 28).
   This soup is suitable for freezing.

Vegetable stock

Good for preparing in advance

Preparation time:
about 90 minutes

3 onions
2 cloves of garlic
2 bunches soup vegetables
about 100 g/3½ oz
   Hamburg parsley
200 g/7 oz cabbage
130 g/4½ oz tomatoes
50 ml /1½ fl oz
   (3 tablespoons) cooking
   oil, e.g. sunflower oil
3 litres/5¼ pints
   (14 cups) water
2 teaspoons salt
2 bay leaves
1 teaspoon peppercorns
1 bunch parsley
2 branches lovage
grated nutmeg

Per serving:
P: 0 g, F: 13 g, C: 1 g,
kJ: 493, kcal: 118

1 Peel the onions and cloves of garlic and chop finely. Prepare the soup vegetables. Peel the celeriac and cut out any bad parts. Peel the carrots and cut off the green leaves and tips. Wash the celeriac and carrots and let them drain. Remove the outer leaves of the leeks, cut off the root ends and dark green leaves. Cut in half lengthways, wash thoroughly and leave to drain. Coarsely chop the celeriac, carrots and leeks.

2 Wash and prepare the Hamburg parsley root, peel, wash and dice. Remove the wilted outer leaves of the cabbage and cut it into quarters. Wash and leave to drain. Cut off the stem and cut the cabbage into strips. Wash the tomatoes and leave to drain.

3 Heat the oil in a large pan. Add the chopped onions and garlic and brown lightly while stirring continuously.

4 Add the remaining prepared vegetables and brown them lightly with the onions and garlic. Now add the water, salt, bay leaves and peppercorns. Bring to the boil and gently simmer uncovered over medium heat for about 60 minutes.

5 Meanwhile, wash the parsley and lovage and pat dry. Pluck the leaves from the stems and chop finely.

6 When the stock is ready, add the herbs and simmer for a few minutes over low heat. Season the stock with nutmeg and strain through a sieve.

Tip: Vegetable stock can be used as a basis for soups, sauces and vegetable dishes.
Vegetable stock can be frozen in small servings.

Cheese and leek soup

Good for preparing in advance (6 servings)

1 Remove the outer leaves of the leeks, cut off the root ends and the dark green leaves. Wash the leeks thoroughly and leave to drain. Then cut into thin rings (photograph 1).

2 Heat the oil in a large pan, add the minced beef and pork mixture and fry it in the hot oil. Use a fork or wooden spoon to smooth any lumps that might form (photograph 2) and season with salt and pepper.

3 Add the leeks and brown them lightly for a few minutes. Add the meat stock, bring the mixture to the boil, cover and cook for about 15 minutes over medium heat.

4 Drain the mushrooms in a sieve and add to the soup. Now stir in the cheese (photograph 3) and allow to melt in the hot soup (which must be off the heat). Season the soup with salt and pepper.

Tip: Serve this soup as a light meal with French bread or rolls.

Preparation time:
about 40 minutes

1 kg/2¼ lb leeks
2 tablespoons cooking
oil, e.g. sunflower oil
500 g/18 oz mince (half
beef, half pork)
salt
freshly ground pepper
1 litre /1¾ pints
(4½ cups) meat stock
1 jar sliced mushrooms
(drained weight 300 g/
10 oz)
200 g/7 oz cream cheese
or processed cheese,
flavoured with herbs

Per serving:
P: 23 g, F: 29 g, C: 7 g,
kJ: 1577, kcal: 378

Vegetable noodle soup
Good value (6 servings)

Preparation time: about 75
minutes, excluding defrosting time

**500 g/18 oz fresh or
  frozen chicken
  trimmings (pieces of
  back, neck, wings)
1.25 litres/2¼ pints
  (5½ cups) water
salt
1.25 kg/2¾ lb vegetables,
  e.g. carrots, kohlrabi,
  green beans, cauliflower,
  broccoli, leeks,
  courgettes, peas
100 g/3½ oz soup
  vermicelli
some chicken or vegetable
  bouillon powder
freshly ground pepper
2 tablespoons chopped
  parsley**

Per serving:
P: 17 g, F: 8 g, C: 17 g,
kJ: 895, kcal: 213

1   Rinse the fresh chicken pieces under cold running water or
    defrost frozen pieces according to the instructions on the
    packet. Add the water to a saucepan, add 1 teaspoon salt, add
    the chicken pieces and bring to the boil, skimming several times.
    Cover and cook over medium heat for about 40 minutes.

2   Meanwhile, clean the vegetables, wash, leave to drain and slice
    or dice. Divide the cauliflower and broccoli into florets, then peel
    and dice the stems.

3   When the cooking time is completed, pour the stock through a
    sieve and carefully skim off the fat with a spoon. Measure
    1.35 litres/2¼ pints (6 cups) stock, making up the quantity with
    water if necessary. Remove the meat from the bones, take off
    the skin, cut the meat into small pieces and reserve. Put the
    stock back into the pot and bring to the boil again.

4   First add the vegetables with longer cooking times, such as the
    carrots, kohlrabi, green beans and cauliflower. Cover and cook
    over medium heat for about 8 minutes.

5   Then add the vegetables with shorter cooking times such as the
    broccoli, courgettes, leeks, peas and the soup vermicelli. Cover
    and cook everything for a further 5-7 minutes.

6   Season the soup with bouillon powder, salt and pepper. Add the
    prepared meat and heat it through. Sprinkle with parsley and
    serve.

Tip: Barely cook the soup vermicelli (follow the instructions on the packet)
because they will continue to cook in the hot soup.
If you cook the chicken stock the day before (point 1) and leave it to cool, by
the next day the fat will have become solid so that it can be removed with a
tablespoon or a skimming spoon.
If you would like more meat in the soup, you can use 4 drumsticks instead of
chicken trimmings.

Variation: The vegetable ingredients can be varied according to season.
Instead of fresh vegetable you can also use 1 kg/2¼ lb frozen soup vegetables
(cooking time according to the instructions on the packaging).

Cooked egg garnish
Classic

Preparation time:
about 35 minutes

2 medium eggs
125 ml/4 fl oz (½ cup)
   milk
salt
grated nutmeg
hot water

Per serving:
P: 5 g, F: 5 g, C: 2 g,
kJ: 286, kcal: 68

1 Whisk the eggs with the milk, salt and nutmeg. Pour this mixture into a well-greased, heat-resistant mould with lid. Cover the mould and put it in a tall, wide saucepan filled with enough hot water to reach half-way up the mould.

2 Cover the pan and cook the egg and milk mixture for 25–30 minutes over a low heat until it is set (the water should only bubble very gently). Now loosen the set egg and milk mixture from the mould and remove it. Let it cool down a little and cut in lozenges or cubes.

Variation: **You can also add a tablespoonful of finely chopped herbs (for instance, parsley and chives), finely grated cheese or tomato purée to the egg and milk mixture.**

Tip: Cooked egg garnish can also be used as an addition to clear soups and stock (for instance, chicken soup, page 12).
You can also make this cooked egg garnish in a microwave oven. Put the mixture in a well-greased glass or china bowl, cover and cook at 450 watts for about 8 minutes.

Meatballs
Classic

Preparation time:
about 15 minutes

40 g/1½ oz (3 table-
   spoons) soft butter or
   margarine
100 g/3½ oz minced meat
   (half beef, half pork)
yolks of 2 medium eggs
40 g/1½ oz (⅜ cup)
   breadcrumbs
salt, pepper
salt water (1 teaspoon salt
   per 1 litre/1¾ pints
   (4½ cups) water) or stock

Per serving:
P: 7 g, F: 16 g, C: 7 g,
kJ: 842, kcal: 201

1 Stir the butter or margarine with a spoon to soften it. Add the minced meat, egg yolks and breadcrumbs and mix thoroughly. Season with salt and pepper.

2 Bring a large quantity of salted water or stock to the boil, enough for the meatballs to be able to move about freely.

3 With wet hands, form the meat mixture into small meatballs. Add to the boiling salted water or stock and cook for about 5 minutes (the liquid should only bubble gently).

Tip: Small meatballs are ideal for adding to stocks (for instance, chicken stock, page 12) or to vegetable soups.
Cooked meatballs are also suitable for freezing. Defrost frozen meatballs thoroughly, then add them to the hot soup to heat up.

Semolina dumplings

For children

1   Pour the milk into a small saucepan, add the butter, salt and nut-
    meg and bring to the boil. Then remove from the heat.

2   Sprinkle the semolina into the milk and stir with a wooden spoon
    to make a smooth mixture. Cook the mixture for about 1 minute.
    Pour the hot mixture into a bowl and stir in the egg.

3   Pour enough salted water or stock into a saucepan to let the
    dumplings move freely around and bring to the boil. Using two
    teaspoons dipped in hot water, make the dumplings from the
    semolina mixture. Put the dumplings in the boiling salted water
    or stock and cook uncovered for about 5 minutes (the liquid
    should bubble very gently).

Tip: Semolina dumplings are ideal for adding to nourishing soups (for
instance, chicken soup, page 12).
You can also add 1–2 tablespoons chopped parsley or mixed herbs (parsley,
dill, tarragon, basil) or 20 g/³/₄ oz (3 tablespoons) grated cheese to the
semolina mixture.

Variation: To make **sweet semolina dumplings**, add 1 pinch of salt and 1
teaspoon sugar to the semolina mixture. Sweet semolina dumplings are
delicious served with cold sweet soup made with fruit or milk soup.

Preparation time:
about 20 minutes

**125 ml/4 fl oz (¹/₂ cup)
    milk**
**10 g/³/₈ oz (2 teaspoons)
    butter**
1 pinch salt
grated nutmeg
**50 g/2 oz (¹/₂ cup) durum
    wheat semolina flour**
1 medium egg
**salt water (1 teaspoon
    salt to 1 litre/1³/₄ pints
    (4¹/₂ cups) water) or
    stock**

Per serving:
P: 4 g, F: 5 g, C: 10 g,
kJ: 424, kcal: 101

Croutons

Easy

1   Cut the crusts off the bread and cut the rest into small cubes.
    Peel a clove of garlic if desired and chop finely.

2   Heat the butter or oil in a pan. Add the diced bread and fry until
    crisp and brown, stirring occasionally.

3   Add the chopped garlic to the pan with the croutons and fry
    briefly but do not let it go brown because it would develop a bit-
    ter taste. Add croutons to soup just before serving.

Tip: Croutons are particularly delicious served with cream soups but they can
also be sprinkled on salads.
Croutons can be prepared in advance. When cool, put them in a well-sealed
container and they will keep for 1 week.

Preparation time:
about 10 minutes

3 slices white bread
1 clove garlic (optional)
**30 g/1 oz (2 tablespoons)
    butter or 30 ml/1 fl oz
    (2 tablespoons) olive oil**

Per serving:
P: 1 g, F: 7 g, C: 7 g,
kJ: 398, kcal: 95

Cream of vegetable soup (basic recipe)
Classic

Preparation times:
about 40 minutes (cream of pea
soup about 30 minutes)

650–1,100 g/1½–2½ lb
vegetables
1 onion
25 g/1 oz (2 tablespoons)
butter or 4 teaspoons
cooking oil, e.g.
sunflower or olive oil
1 litre/1¾ pints (4½ cups)
vegetable stock
salt
freshly ground pepper
spices (optional)
croutons, smoked salmon
pieces, sliced leeks,
prawns (optional
garnishes)

Per serving (broccoli variation):
P: 4 g, F: 6 g, C: 4 g,
kJ: 350, kcal: 84

1 Prepare the vegetables and chop up if necessary. Peel and chop the onion. Heat the butter or oil in a pan, add the chopped onion and fry while stirring.

2 Add the prepared vegetables and fry with the onion while stirring. Then add the vegetable stock and bring to the boil. Cook until done.

3 Now purée the soup and season to taste with salt, pepper and appropriate herbs. Add a garnish before serving if desired.

Cream of broccoli soup: Take 700 g/1½ lb broccoli, remove the leaves, separate the florets, peel the stems, cut into pieces and wash both the florets and the stems. Put the stems and florets with the chopped onion in the saucepan. Add the vegetable stock, cover and cook over medium heat for about 8 minutes until done. Now purée the soup. Season with freshly grated nutmeg and if desired add 1–2 teaspoons peeled, grated, roasted almonds or some chopped parsley.

Cream of carrot soup (photograph opposite, bottom right): Take 700 g/1½ lb carrots, peel and cut off the green leaves and tips. Wash the carrots, leave to drain and cut into slices 1 cm/⅜ in thick. Add the carrots to the stock, cover and cook over medium heat for 12 to 15 minutes, then purée. Season the soup with sugar and ground or freshly grated ginger. If desired add 1–2 teaspoons crème fraîche, 1 teaspoon roasted sesame seeds, some chopped dill or even a few strips of smoked salmon in each bowl.

Cream of pumpkin soup: Cut a pumpkin weighing 1.1 kg/2½ lb into segments and peel. Remove the seeds and fibres and cut the flesh into cubes. Add the stock, cover and cook over medium heat for about 15 minutes until done, then purée. Season the soup with sugar and curry or ground ginger. If desired, add 1–2 teaspoons yogurt or crème fraîche, 1–2 teaspoons pumpkin seeds or sesame seeds or chopped dill in each bowl.

Cream of pea soup (photograph opposite, top left): Take 650 g/1½ lb frozen peas, not defrosted. Add the stock, cover and cook over medium heat for about 8 minutes until done, then purée. Season the soup with grated nutmeg, sugar and cayenne pepper. If desired, add 1–2 teaspoons crème fraîche, 1 teaspoon peeled, chopped roasted almonds, some chopped parsley or chervil or a few prawns to each bowl.

(continued on page 32)

Cream of potato soup (photograph page 31, top right): **Prepare** 1 bunch of soup vegetables for the soup. Peel the celeriac and cut out all the bad parts. Peel the carrots, cut off the green leaves and tips. Wash the carrots and celeriac and leave to drain. Remove the outer leaves of the leeks and cut off the root ends and the dark green leaves. Cut in half lengthways, wash thoroughly and leave to drain. Wash, peel and rinse 400 g/14 oz potatoes. Chop all the vegetables you have just prepared. Add the stock, cover and cook over medium heat for about 15–20 minutes, then purée. Season the soup with grated nutmeg. If so desired, add 1–2 teaspoons crème fraîche, some chopped parsley or chopped chervil and a few croutons to each bowl.

Tip: You can also use mixed vegetables (photograph page 31, bottom left). Vegetable soups should be frozen without their garnish. Just before serving you can add various garnishes to the soup such as croutons (page 29), meatballs (page 28), 50–75 g/2–3 oz raw or cooked ham cut into strips, 75 g/3 oz smoked salmon cut into strips, or 50–100 g/2–3½ oz prawns.

Unripe spelt grain soup

Vegetarian

Preparation time:
about 25 minutes

1 onion
40 g/1½ oz/
   3 tablespoons butter
100 g/3½ oz (1 cup) spelt
   flour
generous 1 litre/1¾ pints
   (4½ cups) vegetable
   stock
125 ml/4 fl oz (½ cup)
   whipping cream
salt, pepper, sugar
grated nutmeg
1 tablespoon chopped
   herbs, e.g. parsley, dill,
   tarragon, chives

Per serving:
P: 4 g, F: 19 g, C: 20 g,
kJ: 1119, kcal: 267

1   Peel the onion and chop finely. Melt the butter in a saucepan, add the chopped onion and fry until pale yellow, stirring all the while. Add the spelt flour and cook briefly, stirring continuously.

2   Now add the vegetable stock little by little, whisking vigorously and making sure that no lumps are formed. Bring the soup to the boil and cook uncovered over low heat for about 10 minutes, stirring occasionally.

3   Add the cream, heat the soup up again and season with salt, pepper, sugar and nutmeg. Stir in the herbs just before serving.

Tip: Garnish with croutons (page 29) before serving.

Mushroom soup
Vegetarian

Preparation time:
about 30 minutes

500 g/18 oz mushrooms (white or brown), or oyster mushrooms
1 onion
35 g/1¼ oz (2 tablespoons) butter or margarine
35 g/1¼ oz (5 tablespoons) plain (all-purpose) flour
1 litre/1¾ pints (4½ cups) vegetable stock
125 ml/4 fl oz (½ cup) double cream
salt, pepper
1 tablespoon chopped basil leaves

Per serving:
P: 7 g, F: 21 g, C: 8 g,
kJ: 1024, kcal: 246

1   Prepare the mushrooms, wiping them clean with kitchen paper and rinsing if necessary. Pat dry and cut into slices or pieces. Peel and dice the onion.

2   Melt the butter or margarine in a saucepan. Add the diced onion and mushroom slices or pieces and fry gently, stirring continuously. Sprinkle the flour on top, stir thoroughly and continue frying for a little while.

3   Add the vegetable stock, stirring vigorously with a whisk, making sure that no lumps are formed. Bring the soup to the boil and cook uncovered over low heat for about 5 minutes, stirring occasionally.

4   Stir in the double cream or crème fraîche. Season the soup with salt and pepper and sprinkle with basil.

Variation: You can change the taste of the soup by adding a little sherry or some curry powder, a pinch of sugar and 1-2 teaspoons lemon juice.

Tomato soup
Easy (6 servings)

Preparation time:
about 50 minutes

1.5 kg/3¼ lb beef tomatoes
2 onions
2 cloves of garlic
4 teaspoons olive oil
500 ml/17 fl oz (2¼ cups) vegetable stock
sugar, salt, pepper
cayenne pepper
1 bay leaf, oregano leaves
some small basil leaves

Per serving:
P: 3 g, F: 4 g, C: 8 g,
kJ: 329, kcal: 78

1   Wash the tomatoes and leave to drain. Cut them into quarters, remove the stalks and cut the flesh into cubes. Peel the onions and garlic and chop finely.

2   Heat the oil in a pan. Add the chopped onions and garlic and fry gently, stirring continuously. Add the diced tomatoes, vegetable stock, sugar, salt, pepper, cayenne pepper, bay leaf and oregano and bring back to the boil. Cover and cook over low heat for about 15 minutes.

3   Remove the bay leaf, then purée the soup and rub through a sieve. Bring the soup back to the boil again and adjust the seasoning by adding the sugar, salt and pepper. Sprinkle with basil.

Variation: You can also serve the soup with **small balls of mozzarella**. To make them, take 250 g/9 oz mozzarella, drain, chop coarsely and purée. Rinse a bunch of basil, pat dry, remove the leaves from the stems, chop up and stir into the puréed mozzarella. Season the mixture with salt and pepper. Make 18-24 mozzarella balls and garnish the soup with them.

Fruit soup (basic recipe)

Refreshing

1 First, prepare the fruit. Wash the cherries, drain, and remove the stalks and stones (photograph 1). Sort the berries, wash if necessary and drain thoroughly. Defrost any frozen berries (reserve the juice and use to make the soup). Wash the plums and leave to drain, cut in half and remove the stones (photograph 2). Wash the apricots and peaches, drain, cut in half and remove the stones. Cut the melon in half, remove the seeds (photograph 3) and peel. Cut the fruit into smaller pieces if necessary.

2 Take 4 tablespoons from the liquid. Pour the remaining liquid into a saucepan and, if desired, add lemon zest, cloves, cinnamon and vanilla sugar. Bring to the boil.

3 Mix together the custard powder and 50 g/2 oz (¼ cup) sugar. Stir in the 4 tablespoons of reserved liquid little by little until you have a smooth mixture. Remove the pan from the heat and stir the mixture into the liquid in the pan with a whisk. Return the pan to the heat and bring the mixture back to the boil.

4 Add the prepared fruit. Bring the sweet and sour cherries to the boil and cook for 2–3 minutes, stirring gently now and again. Bring the frozen fruit to the boil. The fresh berries should be added after the pan has been removed from the heat (soft fruit such as strawberries and raspberries should be added to the cold fruit soup just before serving). Plums, apricots, peaches and melons should be cooked from 1 to 5 minutes depending on their firmness, stirring occasionally.

5 Remove the lemon zest, cloves and/or cinnamon stick. Add sugar and lemon juice to taste. Pour the soup into a glass bowl and leave to cool down.

6 Serve well chilled and, if necessary, add more sugar and lemon juice.

(continued on page 36)

Preparation time:
about 30 minutes, excluding
cooling time

500 g/18 oz fruit, e.g. sweet or sour cherries, assorted berries (fresh or frozen), plums, apricots, peaches or melon
1 litre/1¾ pints (4½ cups) liquid (such as white grape juice, apple juice, apricot or peach nectar, for light fruit; or red grape juice, sour cherry or red currant nectar for dark fruit)
1–3 pieces of lemon peel (untreated)
2–3 cloves (optional)
1 cinnamon stick (optional)
1 sachet vanilla sugar or 2–3 drops natural vanilla essence in 1 tablespoon sugar
40 g/1½ oz custard powder, e.g. vanilla or cream flavour
50–125 g/2–4½ oz sugar
some lemon juice (optional)

Per serving:
P: 2 g, F: 0 g, C: 79 g,
kJ: 1400, kcal: 335

Tip: You can replace half the liquid with red or white wine or water if desired. Cold fruit soups may be garnished with finely chopped lemon balm or peppermint leaves, or sprinkled with finely chopped peeled almonds.

Cold fruit soups are also delicious with sweet semolina dumplings (page 29) or "floating islands" cooked in water (see recipe for milk soup with floating islands, below).

You can also serve it with whipped cream, crème fraîche, yogurt or vanilla ice cream, and pastries such as waffles, sponge fingers or macaroons.

Instead of fresh sour cherries you could also use a jar of sour cherry preserve (drained weight 350 g/12 oz). Leave the sour cherries to drain and reserve the juice; measure the juice and add the other fruit juices or fruit juice-water mixture to bring the liquid up to 1 litre/1¾ pints (4½ cups).

Peaches and apricots should be peeled before use. To do this, blanch the fruit briefly in boiling water (do not let them boil), pour cold water over them and peel off the skin.

Milk soup with floating islands
For children

Preparation time: about 20 minutes

For the soup:
1 packet custard powder, vanilla, almond or cream flavour
60 g/2 oz (¼ cup) sugar
1 pinch salt
1 litre/1¾ pints (4½ cups) milk
1 egg yolk from medium egg
peel of ½ lemon (untreated)

For the floating islands:
1 egg white from medium egg
1 rounded teaspoon sugar

Per serving:
P: 10 g, F: 11 g, C: 36 g,
kJ: 1181, kcal: 282

1 For the soup, mix together the custard powder and sugar with a pinch of salt. Little by little add at least 4 tablespoons of the milk and stir until you obtain a smooth mixture. Stir in the egg yolk. Bring the milk and lemon peel to the boil in a large saucepan.

2 Remove the pan from the heat and stir in the custard and milk mixture using a whisk. Return the pan to the heat and bring back to the boil briefly, stirring continuously. Remove the lemon peel from the mixture.

3 To make the floating islands, whisk egg white with sugar until stiff. Using 2 teaspoons, make little balls from the whisked egg whites, then drop them in the mixture. Cover the pan and cook for about 5 minutes (liquid must only simmer very lightly).

Tip: If desired you can also sprinkle cinnamon sugar on top or add 50 g/2 oz (⅓ cup) of raisins or currants to the mixture. For the lemon zest, wash the lemons in hot water, wipe dry and peel, removing only the yellow part because the white pith underneath has a very bitter taste.

Variation: To make **chocolate flavoured floating islands**, use a packet of chocolate flavoured custard powder and 75 g/3 oz (⅜ cup) sugar but no lemon peel. You can also add a cinnamon stick to the mixture which is removed before serving.

Thick vegetable soup
Vegetarian

1 Peel the carrots, cut off the green leaves and tips. Wash the carrots and leave to drain. Wash the potatoes, peel and rinse. Cut both the carrots and the potatoes into cubes. Top and tail the beans and remove strings if necessary. Wash the beans and cut or break them into pieces.

2 Remove the leaves of the cauliflower and cut out any bad parts. Cut off the woody base and separate the florets. Wash the tomatoes and leave to drain. Make a cross-shaped cut in each tomato, dip briefly in boiling water, then dip in cold water. Peel the tomatoes, remove the stalks and cut into quarters.

3 Peel the onions and dice. Rinse the basil, pat dry, remove the leaves from the sprigs, chop finely and put aside. Then finely chop the stems.

4 Melt the butter, margarine or oil in a pan. Add the diced potatoes and onions together with the beans and brown lightly for about 5 minutes while stirring. Season with salt and pepper. Add the chopped basil stems and vegetable stock. Bring to the boil, cover and cook for about 5 minutes over medium heat.

5 Now add the diced carrots and cauliflower florets, cover and cook for a further 15 minutes.

6 Add the quartered tomatoes and heat them through for about 2 minutes. Season the soup with salt and pepper. Sprinkle with parsley and basil before serving.

Preparation time:
about 70 minutes

375 g/13 oz carrots
375 g/13 oz floury boiling
  potatoes
375 g/13 oz green beans
250 g/9 oz cauliflower
250 g/9 oz tomatoes
2 onions
3 basil sprigs
50 g/2 oz (4 tablespoons)
  butter or margarine or
  40–50 ml (3–4 table-
  spoons) cooking oil, e.g.
  sunflower or olive oil
salt
freshly ground pepper
500 ml/17 fl oz (2¼ cups)
  vegetable stock
2 tablespoons chopped
  parsley

Per serving:
P: 6 g, F: 11 g, C: 23 g,
kJ: 927, kcal: 221

Tip: You can also season the soup with paprika powder or curry.
This vegetable soup is suitable for freezing.
For a less thick soup, increase the amount of stock to
1–1.25 litres/1¾–2¼ pints (4½–5½ cups).
Instead of fresh vegetables 1 kg/2¼ lb of deep-frozen vegetables may be used.
The soup can also be seasoned with vegetarian paste (from a health food shop).

Variation: For thick vegetable soup with meatballs (page 28), meatballs may be added to the soup.

Savoy cabbage soup
Classic

Preparation time:
about 80 minutes

500 g/18 oz beef or lamb
(from the shoulder)
2 onions
30 g/1 oz lard or
2 tablespoons cooking
oil, e.g. sunflower oil
salt
freshly ground pepper
ground caraway or
caraway seeds
750 ml/1¼ pints (3½ cups)
vegetable stock
1 kg/2¼ lb savoy cabbage
375 g/13 oz floury
potatoes
2 tablespoons chopped
parsley

Per serving:
P: 32 g, F: 18 g, C: 18 g,
kJ: 1510, kcal: 360

1   Rinse the meat under running cold water, pat dry and cut into cubes of about 2 cm/¾ in. Peel the onions, cut in half and slice.

2   Heat the lard or oil in a large saucepan. Add the meat and turn it until it is lightly browned.

3   Shortly before the meat is fully browned, add the sliced onions and simmer briefly.

4   Season the meat with salt, pepper and caraway. Add the vegetable stock, bring everything to the boil and cook covered on medium heat for about 30 minutes.

5   In the meantime, remove the coarse outer and withered leaves from the savoy cabbage, cut in quarters, rinse and leave to drain. Cut out the stalk and cut the cabbage into strips. Wash, peel and rinse the potatoes, then cut into dice.

6   When the stock has finished cooking, add the sliced cabbage and diced potato, bring to the boil again and cook covered for about 20 minutes.

7   Season the soup again to taste, sprinkle with parsley and serve.

Tip: 500 g/18 oz of meat will be provided by a shoulder of lamb on the bone weighing about 900 g/2 lb
The soup can be frozen.

Variation: Savoy cabbage soup also tastes good if you use small smoked sausages instead of lamb or beef. To make this, sweat the onion in the lard or oil, add the prepared vegetables, stock, seasonings and sausages, then simmer for about 25 minutes.

Minestrone
Classic

1   Peel the carrots, remove the green leaves and tips, wash and leave to drain. Wash and peel the potatoes, then leave to drain. Cut the ingredients into small dice.

2   Wash and dry the courgettes, cut off the ends and cut the courgettes into slices. Remove the outer leaves of the leeks, cut off the root end and dark green leaves. Cut in half lengthways, wash thoroughly and leave to drain. Cut into slices.

3   Remove the root ends and withered leaves from the celery, pull off the stringy outer threads, wash the sticks, leave to dry and cut into slices.

4   Top and tail the beans, remove any strings, wash and cut or snap into pieces. Peel the onions and cut into rings. Cut the bacon into small dice.

5   Wash the tomatoes, leave to drain, make a cross-shaped cut and dip briefly in boiling water, then dip in cold water. Peel the tomatoes and remove the stalks. Cut the tomatoes in half, remove the seeds and chop into small pieces.

6   Heat the oil in a large saucepan. Add the chopped bacon and sliced onion while stirring. Add the carrots, potatoes, celery and beans and cook gently.

7   Add the vegetable stock, bring all to the boil and cook covered for 10-12 minutes. Then add the courgettes, leeks, peas and noodles or spaghetti, bring to the boil and cook covered for a further 5-7 minutes.

8   Put the tomatoes with parsley and basil into the soup and heat through. Season the soup with salt and paprika, sprinkle with Parmesan and serve.

Tip: The pasta should always be barely cooked (see the instructions on the packet), since it will go on cooking in the hot soup.
Minestrone is frozen without the pasta, which is cooked and added to the soup before serving.
For a vegetarian variation, leave out the bacon and use 2 extra tablespoons of olive oil or butter.

Preparation time:
about 55 minutes

200 g/7 oz carrots
300 g/10 oz firm potatoes
150 g/5 oz courgettes
200 g/7 oz leeks
100 g/3½ oz celery
100 g/3½ oz green beans
2 onions
75 g/3 oz streaky bacon
2 beef tomatoes
2 tablespoons olive oil
1 litre/1¾ pints (4½ cups) vegetable stock
100 g/3½ oz frozen herbs
50 g/2 oz noodles or spaghetti
2 tablespoons chopped parsley
2 tablespoons chopped basil leaves
salt
paprika powder rose-sharp
40 g/1½ oz freshly grated Parmesan

Per serving:
P: 13 g, F: 20 g, C: 29 g,
kJ: 1480, kcal: 353

Old German potato soup
Vegetarian

Preparation time:
about 90 minutes

For the soup:
700 g/1½ lb floury boiling
potatoes
50–75 g/2–3 oz celeriac
250 g/9 oz carrots
1 onion
1 bay leaf
1 clove
40 g/1½ oz (3 table-
spoons) butter
1.5 litres/2¾ pints
(7 cups) hot vegetable
stock
200 g/7 oz leeks
125 ml/4 fl oz (½ cup)
whipping cream or
150 g/5 oz crème
fraîche
salt
freshly ground pepper
dried marjoram leaves
grated nutmeg

For the garnish:
200 g/7 oz chanterelles
1 onion
25 g/1 oz (2 tablespoons)
butter
2 tablespoons chopped
herbs, e.g. chervil,
chives, flat-leaved
parsley

Per serving:
P: 7 g, F: 24 g, C: 27 g,
kJ: 1483, kcal: 354

1 To make the soup, wash the potatoes, peel and rinse. Peel the celeriac and cut out the bad parts. Peel the carrots, cut off the green leaves and tips. Wash the celeriac and carrots and leave to drain. Cut all these prepared vegetables into small cubes or dice. Peel the onion and stud it with the bay leaf and clove.

2 Melt the butter in a pan. Add the diced celeriac and carrots and brown lightly while stirring all the while. Now add the diced potatoes, studded onion and vegetable stock. Cover, bring to the boil and cook over medium heat for about 20 minutes.

3 Meanwhile, remove the outer leaves of the leeks, cut off the root ends and dark green leaves. Cut in half, wash thoroughly, leave to drain and slice. Add the sliced leeks to the soup, cover and cook for about another 10 minutes.

4 Remove the onion, studded with the bay leaf and clove. Remove about one-third of the potato and vegetable mixture from the soup, purée, stir in the crème fraîche and pour the puréed mixture back into the soup. Heat up the soup again and season with salt, pepper, marjoram and nutmeg.

5 For the garnish: Clean the chanterelles with a brush and remove any bad parts. If necessary, rinse the chanterelles and pat dry. Peel the onion and dice finely. Melt the butter in a pan, add the diced onion and fry in the melted butter, stirring continuously. Add the chanterelles and fry for about 5 minutes, stirring frequently.

6 Add the onion-chanterelle mixture to the soup and simmer for about 5 minutes. Sprinkle with herbs just before serving.

Tip: If desired, small Vienna sausages may also be added to the soup. By preparing the chanterelles while the soup is cooking you can reduce the preparation time by 15 minutes. Bottled or canned chanterelles may be used instead of fresh ones.

Lentil soup with smoked sausage
Easy

Preparation time:
about 60 minutes

1 bunch soup vegetables
250 g/9 oz dried lentils
375 g/13 oz firm potatoes
2 onions
2 tablespoons cooking
oil, e.g. sunflower oil
1.5 litres/2¾ pints
(7 cups) vegetable
stock
4 smoked sausages
(chorizo), each about
90 g/3 oz
wine vinegar
salt
freshly ground pepper
some sugar
2 tablespoons chopped
parsley

Per serving:
P: 34 g, F: 31 g, C: 42 g,
kJ: 2444, kcal: 584

1   Prepare the soup vegetables. Peel the celeriac and cut out any bad parts. Peel the carrots and cut off the green leaves and tips. Wash the celeriac and carrots and let them drain. Remove the outer leaves of the leeks, cut off the root ends and dark green leaves. Cut in half lengthways, wash thoroughly and leave to drain. Finely dice the celeriac, carrots and leeks (photograph 1).

2   Put the lentils in a sieve and rinse under cold water. Wash the potatoes, peel and rinse them and then cut into pieces (photograph 2). Peel the onions, cut in half and slice.

3   Heat the oil in a pan, add the prepared potatoes and vegetables and brown lightly. Add the vegetable stock and lentils, bring to the boil, cover and cook over medium heat for about 15 minutes.

4   Add the smoked sausages (photograph 3) and cook for a further 10 minutes.

5   Season the soup with vinegar, salt, pepper and sugar. Sprinkle with parsley before serving.

Tip: If desired, add a bay leaf which is then removed before serving.

Variation 1: You can save time by using bottled or canned lentils. In this case, put the prepared potatoes in 750 ml/1¼ pints (3½ cups) of vegetable stock, cover and cook over medium heat for about 10 minutes. Then add the smoked sausages, cover again and cook for a further 5 minutes. Finally, add the can of lentils and the soup vegetables (800 g/1¾ lb) and cook for a further 5 minutes. Season with salt, pepper, vinegar and sugar.

Variation 2: To make a **vegetarian lentil soup**, increase the amount of potatoes to 500–600 g/18 oz–1¼ lb, leave out the smoked sausages and sprinkle with grated Parmesan just before serving.

Pichelsteiner (meat and vegetable soup)

Classic

1 Rinse the meat under cold running water, pat dry and cut into cubes of 2 cm/¾ in. Peel the onions, cut in half if necessary and slice.

2 Heat the clarified butter, margarine or oil in a pan. Add the cubed meat and brown lightly, stirring continuously (photograph 1). Shortly before the meat has browned sufficiently, add the sliced onions (photograph 2) and fry briefly.

3 Season the meat with salt, marjoram, lovage and pepper. Add the vegetable stock, bring to the boil, cover and cook over medium heat for about 40 minutes.

4 Meanwhile, peel the carrots and cut off the green leaves and tips. Wash the carrots and leave to drain. Wash the potatoes, peel and rinse. Cut both the carrots and potatoes into cubes. Remove the outer leaves of the leeks, cut off the root ends and dark green leaves. Cut in half, wash thoroughly, leave to drain and cut into slices. Remove the dried outer leaves of the white cabbage, cut into quarters, rinse, leave to drain, cut off the base and cut into thin strips (photograph 3).

5 When the meat is done, add the prepared vegetables and potatoes. Bring to the boil, season with salt and pepper, cover and cook for a further 20 minutes.

6 Season with the various herbs and sprinkle with parsley before serving.

Tip: This soup is suitable for freezing.

Preparation time:
about 70 minutes

500 g/18 oz mixed meat from shoulder or neck (lamb, pork, beef)
2 onions
30 g/1 oz (2 tablespoons) clarified butter or margarine or 2 tablespoons cooking oil, e.g. sunflower oil
salt
dried marjoram
dried lovage
freshly ground pepper
500 ml/17 fl oz (2¼ cups) vegetable stock
250 g/9 oz carrots
375 g/13 oz firm potatoes
350 g/12 oz leeks
300 g/10 oz cabbage
2 tablespoons chopped parsley

Per serving:
P: 30 g, F: 17 g, C: 19 g,
kJ: 1469, kcal: 351

Soup with green beans

For guests

Preparation time:
about 80 minutes

**500 g/18 oz braising beef,
e.g. from the shoulder**
1 onion
2–3 sprigs savory
**30 g/1 oz (2 tablespoons)
margarine or clarified
butter, or 2 table-
spoons cooking oil, e.g.
sunflower oil**
salt
freshly ground pepper
**500 ml/17 fl oz (2¼ cups)
vegetable stock**
1 kg/2¼ lb green beans
**500 g/18 oz firm
potatoes**
**1–2 tablespoons chopped
parsley**

Per serving:
P: 33 g, F: 15 g, C: 27 g,
kJ: 1592, kcal: 380

1   Rinse the beef under cold running water, pat dry and cut into cubes of 2 cm/¾ in. Peel and chop the onion. Rinse the savory and pat dry.

2   Heat the margarine, clarified butter or oil in a pan. Add the cubed meat and brown lightly while stirring. Shortly before the meat has browned sufficiently, add the onion and fry briefly.

3   Season the meat with salt and pepper. Add the savory and vegetable stock. Bring to the boil, cover and cook over medium heat for about 40 minutes.

4   Meanwhile, top and tail the green beans removing any strings. Wash the beans and cut or break into small pieces. Wash the potatoes, peel, rinse and cut into pieces.

5   Add the potato and bean pieces and season with salt and pepper. Bring back to the boil, cover and cook for a further 20 minutes.

6   Remove the savory. Season the soup with salt and pepper and sprinkle with parsley before serving.

Tip: This soup is suitable for freezing.

Variation (photograph): A shoulder of lamb may be used instead of beef, and 2–3 tomatoes may also be added. Wash them, leave to drain, make cross-shaped cut, dip briefly in boiling water, then dip them in cold water. Peel the tomatoes, remove the stalks and dice. Add the tomatoes to the soup shortly before the cooking is completed. If desired, sprinkle with basil before serving.

Unripe spelt grain soup with crème fraîche

Easy

Preparation time:
about 45 minutes

2 onions
400 g/14 oz leeks
50 g/2 oz (4 tablespoons)
butter
125 g/4½ oz unripe spelt
grains
1 litre/1¾ pints (4½ cups)
vegetable stock
2 beef tomatoes
150 g/5 oz crème fraîche
salt
freshly ground pepper
1 tablespoon chopped
chives

Per serving:
P: 7 g, F: 23 g, C: 27 g,
kJ: 1447, kcal: 347

1   Peel the onions and dice. Remove the outer leaves of the leeks, cut off the root ends and dark green leaves. Cut in half lengthways, wash thoroughly, leave to drain and cut into strips.

2   Melt the butter in a pan. Add the diced onion and brown lightly, stirring continuously. Now add the strips of leeks and the spelt grains and brown them lightly, too.

3   Add the vegetable stock, bring to the boil, cover and cook for 25 minutes.

4   Meanwhile, wash the tomatoes, drain, make a cross-shaped cut, dip briefly in boiling water, then dip in cold water. Peel the tomatoes, remove the stalks and dice the tomatoes.

5   Stir in the crème fraîche. Add the diced tomatoes and briefly heat them through.

6   Season the soup with salt and pepper and sprinkle with chopped chives before serving.

Tip: This soup is suitable for freezing.

Meat

Preparation/Storage

Meat must be prepared when it is as fresh as possible because its high protein and water content make it highly perishable. When using meat which has not been minced, you must first rinse it under cold running water, pat it dry and then prepare it according to the recipe. Otherwise put the pieces of meat in a china or stainless steel container, cover (for instance with a lid, a plate or clingfilm) and store in the fridge until you use it. In this case you should only rinse the meat just before you are about to prepare it. Coat small amounts of meat with oil before storing in the fridge. This will prevent the meat from drying out and will also make it more tender.

If you do not need to use the meat immediately, you can wrap it up and freeze it. To use the frozen meat, leave it to defrost covered in the fridge and immediately pour away any water resulting from the thawing (because of the danger of salmonella). Once thawed, the meat must be prepared immediately. Never freeze it a second time.

When buying pre-packaged meat, check the best-before date and the recommended storage temperature indicated on the package.

Coating in breadcrumbs

Anything coated in breadcrumbs is protected by its coating from drying out during the frying process. In addition, the breadcrumbs create a delicious, tasty crust. Coating in breadcrumbs is particularly suitable for individual portions

such as schnitzels and chops.

To coat in breadcrumbs: Prepare three shallow bowls. Put flour in the first one, one or more eggs (depending on the amount of meat to be coated) whisked with a fork in the second one, and breadcrumbs in the third one. Rinse the pieces of meat and dab them dry in the flour. Then turn each one over in the egg and press it lightly in the breadcrumbs. Shake off any excess breadcrumbs because they would burn during the frying process. Fry the breadcrumb-coated meat immediately to prevent the coating from becoming soggy. You can also add grated cheese to the breadcrumbs. Or alternatively coat the meat in sesame seeds, grated coconut, crushed corn flakes or finely chopped nut kernels, almonds or sunflower seeds.

Cooking methods

Frying

Frying means cooking and browning in shallow fat. This method of cooking can be used for cooking individual portions such as schnitzels, chops and steaks. The meat can be fried uncoated in its natural state, or coated in flour or in breadcrumbs.

- Heat the fat (edible oil, clarified butter or vegetable fat) in a frying pan.
- Put the seasoned meat (which has first been rinsed in cold running water and then patted dry) in the hot oil or fat so that the pores close up quickly and the meat remains tender.
- Fry the meat until golden brown and crisp on one side.
- Only turn the meat when it comes easily off the bottom of the pan.
- Fry the meat until it is golden brown on both sides.
- Only salt the meat and add the onions after frying because they draw out water.

- Take the meat you have just fried out of the pan and briefly drain it on kitchen paper in order to remove excess fat. Serve immediately or cover and keep in a warm place.
- To make the sauce: Loosen the cooking deposits with a little liquid, such as water, stock, wine or whipping cream, and deglaze. If desired, thicken it with a roux, starch or gravy thickener, for instance.

Roasting in the oven
When roasting in the oven, the meat is cooked and browned in the oven in an uncovered container with or without the addition of fat. This cooking method is particularly suitable for larger pieces of meat such as roasts and poultry.

- Preheat the oven to the temperature indicated in the recipe.
- Put the drip pan in the oven on the bottom shelf and, if desired, add a little water.
- Place the prepared, seasoned roast in the drip pan or on a roasting grid over the drip pan.
- When the roasting juices begin to brown and thicken, and any liquid added has evaporated, add more liquid, preferably hot.
- During the roasting process,

baste the meat with the cooking juices from time to time.
- Another method consists of browning the meat in hot oil in a casserole on top of the cooker. The roast is then transferred to the oven to complete the roasting process. Here, too, it is important to replace the liquid which has evaporated and baste the roast with the cooking juices from time to time.

Earthenware cooking pots or cooking bricks are also ideally suited for roasting in the oven. Put the meat in the earthenware container which has been previously soaked in water, cover with the lid, then put it in the cold oven (please follow the manufacturer's instructions). You can also cook roasts in the oven in roasting bags or in foil (again, follow the manufacturer's instructions).

In order to ensure that the meat remains tender, you can use the low-temperature cooking method, using a meat thermometer to maintain the correct temperature. Brown the meat to be roasted in a casserole on top of the cooker, then cook it uncovered in a very cool

oven, preheated to 80 °C/ 180 °F, or 70 °C/160 °F in a fan oven, for about 4 hours. There is no need to baste with this method. When using this cooking method it is important that the temperature remains absolutely constant. This is why it is essential to use a meat thermometer. At the end of the cooking time the temperature in the centre of the meat should be at least 60 °C/140 °F. This method is only suitable for beef and lamb roasts (for instance leg of lamb, page 98). Other kinds of meat need a higher temperature.

Braising
Braising consists first in browning the meat in hot fat, then simmering it in very little liquid and steam. Braised dishes can be cooked either on top of the cooker or in the oven in a well-sealed casserole.

- Rinse the meat under cold water, pat dry and season. Then brown the meat in hot oil.
- Add the onions, green vegetables (if any) and fry.
- Add some hot liquid (for instance, water, stock or wine). The liquid should only cover one quarter of the meat at the most.

49

- Reduce the temperature, cover and braise on top of the cooker or braise in the preheated oven.
- Add liquid regularly to replace what has evaporated.

Cooking (boiling)

Boiling means cooking meat (for instance, boiled beef, page 56) in a large quantity of boiling liquid (water or stock, sometimes mixed with vinegar or wine).

- Bring sufficient liquid to the boil (with green vegetables if the recipe requires it) in a pan to cover the meat completely or almost completely.
- Rinse the meat under cold water and put the meat in the boiling liquid. The pores of the meat will close immediately so that very little meat juice will be exuded, thus ensuring that the meat remains tender.
- Cook the meat with the lid on so that the temperature remains constant at a simmering point. This means that the liquid should barely bubble.
- The remaining cooking liquid can be used in another dish or frozen for later use.

Testing the cooking

There are several ways to test whether the meat is properly cooked. For instance, you can use a meat thermometer, available in hardware shops or any shop selling household goods, to check the internal temperature. Another way is to judge from the colour of the juice produced when cutting the meat: when the meat is sufficiently cooked, the meat juices run clear and no longer pink or red. You can also check whether meat is cooked by pressing a spoon onto the meat:

soft: the meat is still red inside (the spoon sinks in easily)

springy: the meat is pink inside (the spoon sinks in a little)

firm: the meat is cooked through (the spoon does not sink in).

Carving the meat

- Large pieces of meat such as roasts, and also steaks, should be covered with a large bowl or wrapped in aluminium foil and left to rest for at least 10 minutes before being carved so that the meat juices are distributed throughout the meat.
- Always cut the meat across the fibres. Reserve any meat juices which may be produced while the meat is resting and being carved, and use to make the gravy.

Beef

Depending on the age of the animal, we distinguish between:

- calves (male and female animals not fully grown, up to about 12 months old).
- heifers (15 months to 2 years old)
- oxen (2 to 3 years old).
- cows and bulls (2 years up to over 5 years old).

The meat produced by young animals is bright light red or brick red in colour with small white to light yellow streaks of fat. The cut surface is shiny and the texture is fine to medium-fine. The meat of older animals is dark reddish-brown in colour with yellowish fatty streaks and a coarser texture. Beef must be well hung. Hanging means that the bled meat of the freshly slaughtered animal is hung in a well-ventilated room at a temperature of between 1-3 °C/ 34-37 °F for a period ranging from a few days to a few weeks, depending on the cut of meat and its purpose, to tenderize the meat. But poultry should never be hung because it goes off very quickly.

Suitable cuts for roasting are: Sirloin, fillet, rib roast, topside, silverside, top rump, thick flank and rump roast.

Suitable cuts for braising are:
Topside, rump ox, rolled ribs, rump roast, shoulder-tip and shoulder.

Suitable cuts for frying and grilling are:
Slices cut from the rib (entrecôte steak), sirloin steak, rump steak, fillet steak (châteaubriand), thick flank, rump roast and liver.

Suitable cuts for boiling are:
Chine, neck, breast, ribs, flat or rolled ribs, shoulder, flank, knuckle and tail, lungs, heart, tongue, kidneys.

Cuts of beef

Neck
With marbled muscle meat and strong fibres.

Rib roast
The most tender steaks come from this part of the cut.

Sirloin

From the middle part of the back. Divided into rump steaks and entrecôtes.

Thick flank
Lean muscle meat, ideal for braising, for large roulades and goulash.

Flank
Marbled with sinews and fat.

Fillet

The most expensive cut. Very tender and therefore ideal for steaks.

Top rump
Lean cut from near the tail. Top end of the price range.

Neck and clod

Lower part of the neck.

Topside

Lean cut from the leg, marbled with fine fatty streaks.

Rolled ribs
Cut from behind the front leg.

Knuckle
Lean, containing sinews. The marrow in the bone has a high fat content.

Brisket
This is sold boned and rolled for roasting or braising. Also ideal for casseroles.

Shoulder cut
Tender cut from the front leg. Rather coarse textured, ideal for boiled beef.

Thin flank
Ideal for boiled beef.

Beef steaks

Fillet steak
Particularly tender, this is cut from the middle part of the fillet. Weight: 150-200 g/5-7 oz, thickness 3-4 cm/1¼-1½ in.

Chateaubriand
Double fillet steak. Weight: about 400 g/14 oz (enough for two people), thickness: about 8 cm/3 in. This is eaten very rare.

Rump steak
This is cut from the flat part of the sirloin. It has a thin fatty border which is notched before frying. Weight: 200-250 g/7-9 oz, thickness: 2-3 cm/¾ in-1¼ in.

Topside steak
This is cut from topside. Weight: about 200 g/7 oz, thickness: 2-3 cm/¾ in-1¼ in.

Veal

Veal comes from young animals less than 4 months old and up to 150 kg/330 lb in weight. Veal is delicate in texture with a light red colour (contains iron) and is lean to low in fat.

Suitable cuts for frying and grilling are: Slices of fillet, rump, loin, best end of neck, liver, kidneys.

Suitable cuts for boiling are: Scrag end of neck, breast, knuckle, liver, tongue, heart.

Suitable cuts for roasting are: Leg, knuckle, loin, chine, fillet, breast.

Suitable cuts for braising are: Breast, scrag end, shoulder, knuckle.

Veal cuts

Scrag end

Tender, short-fibered cut, usually sold on the bone.

Topside fillet

Tender cut, ideal for roasting. Cut into slices, it is excellent for schnitzel.

Rack of veal (middle neck, best end)
The fillet is removed and sold separately.

Breast
In fattened calves, this is well covered with meat.

Fillet

High quality roasting cut from the leg. Also ideal for cutlets.

Knuckle

Streaked with lean muscle and sinews.

Pork

Pork usually comes from animals less than one year old, which have not yet reached sexual maturity. It tastes best when freshly slaughtered. In young animals, the meat is pale red to pinkish red with a delicate texture, ranging from lean to slightly marbled with thin fatty streaks. The meat of older animals is a darker red and relatively coarse fibered.

Suitable cuts for boiling are:
Belly, knuckle, tongue, heart, kidneys.

Suitable cuts for frying and grilling are:
Knuckle, fillet, leg (knuckle) end, fillet, leg fillet end, spare rib.

Suitable cuts for braising are:
Shoulder, breast (rib cut), belly, knuckle, liver, kidneys, heart.

Pork cuts

Knuckle
Contains a high proportion of bone and sinews; can be boiled or roasted.

Fillet

Lean, slightly dry, coarse textured cut from the leg. Traditional cut used for schnitzel.

Chine

Tender cut, streaked with fat.

Shoulder

Traditional cut for roasting.

Loin
Relatively lean meat with a regular texture. Prepared as chops with the bones, or as roast or steak without the bones. When boned it can also be salted and smoked and served as smoked loin of pork.

Spare ribs

Continuation of the loin.

Belly
Tender, long-fibered cut, streaked with fat. Some of the leaner cuts are also sold for grilling. It is also processed as streaky bacon.

Tenderloin
Very tender, lean cut. Top of the price range.

Leg knuckle end, hock
Top part of the leg. A cut with a fatty rind.

Ham
Lean, tender cut from the leg. Traditional cut used for preserving and smoking.

Fillet
Particularly tender cut from the leg. Top of the price range.

Lamb

There is fresh lamb (raised in the region) and deep-frozen lamb (mostly from New Zealand). You can buy fresh lamb either from the butcher (if necessary order in advance) or in Turkish and Greek shops. Milk-fed or baby lambs are under 3 months old and have not yet been weaned. The meat is brick-red with a delicate texture and very little fat. Ordinary lambs have been weaned and fattened up and are no more then 1 year old. The meat is brick red with only a little white, yellowish fat and delicate texture.

Mutton: the meat is dark red with a coarse texture, and has a very strong taste and a yellow layer of fat.

Suitable cuts for roasting are: Leg, saddle, loin (chops).

Suitable cuts for braising are: Leg, chine, breast, shoulder, shanks.

Suitable cuts for frying and grilling are: Loin chops, shoulder and leg steaks, fillet, noisettes.

Suitable cuts for boiling are: Scrag end of neck, middle neck, breast, shoulder, belly, knuckle.

Lamb cuts

Neck (scrag end of neck, middle neck, chine)

Tender, short-fibered cut, marbled with fat. Suitable for goulash and minced meat.

Shoulder

Slightly streaked with sinews. Tender and juicy. Middle price range.

Leg

Relatively lean, very tender, juicy cut. Top of the price range.

Loin/saddle

A succulent, juicy cut, usually served as chops or cutlets.

Rib chops
From below the loin. Top of the price range.

Noisettes
Boned rib or loin chops.

Minced meat

Minced meat can be made from any kind of meat. However, minced meat sold in shops is made from beef, pork and lamb, and not from game and poultry. The percentage of fat in mince varies. Mince must be carefully prepared and stored because its considerably increased surface area provides an ideal breeding ground for micro-organisms, so it can go bad very quickly. For this reason it should be processed as quickly as possible after it has been bought.

Types of mince

Ground beef (for beefburgers or steak tartare)
Pure, finely minced beef from which all visible fat and connective tissues have been carefully removed. It has a maximum fat content of 6%.

Minced beef
Beef with a fat content of up to 20%.

Minced pork
Has a maximum fat content of 35%.

Seasoned pork
Minced pork seasoned with various condiments, for instance with spices, salt and onions.

Mixed mince
Consists of 50% minced beef and 50% minced pork and has a maximum fat content of 30%.

In order to ensure a light consistency, you can add and stir into the meat a roll, soaked in milk and pressed to remove excess liquid, or 1 large mashed potato, or 1–2 tablespoons of cooked rice or bulgar (wheat grains), or a few tablespoons of curd cheese, or 2 tablespoons soaked, drained cereals (for instance oats) per 500 g/18 oz mince. Minced meat can be prepared in various shapes, for instance as a meat loaf, "steak hâché", rissoles or meat balls. Always moisten your hands with a little water before handling or shaping the mince.

Rabbit

A young, fattened rabbit is slaughtered when it reaches a weight ranging between 1.3–1.7 kg/2¾–3¾ lb. As well as whole ready-to-cook rabbit, rabbit pieces (particularly legs and saddle) are readily available.

Cutting up a rabbit

- Place the ready-to-cook rabbit on its back on a chopping board.
- Make a cut in the front and back legs using a sharp knife, and detach from the body by pulling the joints downward vigorously and cutting them off.

- Separate the thin flanks from the back, using a sharp knife or kitchen scissors.

Offal

The liver, tongue, heart, brains, sweetbreads (thymus gland), kidneys, tripe, lungs, spleen, udder and stomach of many animals are all edible. Offal is usually low in fat and rich in protein, vitamins and minerals, but it is also high in cholesterol and uric acid. Some kinds of offal are considered delicacies in many countries. But because they can suffer heavy metal pollution (especially the liver and the kidneys), they should not be consumed too often, at most once a month. When buying offal make sure that it comes from young animals because it will be more tender and less polluted.

Boiled beef
Takes some time

Preparation time: about 3 hours

1-1.5 litres/1¾-2¾ pints
   (4-4½ cups) water
1 kg/2¼ lb beef (topside)
1-1½ teaspoons salt
1 bay leaf
2 teaspoons peppercorns
2 large onions
150 g/5 oz carrots
150 g/5 oz kohlrabi
150 g/5 oz celeriac
200 g/7 oz leeks

For the horseradish
sauce:
30 g/1 oz (2 tablespoons)
   butter or margarine
25 g/1 oz (4 tablespoons)
   plain (all-purpose) flour
375 ml/12 fl oz (1½ cups)
   beef stock
125 ml/4 fl oz (½ cup)
   whipping cream
20 g/¾ oz freshly grated
   horseradish
salt
a little sugar
about 1 teaspoon lemon
   juice

1 tablespoon chopped
   parsley

Per serving:
P: 58 g, F: 22 g, C: 12 g,
kJ: 2011, kcal: 480

1   Pour the water into a large saucepan and bring to the boil. Rinse the beef under cold running water and add to the boiling water. Add the bay leaf and season with salt and peppercorns. Bring to the boil again, cover and simmer very gently for about 2 hours (the liquid should not be allowed to bubble but only move very gently).

2   Meanwhile, peel the onions and chop them. Peel the carrots and cut off the green leaves and the tips. Peel the kohlrabi and cele-riac and remove any bad bits. Wash all the vegetables, leave to dry and cut into slices. Remove the outer leaves of the leeks, cut off the root ends and dark leaves. Cut in half lengthways, wash thoroughly and leave to drain and cut into 2 cm/¾ in long pieces.

3   When the meat has cooked, add the prepared vegetables, cover and cook for another 20 minutes.

4   Let the cooked meat rest with the lid on for about 10 minutes so that the meat juices are well distributed. Strain the stock with the vegetables through a sieve, keep the stock and put aside 375 ml/12 fl oz (1½ cups) for the sauce. Cover the vegetables and keep in a warm place.

5   While the meat is resting, melt the butter or margarine for the horseradish sauce in a small pan. Stir in the flour and cook until the mixture turns light yellow, stirring continuously. Add the reserved stock and cream and stir vigorously with a whisk, making sure that there are no lumps. Bring the sauce to the boil, stirring continuously, then simmer uncovered over low heat for about 5 minutes, stirring now and again.

6   Stir in the horseradish. Season the sauce with salt, sugar and lemon juice. Slice the meat and arrange on a preheated dish, pour a little hot stock over it and garnish with the vegetables and parsley. Serve the sauce with the boiled beef.

Tip: Instead of fresh horseradish you can use bottled horseradish sauce. Boiled fillet of beef can be frozen in the stock.

Accompaniment: Potatoes sprinkled with parsley (page 210) and green salad.

Beef olives
Classic

Preparation time:
about 75 minutes

**4 slices beef topside,
    180–200 g/7 oz each**
salt
freshly ground pepper
medium mustard
60 g/2 oz streaky bacon
4 onions
**2 medium-sized pickled
    gherkins**
1 bunch soup vegetables
**2 tablespoons cooking
    oil, e.g. sunflower oil**
**about 250 ml/8 fl oz
    (1 cup) hot water or
    vegetable stock**
**20 g/¾ oz (3 tablespoons)
    plain (all-purpose) flour**
2 tablespoons water

In addition:
**cocktail sticks or kitchen
    string**

Per serving:
P: 42 g, F: 32 g, C: 9 g,
kJ: 2072, kcal: 495

1   Pat the slices of beef dry with kitchen paper, sprinkle with salt and pepper and spread with 2–3 teaspoons of mustard. Cut the bacon into strips. Peel 2 onions, halve and cut into slices. Cut the pickled gherkins into strips.

2   Put the prepared ingredients on the slices of meat. Roll up the slices lengthwise and secure with cocktail sticks or tie with kitchen string.

3   Peel and quarter the remaining 2 onions. Prepare the soup vegetables. Peel the celeriac and cut out any bad parts. Peel the carrots and cut off the green leaves and tips. Wash the celeriac and carrots and let them drain. Remove the outer leaves of the leeks, cut off the root ends and dark green leaves. Cut in half lengthways, wash thoroughly and leave to drain. Cut the prepared ingredients into small pieces.

4   Heat the oil in a saucepan or pan. Brown the beef olives well on all sides. Fry the onions and soup vegetables briefly, then add half the hot water or stock and the beef olives. Braise covered on medium heat for about 1½ hours.

5   While braising, turn the beef olives from time to time and periodically replace the evaporated liquid with hot water or stock. When the beef olives are cooked, remove the cocktail sticks or string, place on a preheated plate and keep warm.

6   Strain the cooking juices through a sieve, make up to 375 ml/ 12 fl oz (1½ cups) water or stock and bring to the boil. Mix the flour with water and stir into the cooking liquid with a whisk, taking care to prevent any lumps from forming. Bring the sauce to the boil and cook uncovered over low heat for about 5 minutes, stirring occasionally. Season the sauce to taste with salt, pepper and mustard.

Accompaniment: **Cauliflower, red cabbage (page 175) or peas (page 162) and carrots (page 158) and boiled potatoes (page 210).**

Tip: **If desired, you can replace about 100 ml/3½ fl oz (½ cup) of the water or vegetable stock with red wine.**

Goulash
Classic

1 Peel the onions, halve and cut into slices. Rinse the beef under cold running water, pat dry and cut into cubes of 3 cm/1¼ in.

2 Heat half the margarine or oil in a pan, add the cubed meat and brown well on all sides. Now add the remaining margarine or oil and the sliced onions (photograph 1) and brown with the meat.

3 Season the meat mixture with salt, pepper and paprika powder and stir in the tomato purée (photograph 2). Add 250 ml/8 fl oz (1 cup) hot water, cover and braise the meat over medium heat for 1¼ to 1½ hours until cooked. If too much liquid has evaporated, add a little water (photograph 3).

4 Season the goulash with salt, pepper, paprika powder and Tabasco.

Tip: Instead of salt, pepper and paprika you can also use ready-made goulash seasoning.
You can add a more sophisticated touch by replacing half the water with red wine.
Instead of beef you could also use lean pork fillet (braising time about 45 minutes) or half beef, half pork.
Goulash is suitable for freezing.

Accompaniment: Noodles or rice with a tomato and onion salad (page 195).

Variation: **Goulash with mushrooms.** Take 200 g/7 oz mushrooms, trim off the ends and cut off any bad parts. Wipe clean with kitchen paper or if necessary rinse and pat dry. Slice and add to the goulash about 10 minutes before the end. Alternatively, drain a jar of sliced mushrooms (drained weight 210 g/7½ oz) in a sieve and add shortly before the end of the cooking time.

Preparation time:
about 90 minutes

500 g/18 oz onions
500 g/18 oz lean beef
   (without bones, e.g.
   topside) or ready-cubed
   braising steak
30 g/1 oz (2 tablespoons)
   margarine or 2
   tablespoons cooking oil,
   e.g. sunflower oil
salt
freshly ground pepper
paprika powder
4 slightly rounded tea-
   spoons tomato purée
about 250 ml/8 fl oz
   (1 cup) hot water
1-2 dashes Tabasco sauce

Per serving:
P: 29 g, F: 10 g, C: 7 g,
kJ: 979, kcal: 234

Sauerbraten (braised beef marinated in vinegar and herbs)

Takes some time

Preparation time: about 3 hours, excluding marinating

750 g/1½ lb beef (such as topside, without bones)

For the marinade:
2 onions
1 bunch soup vegetables
5 juniper berries
15 peppercorns
5 allspice berries
2 cloves
1 bay leaf
250 ml/8 fl oz (1 cup) wine vinegar
375 ml/12 fl oz (1½ cups) water or red wine

30 g/1 oz (2 tablespoons) clarified butter, coconut oil or cooking oil, e.g. sunflower oil
salt
freshly ground pepper
375 ml/12 fl oz (1½ cups) marinade liquid
50 g/2 oz honey cake
some sugar

Per serving:
P: 41 g, F: 16 g, C: 14 g,
kJ: 1641, kcal: 392

1 Rinse the beef under cold running water and pat dry.

2 For the marinade, peel the onions and cut into slices. Prepare the green vegetables: Peel the celeriac and remove any bad bits. Peel the carrots and cut off the green leaves and tips. Wash the celeriac and carrots and leave to drain. Remove the outer leaves of the leeks, cut off the root ends and dark leaves. Cut in half lengthways, wash thoroughly and leave to drain. Finely chop all three vegetables.

3 Mix together the onions and green vegetables with the juniper berries, peppercorns, allspice berries, cloves, the bay leaf, wine vinegar and water or red wine in a bowl. Add the meat to the marinade, cover with a lid and leave in the refrigerator for about 4 days, stirring the meat from time to time.

4 Remove the marinated meat from the marinade and pat dry. Pour the marinade through a sieve, reserve 375 ml/12 fl oz (1½ cups) and put the marinade and vegetables to one side.

5 Heat the clarified butter, coconut oil or cooking oil in a pan or casserole. Add the meat, brown well on all sides and season with salt and pepper. Add the drained vegetables and brown briefly with the meat. Add some of the reserved marinade liquid to the meat. Cover and braise the meat over medium heat for about 30 minutes, stirring now and again and replacing the evaporated liquid by adding more marinade whenever necessary.

6 Chop the honey cake finely, add to the meat and braise for another 1½ hours as described above.

7 Let the cooked meat rest for about 10 minutes with the lid on so that the meat juices are well distributed. Slice the meat and arrange the slices on a preheated dish.

8 Rub the braising residue together with the vegetables through a sieve, heat up again, season with salt, pepper and sugar and serve as sauce with the meat.

Accompaniment: Macaroni or potato dumplings (page 220), red cabbage (page 175) and apple sauce (page 280) or dried fruit. Soak 200 g/7 oz dried fruit in 500 ml/17 fl oz (2¼ cups) apple juice, cover and cook for about 30 minutes. Season with a little salt.

Braised beef
Takes some time

Preparation time: about
2³/₄ hours

750 g/1½ lb beef (flank, boned)
salt
freshly ground pepper
2 onions
100 g/3½ oz tomatoes
1 bunch soup vegetables
30 g/1 oz (2 tablespoons) clarified butter, coconut oil or 2 tablespoons cooking oil, e.g. sunflower oil
1 teaspoon dried thyme
250 ml/8 fl oz (1 cup) vegetable stock
tomato purée
some sugar

Per serving:
P: 40 g, F: 22 g, C: 6 g,
kJ: 1593, kcal: 380

1 Rinse the beef under cold running water, pat dry and rub salt and pepper into it. Peel the onions and dice. Wash the tomatoes, leave to drain, cut into quarters and remove the stalks. Cut the tomatoes into pieces.

2 Prepare the soup vegetables. Peel the celeriac and cut out any bad parts. Peel the carrots and cut off the green leaves and tips. Wash the celeriac and carrots and let them drain. Remove the outer leaves of the leeks, cut off the root ends and dark green leaves. Cut in half lengthways, wash thoroughly and leave to drain. Cut the prepared vegetables into small pieces.

3 Heat the butter, coconut oil or cooking oil in a saucepan or frying pan. Brown the meat well on all sides. Add the prepared vegetables, cook briefly and sprinkle thyme over the meat. Add the vegetable stock, bring to the boil, cover and braise the meat for 2½ hours.

4 While braising, turn the meat from time to time, replacing the evaporated liquid with vegetable stock periodically if necessary.

5 When the meat is done, let it rest covered for 10 minutes so that the meat juices are distributed. Then cut the meat into slices and put on a preheated dish.

6 Purée the cooking liquid with the vegetables or push through a sieve, perhaps adding some vegetable stock. Heat the sauce, season with salt, pepper, tomato puree and sugar and serve with the meat.

Tip: Instead of vegetable stock, you can also use half vegetable stock and half red wine.
Any leftover braised beef can be frozen with the sauce.

Accompaniment: **Potato dumplings (page 220) or boiled potatoes (page 280) and green beans (page 162) or peas (page 162) and carrots (page 158).**

Braised pork
Popular

1 Rinse the pork under cold running water, pat dry and season with salt, pepper and paprika.

2 Prepare the soup vegetables. Peel the celeriac and cut out any bad parts. Peel the carrots and cut off the green leaves and tips. Wash the celeriac and carrots and let them drain. Remove the outer leaves of the leeks, cut off the root ends and dark green leaves. Cut in half lengthways, wash thoroughly and leave to drain. Cut the prepared vegetables into small pieces.

3 Heat the butter or cooking oil in a saucepan or frying pan. Brown the meat well on all sides and sprinkle with marjoram or thyme.

4 Add the soup vegetables and onions (photograph 1), and cook briefly. Add enough hot water to cover the meat and braise covered over medium heat for about 1½ hours. While braising, turn the meat from time to time and periodically replace the evaporated liquid with hot water.

5 When the meat is done, let it rest covered for 10 minutes before slicing it so that the meat juices are distributed.

6 In the meantime rub the cooking liquid with the vegetables through a sieve (photograph 2), and measure 400 ml/14 fl oz (1¾ cups) of liquid, making the quantity up with hot water if necessary. Add the cooking juices from the braised pork, bring to the boil and reduce to the consistency desired. Season with salt, pepper and marjoram or thyme.

7 Carve the meat into slices across the grain (photograph 3), put on a preheated plate and add the sauce.

Accompaniment: **Boiled potatoes (page 210), cauliflower, peas (page 162), and carrots (page 158) or broccoli.**

Preparation time: about 2 hours

**750 g/½ lb pork gammon
from the leg, without
bones
salt
freshly ground pepper
paprika
1 bunch soup vegetables
4 onions
30 g/1 oz (2 tablespoons)
clarified butter or
2 tablespoons cooking
oil, e.g. sunflower oil
dried, chopped marjoram
or thyme
hot water**

Per serving:
P: 41 g, F: 21 g, C: 5 g,
kJ: 1571, kcal: 375

Saxony onion stew
Sophisticated

Preparation time:
about 75 minutes

500 g/18 oz onions
800 g/1¾ lb beef from
the neck
about 600 ml/20 fl oz
(2½ cups) water or
vegetable stock
salt
freshly ground pepper
½-1 teaspoon caraway
seeds
1 bay leaf
about 350 g/12 oz
cucumbers
125 g/4½ oz pumpernickel
1-2 teaspoons chopped
parsley (optional)

Per serving:
P: 41 g, F: 16 g, C: 19 g,
kJ: 1621, kcal: 387

1   Peel the onions, cut into quarters and slice. Rinse the beef under cold running water, pat dry and cut into cubes of about 2 cm/ ¾ in (photograph 1), removing the skin and fat as you do so.

2   Pour the water, seasoned with a scant teaspoon of salt, or the vegetable stock into a large pan and bring to the boil. Add the sliced onion, cubed meat, pepper, caraway and bay leaf, bring the boil, cover and cook over medium heat for about 50 minutes.

3   Meanwhile, peel the cucumber, cut off the ends and dice. Chop the pumpernickel into fine crumbs.

4   Add the pumpernickel (photograph 2) and diced cucumber (photograph 3), season with salt and pepper, cover and cook for a further 10 minutes.

5   Adjust the seasoning with salt and pepper. Sprinkle with parsley before serving if desired.

Accompaniment: **Boiled potatoes or potatoes boiled in their skins (page 210) or German farm bread.**

Cordon bleu
A little more expensive

Preparation time:
about 25 minutes

**8 veal escalopes, each
about 75 g/3 oz
salt
freshly ground pepper
4 slices cheese, each
about 40 g/1½ oz,
e.g. Emmental
4 slices cooked ham, each
about 50 g/2 oz
2 eggs
about 60 g/2 oz (¾ cup)
breadcrumbs
about 40 g/1½ oz
(3 tablespoons)
clarified butter or
margarine**

Per serving:
P: 57 g, F: 28 g, C: 6 g,
kJ: 2117, kcal: 505

1   Rinse the veal escalopes under cold running water, pat dry, tenderize the meat slightly and season with salt and pepper. Put a slice of cheese and ham on each of 4 escalopes, then cover each with another escalope (photograph 1) and press well together.

2   Beat the egg in a soup plate with a fork. Dip each portion first in the egg mixture, then in the breadcrumbs (photograph 2).

3   Heat the clarified butter or margarine in a non-stick pan. Add the meat and fry until golden brown over medium heat for about 10 minutes, turning over carefully from time to time (photograph 3).

Accompaniment: Potato chips (page 215) or croquettes, peas (page 162) and carrots (page 158).

Tip: The slices of cheese and ham should be the same size as the meat. Shake the meat lightly to remove all loose breadcrumbs from the meat before frying to prevent them from browning too quickly, which would make them taste bitter.
You can beat or tenderize the meat with a meat mallet or ask the butcher to tenderize the meat for you.

Variation: Instead of veal you can also use pork or turkey escalopes.

Züricher Geschnetzeltes (thin strips of meat cooked in sauce)

Quick

Preparation time:
about 30 minutes

**600 g/1¼ lb veal, from
  the leg, 2 onions
40 g/1½ oz (3 table-
  spoons) butter or
  4 tablespoons cooking
  oil, e.g. sunflower oil
salt, pepper
15 g/½ oz (2 tablespoons)
  plain (all-purpose) flour
250 ml/8 fl oz (1 cup)
  whipping cream
125 ml/4 fl oz (½ cup)
  white wine
some dashes lemon juice
chervil leaves (optional)**

Per serving:
P: 33 g, F: 35 g, C: 6 g,
kJ: 2079, kcal: 497

1 Rinse the veal under cold running water, pat dry and cut into thin strips. Peel the onions, cut in half and chop finely.

2 Heat half the clarified butter or oil in a pan. Add half the strips of meat and fry for 2-3 minutes, stirring frequently. Season with salt and pepper and remove from the pan. Then fry the rest of the meat in the remaining fat and remove from the pan.

3 Add the chopped onion to the remaining cooking fat and fry for about 2 minutes, stirring continuously. Sprinkle the flour on top and fry briefly with the onion. Now add the cream and white wine. Bring to the boil, stirring continuously and cook for another few minutes over medium to high heat while stirring.

4 Return the meat to the pan and heat up in the sauce (do not allow it to boil because the meat would become tough). Season the Geschnetzeltes with salt, pepper, sugar and lemon juice and garnish with chervil leaves if desired.

Accompaniment: **Rösti (page 212) and green salad.**

Variation: **You can add 250 g/9 oz well cleaned, sliced mushrooms, frying them with the onions (photograph).**

Saltimbocca alla romana

A little more expensive

Preparation time:
about 30 minutes

**4 thin slices veal,
  each 100 g/3½ oz,
  from the leg
4 leaves sage
4 slices Parma ham
salt, pepper
20 g/¾ oz (3 tablespoons)
  plain (all-purpose) flour
1-2 tablespoons cooking
  oil, e.g. sunflower oil**

1 Rinse the veal under cold running water and pat dry. Rinse the sage and pat dry. Place a slice of Parma ham and 1 sage leaf on each slice of veal, fold together and secure with wooden cocktail sticks. Season with salt and pepper on both sides and coat in flour.

2 Heat the oil in a pan, add the meat and fry for 3-4 minutes on one side. Then turn the meat and fry for a further 3-4 minutes. Arrange the meat on a preheated dish, cover and keep in a warm place.

(continued on page 70)

For the sauce:
**125 ml//4 fl oz (½ cup)
white wine or vermouth
125 g/4½ oz double
cream
salt, pepper, sugar**

In addition:
wooden cocktail sticks

Per serving:
P: 24 g, F: 23 g, C: 4 g,
kJ: 1442, kcal: 346

3   For the sauce, loosen the cooking deposits from the bottom of
the pan with white wine or vermouth and boil it down a little.
Stir in the double cream, heat up the sauce and season with salt,
pepper and sugar.

4   Finally, stir in the meat juices and pour the sauce over the meat.

Tip: Instead of veal you can also use pork or turkey escalopes.

Accompaniment: Rice seasoned with saffron.

Pork chops coated in breadcrumbs
Q u i c k

Preparation time:
about 30 minutes

**4 pork chops, each about
200 g/7 oz
salt
freshly ground pepper
paprika
1 egg
20 g/¾ oz (3 table-
spoons) plain (all-
purpose) flour
40 g/1½ oz (⅜ cup)
breadcrumbs
50 g/2 oz (4 tablespoons)
clarified butter,
margarine or 3 table-
spoons cooking oil,
e.g. sunflower oil**

Per serving:
P: 45 g, F: 14 g, C: 9 g,
kJ: 1431, kcal: 342

1   Rinse the pork chops under cold running water, pat dry and
sprinkle with salt, pepper and paprika.

2   Beat the egg with a fork in a deep plate. Coat the chops first in
flour (photograph 1), then in the beaten egg (photograph 2) and
finally in the breadcrumbs (photograph 3). Press the breadcrumbs firmly onto the chops and shake off any loose crumbs.

3   Heat the clarified butter, margarine or oil in a pan, add the chops
and fry for 8 minutes on each side. Arrange on a preheated dish.

Accompaniment: Potatoes sprinkled with parsley (page 210), mixed
vegetables with mushroom sauce (page 142).

Tip: Instead of pork chops you can also use veal chops (fry for 5–6 minutes on
each side).
Garnish the chops with lemon segments and parsley.

Variation: For **plain pork chops**, rinse the chops as above, pat dry, season
and fry for about 7 minutes on each side.

Pork escalopes
Classic

1 Peel and chop the onion. Remove the stalks from the mushrooms and cut off any bad parts, rub with kitchen paper, rinse if
necessary, pat dry and cut into slices.

2 Rinse the veal under cold running water, pat dry, sprinkle with
salt, pepper and paprika and turn in the flour. Shake off any
loose flour.

3 Heat the clarified butter, margarine or oil in a pan. Fry the
escalopes on both sides over medium heat for 10-12 minutes
(according to the thickness of the escalopes), turning occasionally. When cooked, remove the escalopes from the pan and keep
in a warm place.

4 Cook the diced onion in the remaining fat, stirring occasionally.
Add the sliced mushrooms to the chopped onion. Stir in the
crème fraîche, season with salt and pepper and cook uncovered
for 2-3 minutes over low heat.

5 Mix in the parsley. Pour the sauce over the escalopes.

Tip. Instead of cultivated mushrooms, you can also prepare the escalopes
with 1 jar or can of wild mushrooms, drained weight 290 g (10 oz).

Accompaniment: Potato chips (page 215) or fried potatoes (page 216) and
green salad.

Variation: For **Zigeunerschnitzel**, prepare the escalopes as in points 2-3
above. Add 1 jar (500 g/18 oz) zigeuner sauce to the cooking liquid, heat
through and pour over the escalopes.

Preparation time:
about 35 minutes

1 onion
250 g/9 oz mushrooms
4 escalopes of pork, each
    about 200 g/7 oz
salt
freshly ground pepper
paprika
40 g/1½ oz plain (all-
    purpose) flour
50 g/2 oz (4 tablespoons)
    clarified butter,
    margarine or 4 table-
    spoons cooking oil,
    e.g. sunflower oil
150 g/5 oz crème fraîche
1 tablespoon chopped
    parsley

Per serving:
P: 49 g, F: 28 g, C: 6 g,
kJ: 1931, kcal: 463

Cured rib of pork, Kassel style
Easy (6 servings)

Preparation time:
about 90 minutes

**1.5 kg/3¼ lb Kasseler
pork loin and rib, salted
and smoked, with its
bones removed by the
butcher, and chopped**
1 onion
1 tomato
1 bunch soup vegetables
1 small bay leaf
**125 ml/4 fl oz (½ cup) hot
water**
**sauce thickener
(optional)**
salt
freshly ground pepper

Per serving:
P: 44 g, F: 16 g, C: 3 g,
kJ: 1390, kcal: 332

1 Wash the meat under cold running water, pat dry and score the fatty skin on top in a criss-cross pattern (photograph 1). Preheat the oven.

2 Peel the onion. Wash the tomatoes, cut into quarters and remove the stalk. Prepare the soup vegetables: peel the celeriac and remove the bad parts, peel the carrots and cut off the green leaves and the tips. Wash the celeriac and carrots and drain. Remove the outer leaves of the leeks, cut off the root ends and dark leaves. Cut in half lengthways, wash thoroughly and leave to drain. Chop all the vegetables finely.

3 Place the meat in a roasting tin rinsed in water, with the fatty skin on top (photograph 2). Add the diced vegetables, bay leaf and bones. Put uncovered in the oven.

Top/bottom heat: **about 200 °C/400 °F (preheated)**,
Fan oven: **about 180 °C/350 °F (not preheated)**, Gas mark **6 (not preheated)**,
Cooking time: **about 50 minutes.**

4 When the cooking juices begin to turn brown, add a little hot water (photograph 3). Add more hot water, little by little, as the liquid evaporates and baste the roast with the cooking juices from time to time.

5 Remove the cooked roast and bones from the roasting tin. Cover the meat and leave it to rest for about 10 minutes so that the meat juices are well distributed throughout the roast. Then slice the meat and arrange on a preheated dish.

6 To make the sauce: Loosen cooking deposits stuck to the bottom of the roasting tin with a little water and rub them and the vegetables through a sieve. Pour back into the roasting tin and bring back to the boil. Thicken the sauce with sauce thickener if desired and bring back to the boil briefly. Season the sauce with salt and pepper and serve with the meat.

Accompaniment: Boiled potatoes or potato purée (page 218) and sauerkraut (page 172).

Tip: You may also add 1–2 tablespoons of crème fraîche to the sauce. The meat is also delicious cold with barbecue sauce or chutney and potato salad (page 200).
This dish is suitable for freezing.

Knuckle of pork with sauerkraut
Classic

1 Rinse the meat under cold running water. Put in a pan filled with water, bring to the boil, cover and simmer for about 90 minutes.

2 Meanwhile, slightly separate the sauerkraut. Peel the onion. When the meat is cooked, remove from the pan and strain the cooking liquid through a sieve. Reserve this liquid and pour about 500 ml/17 fl oz (2¼ cups) of it back into the pan. The amount of liquid will depend on the sauerkraut.

3 Add the sauerkraut, onion, bay leaf, cloves and juniper berries to the cooking liquid together with the meat. Bring to the boil, cover and cook over medium heat for about 30 minutes. Add a little more of the cooking liquid if necessary.

4 Meanwhile, wash the potato, peel, rinse and cook. When the potato is cooked, grate it and add to the sauerkraut. Bring to the boil briefly so that the liquid thickens. Season with salt, pepper and sugar. Serve the knuckle of pork with the sauerkraut.

Tip: For cooking the sauerkraut, you can replace 125 ml/4 fl oz (½ cup) of the stock made from the knuckle of pork with dry white wine.

Accompaniment: Potato purée (page 218) or boiled potatoes (page 210).

Preparation time: about 2¼ hours

1.5 kg/3¼ lb knuckle of pork, salted (2–3 pieces, if necessary ordered from the butcher in advance)
about 1.25 litres/2¼ pints (5½ cups) water
750 g/1½ lb sauerkraut, fresh or canned
1 onion
1 bay leaf
3 cloves
5 juniper berries
1 medium floury potato
salt
freshly ground pepper
some sugar

Per serving:
P: 58 g, F: 36 g, C: 6 g, kJ: 2467, kcal: 589

Liver with onions
Classic

Preparation time:
about 40 minutes

5 onions
500 g/18 oz liver
20 g/¾ oz (3
   tablespoons) plain (all-
   purpose) flour
50 g/2 oz (4 tablespoons)
   clarified butter,
   margarine or 4 table-
   spoons cooking oil, e.g.
   sunflower oil
salt
freshly ground pepper
dried chopped marjoram

Per serving:
P: 26 g, F: 18 g, C: 10 g,
kJ: 1260, kcal: 301

1 Peel the onions, cut into thin slices or rings. Rinse the liver under cold running water, pat dry and cut into slices 1-1.5 cm/⅜-½ in thick. Dip the liver in flour so that it is coated on both sides (photograph 1). Shake off any loose flour.

2 Heat 30 g/1 oz (2 tablespoons) clarified butter, margarine or oil in a pan. Add the slices of liver and fry for 3-4 minutes (photograph 2) until the under side has browned. Turn over, season the browned side with salt, pepper and marjoram and fry for another 3-4 minutes. Now season the other side. Arrange the slices of liver on a preheated dish and keep in a warm place.

3 Heat the rest of the clarified butter, margarine or oil in the pan with the cooking juices. Add the onion rings or slices and brown for 8-10 minutes, stirring continuously. Season the onion rings with salt and pepper and add to the liver.

Tip: You can make this dish with pig's liver, beef liver or calf's liver. The various kinds of liver all have a different taste and texture. Calf's liver has the most delicate taste and is more tender than pig's liver, needing less cooking. Beef liver has the strongest taste and a firmer consistency. The cooking time also depends on the thickness of the slices. Liver should never be cooked over high heat because this would quickly make it tough and dry.

Accompaniment: **Potato purée (page 218) and apple sauce (page 280)**

Variation: **For "Berlin-style" liver,** fry 2 medium-sized apples cut into rings or segments with the onions.

Königsberger meatballs
Good value (8-10 pieces)

1 Soak the roll in cold water for 10 minutes (photograph 1). Peel and finely chop the onion. Squeeze the roll well to expel the liquid. Mix the roll with the mince, chopped onion, egg or egg white and mustard; season with salt and pepper.

2 Mould the mixture into 8-10 meatballs with wet hands (photograph 2). Put the meatballs in the boiling vegetable stock, bring to the boil again, skim if necessary and simmer uncovered over low heat for about 15 minutes, keeping the water gently moving. Pour the cooking liquid through a sieve and reserve 500 ml/ 17 fl oz (2¼ cups) of it for the sauce.

3 To make the sauce, melt the butter or margarine in a pan. Add the flour while stirring and cook until it is heated through and bright yellow. Gradually whisk in the hot stock, being careful to avoid forming any lumps. Bring the sauce to the boil and gently cook uncovered over low heat for about 5 minutes, stirring occasionally.

4 Mix the egg yolk with the milk and stir slowly into the sauce, but do not cook any longer. Add the capers with the liquid in which they were preserved. Season to taste with salt, pepper, sugar and lemon juice. Put the meatballs in the sauce (photograph 3), and cook over low heat for about 5 minutes. Sprinkle the Königsberger meatballs with dill and serve.

Tip: Sauce lovers should make 1½ times the quantity of sauce. The meatballs can be frozen in the stock. Prepare the sauce after the meatballs have defrosted.

Accompaniment: **Boiled potatoes (page 210), and pickled beetroot from the jar.**

Preparation time:
about 50 minutes

1 day-old bread roll
1 onion
500 g/18 oz minced meat, half beef, half pork
1 medium egg or white of 1 medium egg
2 level teaspoons medium strong mustard
salt
freshly ground pepper
750 ml/1¼ pints (3½ cups) vegetable stock

For the sauce:
30 g/1 oz (2 tablespoons) butter or margarine
30 g/1 oz (¼ cup) flour
500 ml/17 fl oz (2¼ cups) cooking liquid from the meatballs
yolk of 1 medium egg
4 teaspoons milk
1 small jar of capers, drained weight 20 g/ ¾ oz
salt
freshly ground pepper
some sugar
lemon juice
some dill

Per serving:
P: 28 g, F: 30 g, C: 13 g,
kJ: 1819, kcal: 434

Knuckle of pork
For guests (6 servings)

Preparation time: about
3 ½ hours

**4 salted pork knuckles,
each about 800 g/
1¾ lb, with bones
freshly ground pepper
250 ml/8 fl oz (1 cup) hot
water for the fat-
collecting roasting tin
about 1 litre/1¾ pints
(4½ cups) hot water, or
half vegetable stock
and half water
3 onions
100 ml/3½ fl oz (½ cup)
light beer
dark sauce thickener
(optional)**

Per serving:
P: 78 g, F: 34 g, C: 1 g,
kJ: 2616, kcal: 622

1 Preheat the oven. Rinse the meat under cold running water, pat dry and rub with pepper. Slide a fat-collecting roasting tin onto the third shelf from the bottom and pour 250 ml/8 fl oz (1 cup) of water into it. Place the knuckles on a grid and slide this grid into the oven above the fat-collecting roasting tin.

Top/bottom heat: about 180 °C/350 °F (preheated),
Fan oven: about 160 °C/325 °F (not preheated), Gas mark 4 (not preheated),
Cooking time: about 2¼ hours.

2 Add hot water or vegetable stock now and again to replace the evaporated liquid (the fat-collecting roasting tin should always be filled with liquid to a height of 1 cm/⅜ in). Turn the meat occasionally and baste with the cooking juices.

3 Peel the onions, cut into quarters and add to the liquid in the fat-collecting roasting tin, then **cook for another 60 minutes at the temperature indicated above.** Baste the knuckle with the beer from time to time.

4 Remove the cooked meat from the bone and arrange on a pre-heated dish.

5 Skim the fat off the cooking juices with a spoon, put aside 500 ml/17 fl oz (2¼ cups) of the cooking juices and top up if necessary with water or stock. Thicken with sauce thickener if desired and season with pepper. Serve the sauce with the meat.

Accompaniment: Sauerkraut (page 172) or white cabbage salad and potato purée (page 218), potato dumplings (page 220) or farm-baked bread.

Tip: You can make the sauce spicier by adding a little mustard. This will also make the sauce more digestible.
The knuckle can also be seasoned with dry marjoram leaves or caraway seeds.
If you prefer the rind crisper, raise the oven temperature by 20–40 °C/70–100 °F for the last 15 minutes.
No more than six knuckles should be cooked in the oven at the same time.

Rissoles (meatballs)
Easy

Preparation time: about 35
minutes excluding cooling time

1 day-old bread roll
2 onions
1-2 tablespoons cooking
   oil, e.g. sunflower oil
600 g/1¼ lb minced meat,
   half beef, half pork
1 medium egg
salt
freshly ground pepper
paprika
40 g/1½ oz (3 table-
   spoons) clarified butter,
   margarine or 3 table-
   spoons cooking oil,
   e.g. sunflower oil

Per serving:
P: 31 g, F: 37 g, C: 7 g,
kJ: 2019, kcal: 482

1   Soak the bread roll in cold water. Peel the onion and chop finely. Heat the oil in a pan, add the chopped onion and fry for 2-3 minutes until transparent. Then remove the onions from the pan, drain on kitchen paper and leave to cool down a little.

2   Squeeze the bread roll to remove as much water as possible (photograph 1) and add to the mince together with the chopped onion and egg. Mix well (photograph 2) so that all the ingredients are well blended and season with salt, pepper and paprika. Wet your hands and form the mixture into 8 rissoles (photograph 3).

3   Heat the clarified butter, margarine or oil in a pan. Add the rissoles and fry on both sides over medium heat for about 10 minutes until brown, turning occasionally.

Tip: You can add 1-2 tablespoons chopped parsley to the onions or stir 1 teaspoon mustard into the meat mixture. Rissoles are suitable for freezing.

Accompaniment: **Potato purée (page 218) and carrots (page 158).**

Rabbit in olive sauce
With alcohol

1 Rinse the rabbit pieces under cold running water and pat dry. Separate the back from the stomach flaps (photograph 1) and remove the skin from the back (photograph 2). Season the rabbit pieces with salt and pepper.

2 Rinse the rosemary under cold running water, pat dry and remove the leaves from the stems. Peel the carrots and cut off the green leaves and tips. Peel the celeriac and remove the bad parts. Wash the carrots and celeriac, leave to drain and cut into pieces. Peel the onions and chop.

3 Wash the tomatoes, drain, make cross-shaped cuts, dip briefly in boiling water and then dip in cold water. Peel the tomatoes, remove the stalks and chop coarsely. Stone the olives and cut into quarters.

4 Heat the oil in a pan or casserole, add the rabbit pieces and brown on all sides, turning them over frequently. Remove the back from the pan. Add the prepared vegetables and rosemary and fry for 2–3 minutes.

5 Add the white wine and stock. Bring to the boil, cover and cook over medium heat for about 25 minutes. Return the back to the pan, cover again and braise for a further 25 minutes.

6 Remove all the rabbit pieces from the pan, arrange on a dish, cover and keep in a warm place. Purée the sauce (photograph 3) and stir in the olives and crème fraîche. Season with salt and pepper and serve with the meat.

Tip: You can make the sauce even creamier by adding 20 g/³⁄₄ oz olive paste (from a jar or tube) when you stir in the wine and stock.
This dish is suitable for freezing.

Accompaniment: **Ciabatta and roasted vegetables (page 158).**

Preparation time:
about 75 minutes

1 rabbit, about 1.5 kg/
3¼ lb, cut into 5 pieces,
salt
freshly ground pepper
1–2 branches rosemary
200 g/7 oz carrots
100 g/3½ oz celeriac
2 onions
150 g/5 oz tomatoes
100 g/3½ oz black olives
or 50 g/2 oz stoned
olives
3 tablespoons olive oil
125 ml/4 fl oz (½ cup)
white wine
250 ml/8 fl oz (1 cup)
chicken or vegetable
stock
75–150 g/2½–5 oz crème
fraîche

Per serving:
P: 64 g, F: 46 g, C: 6 g,
kJ: 2984, kcal: 714

Grilled lamb cutlets (photograph)
Easy

Preparation time: about 20 minutes, without marinating time

**8 double lamb chops,
  each 100 g/3½ oz
2 small cloves garlic
2 tablespoons cooking
  oil, e.g. olive oil
pepper, salt**

Per serving:
P: 37 g, F: 31 g, C: 0 g,
kJ: 1783, kcal: 426

1 Trim the fat off the cutlets if necessary and notch the fatty edge. Rinse the cutlets under cold running water and pat dry.

2 Peel the cloves of garlic, press through a garlic press and mix with the oil and pepper. Coat the cutlets with this mixture and leave to marinate in the refrigerator for about 60 minutes. Preheat the grill shortly before the cutlets have finished marinating.

3 Place the cutlets on the grid lined with aluminium foil. Slide it under the preheated oven grill and grill for 3 minutes each side. Season the cooked cutlets with salt.

Accompaniment: **Green beans (page 162) and warm unleavened bread.**

Leg of lamb
For guests (4-6 servings)

Preparation time: about 2 hours

**2 onions
150 g/5 oz tomatoes
1 leg of lamb with bone,
  1.5 kg/3¼ lb
salt
freshly ground pepper
1-2 cloves of garlic
3 tablespoons cooking oil,
  e.g. olive-oil
1-2 teaspoon herbes de
  Provence
about 375 ml/12 fl oz
  (1½ cups) vegetable
  stock or half red wine
  and half vegetable
  stock)**

Per serving:
P: 49 g, F: 19 g, C: 2 g,
kJ: 1552, kcal: 370

1 Preheat the oven. Peel the onions and cut into quarters. Wash the tomatoes, dry, cut into quarters and remove the stalks. Rinse the meat under cold running water, pat dry and rub with salt and pepper. Peel the cloves of garlic and push through a garlic press.

2 Heat the oil in a roasting tin. Add the leg of lamb and brown on all sides. Coat the meat with the garlic paste and sprinkle with herbes de Provence. Remove the lamb from the roasting tin.

3 Put the quartered tomatoes and onions in the roasting tin and fry in the remaining cooking fat for 3-4 minutes. Return the lamb to the roasting tin and add one-third of the vegetable stock or red wine and stock mixture. Put the roasting tin back in the oven and cook uncovered.

Top/bottom heat: **about 180 °C/350 °F (preheated),**
Fan oven: **about 160 °C/325 °F (not preheated),** Gas mark **4 (not preheated),**
Cooking time: **75-90 minutes.**

4 Replace the evaporated liquid little by little with the remaining stock or red wine-stock mixture.

5 Remove the meat from the roasting tin, cover and leave to rest for 10 minutes. Slice the meat and arrange on a preheated dish. Strain the cooking juices with the vegetables through a sieve, adding more stock or wine if necessary. Season with salt and pepper and serve the meat hot.

Poultry

Poultry is relatively high in protein and low in fat compared to other kinds of meat.

Because poultry may be infected with salmonella there are a few rules which must be observed when preparing and cooking poultry:
• Always store poultry in a refrigerator that is sufficiently cold, or in the freezer.
• All objects that have been in contact with poultry must be washed thoroughly after use.
• Throw away the water immediately after defrosting poultry.
• Other food should never come into contact with uncooked poultry or with the water released when poultry is defrosted.
• Always wash your hands very carefully after handling uncooked poultry.
• Always cook poultry thoroughly. Poultry is cooked when the juices that run out are colourless and the legs separate easily from the body. A meat thermometer can be used to check the temperature at the centre of the chicken. When measuring the temperature in this way, be careful not to position the thermometer too close to a bone because this would falsify the result.

Chicken

Small chicken   Roasting chicken   Boiling fowl

Small chicken
Fattened chicken 5–7 weeks old. The breastbone is still flexible and the weight is between 800 g–1.2 kg/1¾–2½ lb. They can be bought fresh or deep-frozen. Chickens are also available which have been fed on a particular food, for instance, corn. The meat of these chickens is particularly tasty.

Roasting chicken
Fattened chicken about 8–9 weeks old, slaughtered before it reaches sexual maturity. The breastbone is still flexible and the weight ranges between 1.2 kg–1.5 kg/2½–3¼ lb.

Boiling fowl
Laying hens that are slaughtered between 12 and 15 months old. The breastbone has become cartilaginous. Boiling fowls have not been fattened but will have been kept for laying eggs. The weight varies between 1 kg/2¼ lb and 2 kg/4½ lb depending on the breed. Boiling fowls can be used for making chicken stock and casseroles.

Guinea fowl
A breed of domestic fowl with dark meat and a fine, delicate texture and aromatic flavour. It weighs 1.0–1.3 kg /2¼–2¾ lb when slaughtered. It can be cooked in a variety of ways.

Duck

Fattened duck
Fattened bird 7–8 weeks old, slaughtered before the plumage has matured. The breastbone is still flexible and the cartilage has not yet become ossified. Weight 1.6–1.8 kg/3½–4 lb.

Young ducks
About 6 months old, these are

slaughtered after the first plumage has matured. The breastbone will still be soft. Weight 1.5-2.0 kg/3¼-4½ lb.

Ducks
Birds over 1 year old, slaughtered after sexual maturity. The breastbone has now become ossified. Weight 1.8-2.5 kg/4-5½ lb.

Barbary duck
Raised in the wild with very little fat and strong flight muscles, in other words, with a high percentage of breast meat. Roasting ducks weigh about 1.6 kg/3½ lb while drakes usually weigh about 3 kg/6½ lb. They are usually sold already cut up, for instance as duck breasts.

Goose

Table goose
Young goose, 11–12 weeks old, slaughtered before its plumage reaches maturity. The breastbone is still soft. Weight 2-3 kg/4½-6½ lb.

Young goose
About 6–7 months old, slaughtered after its plumage reaches maturity for the first time. The breastbone and cartilage are still soft. Weight 3-4 kg/6½-9 lb.

Goose
Over 1 year old, slaughtered after it has reached sexual maturity. The breastbone has become ossified. Weight 4-7 kg/9-15½ lb.

Tip
Ducks and geese are birds with a high proportion of fat and are only suitable for roasting.

Turkey

Turkey cock
Turkeys are usually sold as young animals, no more than 1 year old. The breastbone is still soft while the meat is low in fat and rich in protein. After a relatively long period of fattening, they weigh between 5-11 kg/11-24 lb. Turkey is also sold in pieces, such as turkey legs and turkey escalopes.

Young turkey (baby turkey)
The young turkey is slaughtered at the age of 9–13 weeks after a short period of fattening. Weight between 3-6 kg/6½-13 lb (baby turkey about 1.6 kg/3½ lb).

Quail
Quails are small wildfowl that are now mainly farmed. Often stuffed and roasted, they are served as a starter or entrée. A quail weighs about 150 g/5 oz.

Poultry pieces
All of the more common kinds of poultry are also sold as pieces, fresh, chilled or deep-frozen. You can buy pieces separately, such as a half-breast, breast fillet (escalope, only from chicken and turkey), leg (including the thigh and lower leg), thigh, lower leg and wing. The breast and leg have the most meat but they are also the most expensive. The breast meat of chicken and turkey can also be served

Duck   Turkey   Goose

as thin strips or slices or used as a basis for oriental dishes.

Preparation

Fresh poultry should be put in the refrigerator as soon as possible after purchase. When buying frozen poultry to be stored in the freezer at home, make sure that it thaws as little as possible on the way home. Putting the poultry in a cool bag while transporting it is recommended. When you get home the poultry should be put in the freezer immediately.

Freezing

When deep-freezing fresh poultry yourself, there are a few rules to be observed:
- The poultry must be packed with great care and the freezer bag must not be damaged so that freezer burn does not occur.
- Freeze the poultry in such a way that it freezes to the centre as quickly as possible. This is because if the freezing process is too slow, large ice crystal will develop which will damage the cellular structure of the meat; the meat will then lose much of its juice during thawing and become tough as a result.

Defrosting

Deep-frozen poultry should be defrosted slowly (preferably in a refrigerator but otherwise at room temperature) so as not to damage the cell structure which would toughen the meat.
- Completely remove the packaging and throw it away.
- Place the poultry in a metal sieve inside a container, or in a large bowl on top of an inverted soup plate so that the liquid produced while the poultry is defrosting can flow away (the poultry must not be in contact with that liquid).
- During the defrosting process the container should be covered with a lid, plate, aluminium foil or clingfilm.
- Throw away the water resulting from the defrosting and make sure that no other food comes into contact with that liquid (because of the risk of salmonella).
- Finally, wash your hands, the work surfaces and the dishes used.

Jointing

This refers to the cutting up of poultry into pieces, which is done so that the various pieces which require different

cooking times can be cooked properly. A leg, for instance, needs to cook longer than breast meat.

For example, a chicken:
- Place the prepared chicken on its back and cut off the legs and wings with a sharp knife.
- Cut the breast meat along the breastbone as far down as the bone, cutting the breastbone with poultry shears.
- Cut the back along the backbone (use poultry shears), cut out the backbone and halve the breast.
- Cut the legs at the joint using a knife or poultry shears.

Dressing

When poultry is to be cooked whole, all the protruding parts, such as the legs and the wings, must be tied close to the body with kitchen string to prevent them from drying out.

Method:
- Cut off the legs. With a sharp carving knife, make a cut into the meat as far as the joint, twist the joint slightly and cut through the tendons.
- Cut off the wings with a sharp knife, then cut at the joints.
- Loosen the breast meat on both sides of the bone using a knife and slice into portions.
- Arrange the meat on a previously warmed dish.

Method:
- Place the prepared poultry on its back, bend the tips of the wings towards the back and slide under the body. If the tips of the wings have been cut off, tie the wings together under the body with string.
- Tie the legs together with string, cross-wise or all around.

Stuffing

Large birds such as turkeys and geese are particularly suited for stuffing. The stuffing is then served as an accompaniment to the meat, which is also more aromatic as a result.

Method:
- Place the prepared fowl on its back.
- Put the stuffing in the abdominal cavity.
- Sew up the opening with string or secure with wooden cocktail sticks and tie crossways with string.

Carving

Carving is the process of cutting up the cooked fowl into individual servings.

Chicken fricassée

Classic

Preparation time: about 1¼ hours, excluding cooling time

1.5 litres/2¾ pints (7 cups) water
1 bunch soup vegetables
1 onion
1 bay leaf
1 clove
1 oven-ready chickens 1–1.2 kg/2¼–2½ lb
1½ teaspoons salt

For the sauce:
25 g/1 oz (2 tablespoons) butter
30 g/1 oz (¼ cup) plain (all-purpose) flour
500 ml/17 fl oz (2¼ cups) chicken stock
1 can asparagus pieces, drained weight 175 g/ 6 oz
1 tin mushrooms, drained weight 150 g/5 oz
3 tablespoons white wine
about 1 tablespoon lemon juice
1 teaspoon sugar
2 egg yolks from medium eggs
3 tablespoons whipping cream
salt
freshly ground pepper
Worcestershire sauce

Per serving:
P: 41 g, F: 24 g, C: 8 g,
kJ: 1788, kcal: 427

1 Bring the water to the boil in a large saucepan. Meanwhile, prepare the soup vegetables. Peel the celeriac and remove any bad parts. Peel the carrots and cut off the green leaves and the tips. Wash the carrots and celeriac and leave to drain. Remove the outer leaves of the leeks, cut off the root ends and dark leaves. Cut in half lengthways, wash thoroughly and leave to drain. Coarsely chop all the vegetables. Peel the onion and stud it with a bay leaf and a clove.

2 Wash the chicken inside and outside under cold running water, put into the boiling water, bring back to the boil and skim.

3 Now put the prepared vegetables into the saucepan with the chicken, cover and cook for about 60 minutes over low heat.

4 Take the chicken out of the stock and allow to cool a little. Strain the stock through a sieve, remove the fat if necessary and reserve 500 ml/17 fl oz (2¼ cups) of the stock to make the sauce. Loosen the meat from the bones, remove the skin and cut the meat into large pieces.

5 To make the sauce, melt the butter in a pan. Stir in the flour and cook until the mixture turns pale yellow, stirring all the time. Add the reserved stock and beat vigorously with a whisk to obtain a smooth mixture without lumps. Bring the sauce to the boil and cook gently for about 5 minutes without a lid, stirring occasionally.

6 Drain the asparagus pieces and mushrooms in a colander and add to the sauce together with the chicken. Bring back to the boil briefly. Add the white wine, 2 teaspoons lemon juice and sugar.

7 Whisk the egg yolk into the cream and fold carefully into the fricassee to thicken, but do not let the sauce boil any more. Season the fricassee with salt, pepper, Worcestershire sauce and lemon juice.

Accompaniment: Rice or noodles and salad.

Tip: Instead of canned or bottled asparagus you can also buy deep-frozen asparagus. Instead of the tinned mushrooms, 150 g/5 oz fresh mushrooms may be used: clean, slice and fry in 1 tablespoon butter before adding to the sauce (photograph).
The rest of the stock can be used to make soup or incorporate in a sauce. The stock can also be frozen.

4   Remove the cooked chicken from the roasting tin. Cover and leave to rest for 5–10 minutes.

5   If necessary, add some water to the cooking deposits, and if desired, rub through a sieve together with the vegetables. Season with salt, pepper and paprika. Carve the chicken into pieces with a knife or poultry shears and arrange on a dish. Serve with the sauce.

Accompaniment: Potato chips (page 215) and broccoli.

Chicken breast with mozzarella
Quick

Preparation time:
about 30 minutes

4 chicken breast fillets
   without skin, about
   150 g/5 oz each
salt
freshly ground black
   pepper
2 large tomatoes
125 g/4½ oz mozzarella
   cheese
2 tablespoons cooking
   oil, e.g. sunflower oil
some small basil leaves

Per serving:
P: 42 g, F: 9 g, C: 1 g,
kJ: 1047, kcal: 250

1   Preheat the oven grill. Rinse the chicken fillets under cold running water, pat dry and sprinkle with salt and pepper.

2   Wash the tomatoes, remove the stalk ends and cut each tomato into four slices. Drain the mozzarella and cut into 8 slices.

3   Heat the oil in a heat-resistant pan and fry the breast fillets on both sides for about 10 minutes.

4   Arrange two slices of tomatoes on each breast fillet, sprinkle with pepper, then cover each breast fillet with 2 slices of mozzarella and sprinkle with pepper.

5   Put the pan on the shelf under the preheated oven grill and grill the breast fillets for 5–10 minutes until the cheese begins to melt. (Instead of a heat-resistant pan, the breast fillets can be put in a soufflé dish after frying them in a frying-pan.)

6   Garnish the grilled fillets with basil leaves before serving.

Accompaniment: Buttered rice or garlic toast and iceberg salad (page 190).

Tip: If an oven grill is not available, you can put the pan or soufflé dish in the oven preheated to a temperature of about 220 °C/425 °F (top/bottom heat), 200 °C/400 °F (fan oven) or Gas mark 7 and cook until the cheese begins to melt.

Chicken legs (photograph bottom left)
Popular

Preparation time:
about 55 minutes

**4 drumsticks, each about
250 g/9 oz**
½ **teaspoon salt**
**1 pinch freshly ground
pepper**
1 teaspoon paprika
**1-2 tablespoons cooking
oil, e.g. sunflower oil**

Per serving:
P: 34 g, F: 21 g, C: 0 g,
kJ: 1369, kcal: 327

1 Preheat the oven. Rinse the chicken legs under cold running water, pat dry, cut off any bits of the back that may still be attached and remove any remaining fat and skin.

2 Stir the salt, pepper and paprika into the oil. Rub this mixture on the chicken legs and place in a roasting tin. Put the roasting tin on the middle shelf in the oven.

Top/bottom heat: about 200 °C/400 °F (preheated),
Fan oven: about 180 °C/350 °F (preheated), Gas mark 6 (preheated),
Cooking time: about 45 minutes.

Accompaniment: Potato chips (page 215), potato salad (page 200) or fried potatoes (page 216) with peas (page 162) or carrots (page 158).

Variation 1: **Tandoori chicken legs** (photograph bottom right)
Stir 125 g/4½ oz natural yogurt (3.5% fat) until smooth. Peel 1 clove of garlic, press through a garlic press and stir into the yogurt. Add ½ teaspoon salt, 1-1½ teaspoons sweet paprika, ½-1 teaspoon Madras curry, a scant ½ teaspoon ground cinnamon, a small pinch of cayenne pepper and a pinch of ground cloves; stir well. Prepare the chicken legs as described in point 1 and rub them with this marinade, put in a shallow dish, cover and leave for at least 2 hours or overnight in the refrigerator. Now put the chicken legs in a roasting tin as described above, coat again with the marinade and roast as indicated above. If you like you can baste the chicken legs again with the marinade half-way through the roasting process and sprinkle them with sesame seeds.

Variation 2: **Hot chilli chicken legs** (photograph top left)
Mix together 1 crushed clove of garlic, 1 teaspoon balsamic vinegar, 1 teaspoon liquid honey and 1 tablespoon vegetable oil (e.g. sunflower oil) and 4 heaped tablespoons hot chilli sauce; stir well. Prepare the chicken legs as described in point 1 and rub them with this marinade, put in a shallow dish, cover and leave for at least 2 hours or overnight in the refrigerator. Now put the chicken legs in a roasting tin as described above, coat them again with the marinade and roast as described above. Baste the chicken legs from time to time with the marinade while they are roasting.

Variation 3: **Chicken legs with a herb crust** (photograph top right).
Prepare the chicken legs as described in point 1 and rub with salt, pepper and sweet paprika. Mix together 4–5 tablespoons chopped mixed herbs (fresh or deep-frozen, e.g. parsley, tarragon, chives) with 6 tablespoons breadcrumbs. Now coat the chicken first in flour, then in 1 beaten egg and finally in the breadcrumbs, pressing to ensure that the breadcrumbs stick to the chicken legs. Put the chicken legs in a roasting tin as described above, sprinkle them with 3–4 tablespoons vegetable oil (e.g. sunflower oil) and roast as indicated above.

Turkey thigh with vegetables
For guests

Preparation time: about 1 ³/₄ hours

3 tablespoons cooking oil,
   e.g. sunflower oil
1 turkey leg with bones,
   about 1 kg/2¼ lb
salt
freshly ground pepper
1 litre/1³/₄ pints (4½ cups)
   hot water or vegetable
   stock
500 g/18 oz onions
200 g/7 oz carrots
200 g/7 oz celeriac
1 small root Hamburg
   parsley
200 g/7 oz leeks
250 g/9 oz tomatoes
1-2 branches rosemary or
   thyme
150 g/5 oz sour cream
15 g/½ oz (2 tablespoons)
   plain (all-purpose) flour
1-2 tablespoons chopped
   parsley (optional)

Per serving:
P: 44 g, F: 35 g, C: 16 g,
kJ: 2338, kcal: 559

1   Put the oil in a roasting tin, place the tin on the middle shelf in the oven and preheat the oven.

2   Rinse the turkey thigh under cold running water, pat dry, rub with salt and pepper, put in the hot roasting tin and roast.

Top/bottom heat: about 200 °C/400 °F (preheated),
Fan oven: about 180 °C/350 °F (preheated), Gas mark 6 (preheated),
Cooking time: about 70 minutes.

3   As soon as the roasting juices begin to brown, add a little hot water or vegetable stock. Baste the turkey thigh now and again with the roasting juices and add more water or stock to replace the evaporated liquid.

4   Meanwhile, peel and chop the onions. Peel the carrots and cut off the green leaves and the tips. Peel the celeriac and remove the bad parts. Clean the parsley root and peel. Wash the vegetables and leave to drain. Cut the carrots into slices 1.5 cm/½ in thick. Coarsely chop the celeriac and parsley root.

5   Remove the outer leaves of the leeks, cut off the root ends and dark leaves. Cut in half lengthways, wash thoroughly, leave to drain and cut into pieces 3 cm/1¼ in long. Wash the tomatoes, wipe dry, remove the stalk ends and dice.

6   Rinse the sprigs of rosemary and thyme, pat dry, remove the leaves from the stems and chop coarsely. Add the chopped onions and prepared vegetables to the turkey thigh in the roasting tin. Add a little water or stock if necessary and season with salt, pepper, rosemary or thyme and **roast for another 20 minutes at the same oven temperature as indicated above.**

7   Arrange the turkey thigh and vegetables on a preheated dish and keep in warm place. Put the roasting tin on a ring of the hob, loosen the bits stuck to the bottom with a little water, strain through a sieve, add enough water to make up 400 ml/14 fl oz/1³/₄ cups, pour into a saucepan and bring to the boil.

8   Stir the flour into the sour cream and add this mixture to the boiling liquid, stirring with a whisk and making sure that there are no lumps. Bring the sauce to the boil and simmer gently uncovered over a low heat for about 5 minutes, stirring occasionally. Season the sauce with salt and pepper and serve with the vegetables and turkey. Sprinkle with parsley if desired.

Accompaniment: **Boiled potatoes (page 210) or rice.**

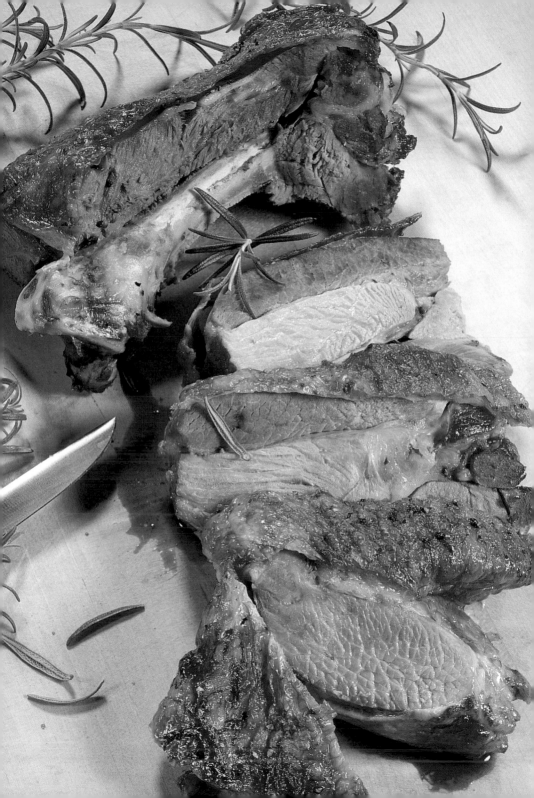

Fried duck
Classic

Preparation time:
2 $^1/_2$–2 $^3/_4$ hours

**1 oven-ready duck,
2–2$^1/_2$ kg/4$^1/_2$–5$^1/_2$ lb
salt
freshly ground pepper
about 850 ml/30 fl oz
(4 cups) water**

For the sauce:
**1 teaspoon plain (all-
purpose) flour
50 ml/1$^1/_2$ fl oz (3 tablespoons) cold water**

In addition:
kitchen string

Per serving:
P: 82 g, F: 53 g, C: 2 g,
kJ: 3388, kcal: 805

1   Preheat the oven top and bottom. Rinse the duck inside and out under cold running water, then pat dry. Remove the fat from the cavity if necessary and rub the inside and outside of the duck with salt and pepper.

2   Tie together the two legs and the two wings. Pour 50 ml/1$^1/_2$ fl oz (3 tablespoons) water into a roasting tin. Put the duck in it breast down and uncovered put on a shelf in the oven.

Top/bottom heat: **about 180 °C/350 °F (preheated),**
Fan oven: **about 160 °C/325 °F (not preheated),** Gas mark **4 (not preheated),**
Cooking time: 2$^1/_4$–2$^1/_2$ hours.

3   Meanwhile rinse the stomach, heart and neck and place in a pan filled with 750 ml/1$^1/_4$ pints (3$^1/_2$ cups) water. Add 1 teaspoon salt, bring to the boil, cover and cook for about 30 minutes over low heat. Then pour through a sieve and reserve the cooking liquid.

4   During the roasting time prick the duck under the wings and legs several times so that the fat runs out. After roasting for 30 min-utes remove the accumulated fat from the roasting tin; repeat at intervals several times. When the cooking deposits begin to brown add a little of the stock. Replace the evaporated liquid with stock. After about 60 minutes of roasting, turn over the duck.

5   Stir $^1/_2$ teaspoon salt into 100 ml/3$^1/_2$ fl oz ($^1/_2$ cup) water. About 10 minutes before the end of the roasting time, pour over the duck and increase the temperature by about 20 °C/70 °F so that the skin becomes crisp.

6   Remove the cooked duck from the roasting tin, cover and leave to rest fo 5–10 minutes.

7   Loosen the cooking deposits with some hot water, pour through a sieve, remove the fat, make up the quantity to 375 ml/12 fl oz (1$^1/_2$ cups) with water, put in a pan and bring back to the boil. Mix the flour with some cold water and stir it into the cooking liquid with a whisk, being careful to avoid making any lumps. Bring the sauce to the boil and cook gently uncovered over low heat for about 5 minutes, stirring occasionally. Season the sauce to taste with salt and pepper.

8   Carve the duck into pieces, arrange on a preheated dish and serve with the sauce.

Accompaniment: **Potato dumplings (page 220) and red cabbage (page 175).**

Duck legs with pointed cabbage
For guests

1   Rinse the duck legs under cold running water, pat dry and sprinkle with salt and pepper.

2   Heat a pan without any fat, add the duck legs and brown them all around. Add a little hot stock, cover and braise over medium heat for about 60 minutes, gradually adding more hot stock as the liquid evaporates while turning the duck legs now and again.

3   Meanwhile, remove the outer leaves of the cabbage, cut into quarters, wash and leave to drain. Now remove the stalk and cut the cabbage into strips. Peel and chop the shallot or onion.

4   Heat the clarified butter or oil in a pan. Add the chopped shallot or onion and fry until golden. Add the cabbage, white wine and season with salt and pepper. Cover and braise the cabbage for 8-15 minutes until cooked, stirring occasionally.

5   Take the duck legs out of the pan, cover and let rest for about 10 minutes.

6   Remove some fat from the cooking juices using a spoon, then add the cabbage with the cooking liquid to the braising juices and cook briefly. Season with salt and pepper and stir in the parsley. Put the cabbage on a dish and arrange the duck legs on top.

Accompaniment: **Potato dumplings (page 220).**

Tip: Instead of pointed cabbage you can also use Savoy cabbage.

Preparation time:
about 80 minutes

4 duck legs, each about
    200 g/7 oz
salt
freshly ground pepper
about 100 ml/3½ fl oz
    (½ cup) hot vegetable
    or chicken stock
500 g/18 oz pointed
    cabbage
1 shallot or onion
20 g/¾ oz (1½ table-
    spoons) clarified butter
    or 3 teaspoons cooking
    oil, e.g. sunflower oil
125 ml/4 fl oz (½ cup)
    white wine
1-2 tablespoons chopped
    parsley

Per serving:
P: 35 g, F: 44 g, C: 3 g,
kJ: 2374, kcal: 568

Breast of duck with orange sauce
With alcohol

Preparation time:
about 35 minutes

**2 duck breast fillets,
about 300 g/10 oz each**
salt
freshly ground pepper
2 teaspoons honey
**15 g/½ oz (1 tablespoon)
butter**
**3-4 teaspoons orange
liqueur, e.g. Grand
Marnier**

For the orange sauce:
1 untreated orange
150 g/5 oz crème fraîche
salt
freshly ground pepper
some honey

Per serving:
**P: 28 g, F: 37 g, C: 11 g,
kJ: 2118, kcal: 507**

1   Rinse the duck breasts under cold running water, pat dry and sprinkle with salt and pepper.

2   Heat a frying pan without any fat. Put the fillets in the pan with the fatty side downwards and fry for about 6 minutes. Then turn the fillets and fry on the other side for another 6 minutes (photograph 1).

3   Shortly before the duck fillets are cooked, coat the skin of the duck fillets with honey, using a pastry brush (photograph 2) and add some butter. Pour the orange liqueur over the fillets and then remove them from the pan. Place on a preheated dish and keep in a warm place.

4   To make the orange sauce, wash the orange under hot running water, wipe dry, peel thinly and cut the peel into very fine strips, or peel the orange with a zester. Cut the orange in half and squeeze it.

5   Skim the fat off the cooking juices with a spoon or pour it off. Scrape the bits at the bottom of the pan while adding the orange juice and zest to the cooking juices. Stir in the crème fraîche and bring to the boil. Season the sauce with salt, pepper and honey. The cooking juices from the duck fillets may also be added. Serve the sauce with the duck fillets.

Accompaniment: Tagliatelle or pommes duchesse (page 219).

Tip: You can also flambé the duck fillets with orange liqueur. To do this, heat 4-5 tablespoons orange liqueur in small saucepan, set light to the alcohol and pour over the duck fillets (photograph 3).

Game

Game is divided as follows:

Roe deer has delicious red-brown venison and is available on the market as fresh meat during the shooting season, between May and February.

Red deer has very tender, fine-fibered dark venison (young specimens up to 3 years old) and is available on the market as fresh meat during the shooting season, between June and February. During the rutting period the meat often has a strong, distinctive taste.

Fallow deer produces more tender venison than red deer but it is also more marbled with fatty streaks. Its taste very much resembles that of roe deer. The hunting season starts in July and continues until February. As well as being shot, fallow deer can also be bred.

Wild boar In the case of wild boar it is important that the meat comes from young animals (young boars). The meat of older boars is tougher, fatter, more difficult to digest and has a layer of bacon fat. The shooting season for young boars is from June until January.

Hares up to 8 months old have very tender, red-brown meat. The quality of the meat depends on the age of the ani-

mal and its environment. The shooting season is from October to January.

Pheasants, which are often sold ready-to-roast, are the size of chicken and have tender, juicy meat, especially young animals. The shooting season is from October until January. Pheasants are also often bred.

Partridges are the size of pigeons and produce very tender meat with a delicate taste. This is especially true when the animal is young. The shooting season is from September until December.

Preparation

The game offered in shops is usually already skinned and cut into pieces. The cuts usually available are the following:
- Saddle, leg, whole hare for roasting.
- Shoulder, foreleg for braising.
- Neck, belly, breast for stewing.

Game should always be well cooked.

Skinning

Game (except for wild fowl) must be skinned before it can be prepared. For this you will need a pointed, very sharp knife which you will slide with

great care under the sinewy skin and make an incision. Then gently pull the end of the cut sinew using your hand, slightly lifting the knife with the blade upwards and pulling off the skin in large strips.

Marinating/pickling

"Marinating" refers to the process of pickling the meat to alter the taste of the meat or to reduce its strong, "gamy" taste. Marinating is especially common in the case of older animals and cheaper cuts. The meat (frozen meat should be defrosted first) is marinated for a period of 12 hours to 4 days. This makes the meat more tender and juicier while reducing the strong gamy taste, as the meat absorbs the flavours of the marinade. Besides the usual main ingredients such as vinegar, wine or buttermilk, marinades also include condiments and onions. Condiments should only be added in small amounts in order to avoid excessive seasoning. Do not add salt to the marinade – it would dry out the meat. The meat should be completely covered by the marinade. Cover the container and refrigerate.

Basic recipe for a red wine marinade:

Take 200 g/7 oz onions, 150 g/ 5 oz carrots and 150 g/5 oz celeriac. Wash and chop coarsely. Add 2 sprigs of thyme, 1 tablespoon slightly crushed juniper berries, 1 tablespoon black peppercorns, 4 cloves and 2 bay leaves. Mix all together and arrange on top of the meat. Mix together 1 litre/1¾ pints (4½ cups) red wine and 40 ml/1½ tablespoons port and pour over the meat and vegetables.

Barding and larding

Larding consists of inserting strips of bacon into a large cut of meat with a larding needle. This may damage the meat

fibres, allowing the meat juices to run out and causing the meat to dry out. If buying already larded game, check that the bacon is fresh because it can easily go rancid while being stored.

In order to prevent the meat from drying out during the cooking process, lean game is wrapped in (barded with) slices of fatty or streaky bacon and the bacon is secured with kitchen string. The bacon can then be removed after cooking and the meat remains tender and juicy.

Very lean wild fowl should also be barded to prevent it from drying out.

The bacon is removed after cooking and can also be eaten

Carving saddle of hare and venison
Roast saddle of hare or venison is carved into individual servings as follows:
- Place the saddle on a carving board with the bone downwards.
- Cut along the bone with a sharp knife, then detach the bone underneath.
- Remove the small fillets on the underneath of the bone.
- Cut the meat which you have detached from the bone in pieces or slices and arrange on a preheated dish with the fillets.
If you do not have much time

you can also detach the saddle from the bone when still raw and briefly fry .

Frozen game
Deep-frozen game is available all year round in the shops. The meat will have become more tender as result of the freezing process. Frozen game may be kept at a temperature of -18 °C/0 °F for one year and wild fowl for 8–10 months. Frozen game should be defrosted in the refrigerator, covered, and the defrosted meat prepared immediately.

Saddle of venison, Baden style
With alcohol

Preparation time: about 90 minutes

1 saddle of venison with bones, weighing about 1.6 kg/3½ lb
salt
freshly ground pepper
75 g/3 oz sliced streaky bacon
1 onion
50 g/2 oz celeriac
100 g/3½ oz carrots
5 juniper berries
125 ml/4 fl oz (½ cup) dry red wine or vegetable stock
2-3 pears, e.g. Williams Christian
200 ml/7 fl oz (⅞ cup) sweet white wine
juice of 1 lemon
200 ml/7 fl oz (⅞ cup) dry red wine
250 ml/8 fl oz (1 cup) whipping cream
180 g/6½ oz cranberry preserve
dark sauce thickener (optional)

Per serving:
P: 67 g, F: 31 g, C: 29 g,
kJ: 2925, kcal: 699

1 Preheat the oven. Rinse the saddle of venison under cold running water, pat dry and remove the skin (photograph 1). Rub the meat with salt and pepper and place it in a casserole rinsed in water, and cover with slices of bacon.

2 Peel and finely chop the onions. Clean the celeriac and carrots, peel, wash, leave to drain and dice. Place the casserole without lid in the oven. As soon as the juices begin to brown, add the juniper berries and red wine or vegetable stock.

Top/bottom heat: **about 200 °C/400 °F (preheated),**
Fan oven: **about 180 °C/350 °F (not preheated),** Gas mark **6 (not preheated),**
Cooking time: **35-50 minutes.**

3 Meanwhile, wash the pears, cut in half and remove the core, preferably with a scoop-shaped melon baller (photograph 2). Add the pear halves to the white wine and lemon juice, bring to the boil and cook over medium heat for about 10 minutes. Take the pears out of the liquid with a skimming ladle and leave to cool.

4 Take the cooked meat out of the roasting tin, cover and let rest for about 10 minutes. Deglaze the cooking juices with red wine and strain with the vegetables through a sieve, bring to the boil and stir in the cream. Add 2 tablespoons cranberry sauce, bring back to the boil and allow to bubble for 3-5 minutes. You can add the meat juices which have run out of the resting meat to the sauce. Thicken the sauce with gravy thickener if you like, and season again with the various condiments.

5 Remove the slices of bacon. Loosen the meat from the bone, cut into slices and put back on the bone (photograph 3) and arrange on a preheated dish.

6 Fill the pear halves with the rest of the cranberry sauce and place around the saddle. Serve the sauce separately.

Accompaniment: Spätzle (page 226), mushrooms and red cabbage (page 175).

Haunch of venison
Suitable for freezing (6 servings)

Preparation time: about 3 hours, excluding marinating time

1.5 kg/3¼ lb haunch of
venison with bones
2 tablespoons cooking
oil, e.g. sunflower oil
1 teaspoon each dried
marjoram and thyme
1 teaspoon dried
rosemary
100 g/3½ oz thinly sliced
fatty bacon
salt
freshly ground pepper
about 150 ml/5 fl oz
(⅝ cup) hot game or
vegetable stock
1 onion
100 g/3½ oz carrots
150 g/5 oz leeks

For the sauce:
125 ml/4 fl oz (½ cup) red
wine
250 ml/8 fl oz (1 cup)
game or vegetable
stock
100 ml/3½ fl oz (½ cup)
whipping cream
20 g/¾ oz (3 table-
spoons) plain (all-
purpose) flour
2 tablespoons cold water
2 tablespoons cranberries
(from the jar)
some small thyme leaves

Per serving:
P: 46 g, F: 19 g, C: 6 g,
kJ: 1640, kcal: 392

1 Rinse the meat under cold running water, pat dry and remove the skin. Stir the marjoram, thyme and rosemary into the oil and coat the haunch with this mixture. Cover and leave in the refrigerator overnight.

2 Preheat the oven. Arrange half the bacon slices in a roasting pan, pre-rinsed with water. Sprinkle salt and pepper over the venison, place it on top of the bacon slices in the roasting pan and cover with the rest of the bacon slices. Put the roasting pan without lid in the oven.

Top/bottom heat: about 200 °C/400 °F (preheated),
Fan oven: about 180 °C/350 °F (not preheated), Gas mark 6 (not preheated),
Cooking time: about 60 minutes.

3 As soon as the cooking juices begin to brown add 150 ml/5 fl oz (⅝ cup) hot game or vegetable stock. Baste the meat from time to time with the cooking juices and replace the evaporated liquid with hot water or hot stock whenever necessary.

4 Meanwhile, peel the onions. Peel the carrots and cut off the green leaves and the tips. Remove the outer leaves of the leeks, cut off the root ends and dark leaves. Cut in half lengthways, wash thoroughly and leave to drain. Coarsely chop all the vegetables. After the 60 minutes roasting time, add the vegetables to the roasting pan with meat and cook for a further 60-90 minutes.

5 Allow the cooked venison to rest covered for about 10 minutes to ensure that the meat juices are well distributed. Remove the slices of bacon, cut into slices and arrange on a preheated dish.

6 To make the sauce, deglaze the cooking juices with red wine and game or vegetable stock. Strain this liquid with the vegetables through a sieve, add the cream and bring back to the boil. Mix flour and water together and stir well to obtain a smooth consistency. Add to the boiling liquid, stirring continuously to make sure that no lumps are formed. Simmer gently without a lid for about 5 minutes, stirring occasionally. Add the cranberries, thyme and if you like the meat juices that have run out from the meat while it was resting. Season the sauce and serve with the meat.

Accompaniment: Boiled potatoes (page 210) or potato dumplings (page 220) and red cabbage (page 175) or Brussels sprouts (page 175).

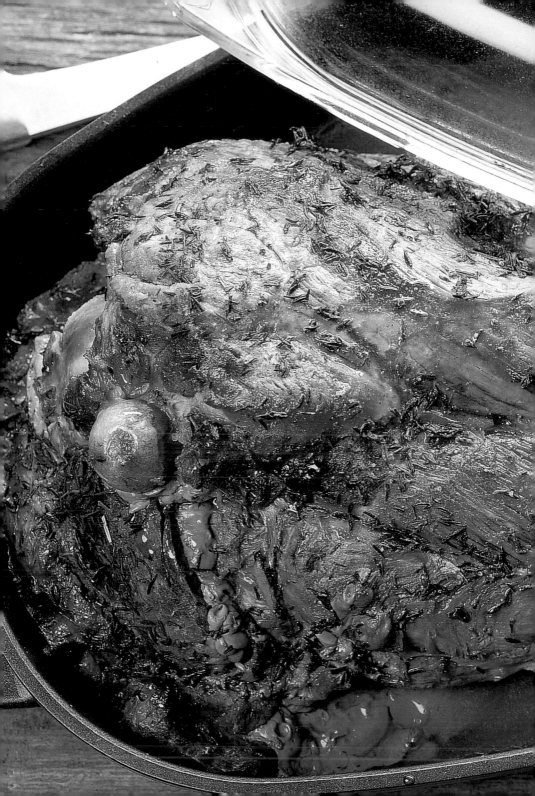

Venison ragout

For guests

Preparation time:
about 90 minutes

**800 g/1¾ lb venison
from the leg, boned,
e.g. deer, boar
75 g/3 oz streaky bacon
1 onion
30 g/1 oz (2 tablespoons)
clarified butter or
2 tablespoons cooking
oil, e.g. sunflower oil
salt
freshly ground pepper
10 g/⅓ oz (1½ table-
spoons) plain (all-
purpose) flour
4 juniper berries
3 cloves
2 pinches dried thyme
250 ml/8 fl oz (1 cup)
vegetable stock or
game stock
250 g/9 oz mushrooms or
chanterelles
4 teaspoons red currant
jelly
4 teaspoons port
50 g/2 oz (4 tablespoons)
cold butter flakes**

Per serving:
P: 47 g, F: 25 g, C: 8 g,
kJ: 1880, kcal: 449

1   Rinse the meat under cold running water, pat dry, remove the skin and cut into cubes of about 2.5 cm/1 in (photograph 1). Finely dice the bacon. Peel and chop the onion.

2   Heat the clarified butter or oil in a pan. Add the diced bacon and fry until golden brown. Now add the cubed meat, brown well on all sides and season with salt and pepper.

3   Add the chopped onion and brown with the meat. Sprinkle flour over the meat. Add a good half of the hot vegetable or game stock to the pan together with the juniper berries, cloves and thyme. Bring to the boil while stirring, then cover and cook the meat over medium heat for about 55 minutes. Replace the evaporated liquid with vegetable or game stock whenever necessary.

4   Meanwhile, cut the stalks off the mushrooms (photograph 2) and remove any bad parts, wipe clean with kitchen paper, rinse if necessary and pat dry (large mushrooms should be halved or quartered). Add the mushrooms to the ragout and cook for another 5 minutes.

5   Stir in the red currant jelly (photograph 3), beat in the butter flakes and season the ragout with salt and pepper.

Accompaniment: Boiled potatoes (page 210), potato dumplings (page 220) or Spätzle (page 226), red cabbage (page 175) or Brussels sprouts (page 175) and cranberry sauce.

Tip: Marinating the meat overnight in buttermilk will make the meat more tender and reduce the strong taste of game. Then pat thoroughly dry and cut into cubes.
The sauce may also be thickened with dark gravy thickener instead of butter.

Pheasant with sauerkraut and wine
A little more expensive

Preparation time:
about 1¾ hours

1 onion
1 can sauerkraut, drained
   weight 770 g/1¾ lb
1 small bay leaf
a few peppercorns
a few juniper berries
salt
250 ml/8 fl oz (1 cup)
   white wine
1 oven-ready pheasant of
   about 1 kg/2¼ lb
6 slices streaky bacon
200 g/7 oz black grapes
200 g/7 oz white grapes
some sugar

chervil or parsley
tomato segments

Per serving:
P: 58 g, F: 16 g, C: 19 g,
kJ: 2108, kcal: 503

1 Preheat the oven, top and bottom. Peel and chop the onion, then mix it well with the sauerkraut, bay leaf, peppercorns and juniper berries. Season with salt, put in an ovenproof dish or casserole and pour the wine over it.

2 Rinse the pheasant inside and out under cold running water, wipe dry, cut into quarters and rub with salt inside and out. Position it on the sauerkraut so that as much as possible is covered by the pheasant. Arrange the bacon slices over the pheasant. Cover the soufflé dish or roasting pan and put in the oven.

Top/bottom heat: about 200 °C/400 °F (preheated),
Fan oven: about 180 °C/350 °F (not preheated), Gas mark 6 (not preheated),
Cooking time: about 25 minutes.

3 At this point, remove the lid and **cook for a further 30 minutes at the same oven temperature.**

4 Meanwhile, wash the grapes, drain, cut in half and remove the pips.

5 Remove the cooked pheasant pieces from the ovenproof dish or casserole, cover and let rest for 10 minutes.

6 Add the grapes to the sauerkraut, mix well and season with sugar. Cover the ovenproof dish or casserole with a lid and return to the oven. **Cook for about another 10 minutes at the same oven temperature.**

7 Arrange the pheasant pieces on the sauerkraut on a preheated dish and garnish with chervil or parsley and tomato segments.

Accompaniment: Potato purée (page 218)

Tip: Instead of pheasant you can also use partridge.

Fish and seafood

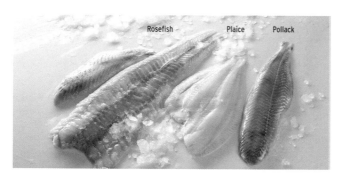

Rosefish   Plaice   Pollack

Fish is divided into sea fish and freshwater fish. Sea fish, which as the name implies, live in the sea and include fish such as rosefish, haddock, cod, turbot, brill and halibut, plaice, pollack, sole, tuna fish, salmon, mackerel and herring. After being caught, the fish are chilled on ice (not frozen) and immediately dispatched to the shops. In the case of longer fishing trips the fish are processed on board the fishing boat (for instance, filleted) and deep-frozen.

Freshwater fish live in rivers, streams, lakes and ponds and include eel, pike, rainbow trout, salmon trout, carp, whitefish, zander, tench and catfish. Freshwater fish are often kept live in a small water-tank before being killed to ensure freshness.

Characteristics of freshness
To check that a fish is fresh, make sure that:
1. the eyes are clear and firm with outward-curved lenses.
2. the gills are brilliant red without mucus (lift the gills slightly to see underneath).
3. the skin is very shiny and covered with transparent mucus (this turns blue in the stock when cooking).
4. the scales are firm.
5. the smell is fresh (in the case of sea fish, it smells of seawater or seaweed).

In the case of filleted fish or fish that has been cut up into pieces, it is more difficult to see whether it is fresh. The main criteria of freshness are a fresh smell and smooth, shiny flesh.

Deep-frozen fish is processed and frozen on the fishing boat immediately after being caught so that it is very fresh when it arrives in the shops.

Storage

Fresh fish should be placed immediately on a glass or china dish (perhaps on a saucer turned upside down so that any liquid oozing from the fish can run away), cover with clingfilm and keep refrigerated. The fish should be cooked the same day if possible.

Deep-frozen fish stored at -18 °C/-0.4 °F can be kept for 2–5 months depending on the fat content (respect the best-before date). It will defrost at room temperature in just a few hours, after which it must be processed immediately.

Preparation of freshwater fish

Usually freshwater fish is sold ready for cooking, in other words it will have been gutted, the scales partly removed, or filleted.

To remove the scales
1. Hold the tail of the fish firmly with one hand, if necessary using a towel or kitchen paper.
2. Using a flat, broad knife or scaler, scrape off the scales going from the tail towards the head. The scales are less likely to go all over the place

if you scrape them off under running water.

Removing the skin
Example: sole

1. Make an incision at the tail fin using a sharp knife.
2. Hold the tail fin down with a cloth.
3. Pull the skin steadily in the direction of the head.
4. Turn the fish over and repeat the operation on the other side.

Filleting fish
Example: sole

1. Having first removed the skin, cut the fish along the backbone from the head to the tail using a sharp knife.
2. Carefully lift the two fillets from the bones using a flat knife.
3. Turn the fish over and remove the two fillets on the other side in the same way.

In the case of round fish there are only two fillets:
1. Make a deep cut along the backbone from the head to the tail.
2. Make an incision behind the gills.
3. Lift the complete fillet away from the bones.
4. Using a knife, remove the bones from the fillet underneath.

5. Remove the skin of the fillets using a knife.

The three-step system

1. Cleaning
Rinse the whole fish or fish fillets under cold running water (in the case of whole fish, rinse it inside and out) and pat dry. In the case of a whole fish which will be cooked in stock, be careful not to damage the mucous membrane when rinsing and wiping the fish dry.

2 Pickling
In the past, fish used to be sprinkled with lemon juice, vinegar or white wine and left covered in the refrigerator to marinate for about 10-15 minutes. The purpose was to absorb the smell and firm up the flesh. Today pickling fish is no longer necessary because fresh fish correctly stored does not produce a fishy smell. Moreover, pickling has a tendency to dry out the flesh.

3 Salting
Whole fish and fish fillets should only be salted immediately before cooking because the salt draws out the fish juices, making the flesh dry. Fish which is going to be marinated should not be salted.

Fish smells

Fish smells can easily be prevented by following a few simple rules:

- Store the fish in a covered container in the refrigerator until it is used.
- Wash your hands and all the objects which have come into contact with the fish in cold water, or better still, rub with lemon juice or vinegar.
- Rinse used dishes in cold water first and only then wash them up carefully in hot water.

Cooking methods

The following cooking methods are suitable for preparing fish:

Poaching in stock, braising, steaming, frying, baking, deep-frying and smoking.

Fish is cooked when:

- the fins and bones can easily be removed.
- the eyes bulge out and appear cloudy.
- the skin can easily be pulled off.
- the flesh separates in flakes when pressed with a fork.

Cockles/scallops/mussels

Cockle   Pilgrim scallop

Common mussel

Cockles, mussels and oysters live in the sea. Their compressed bodies are surrounded by two shells which are held together on one side by a hinge-like joint. Their meat is tender and rich in protein but it goes off very quickly. This seafood is mostly available in the cooler seasons (the months with an "r"). There are also available deep-frozen or in cans. They are several kinds of these bivalves, for instance Pilgrim scallops, scallops, Venus mussels and common mussels.

Buying

- Only buy fresh mussels with closed shells. Throw away any that are already open because they are bad.
- Fresh mussels have a fresh seawater smell.

Preparing mussels

1. Wash the mussels thoroughly in plenty of cold water and brush each one separately until it no longer feels sandy. Any mussels which open while being washed are not edible!

2. Remove any filaments.

3. Put the mussels in the boiling liquid, cover and heat (do not boil) for about 10 minutes until they open, stirring occasionally. Any mussels that do not open

during this cooking process are not edible.

4. Remove the mussels from the cooking liquid with a skimming ladle and arrange in a preheated dish.

Crustaceans

Crustaceans are arthropods that live in stretches of water. The external skeleton is strengthened to varying degrees by deposits of calcium carbonate. Crustaceans discard their shells several times during the growing period. They breathe through gills. The shell contains a red dye that turns the shell of these brown-black animals a reddish colour.

Short-tailed crustaceans
Deep-sea prawns, Norway lobsters, giant prawns, North sea prawns.

Removing prawns from their shells

- Hold the cooked prawn by the head in one hand and grasp the tail with the other.
- Press the head and tail gently against each other, then twist and pull off the head.
- Squeeze the shell gently and remove the meat from it.
- In the case of giant prawns or scampi, the intestines must also be removed. These look like dark filaments and are situated below the upper back. Pull the intestines out either

with a knife or a wooden cocktail stick, or cut the prawn open along the back and remove the filaments of the intestines.

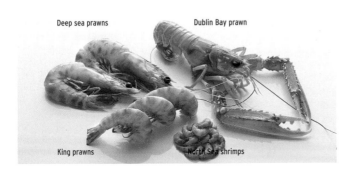

Deep sea prawns   Dublin Bay prawn

King prawns   North Sea shrimps

Fried fish fillet
For children

Preparation time:
about 30 minutes

**4 fish fillets of 200 g/
7 oz each, e.g. cod,
pollack or rosefish**
salt
freshly ground pepper
1 egg
4 teaspoons cold water
**40 g/1½ oz (6 table-
spoons) plain (all-
purpose) flour**
**50–75 g/2–3 oz (¼–1 cup)
dried breadcrumbs**
**75 ml/3 fl oz (⅜ cup)
cooking oil, e.g.
sunflower oil**
lemon slices (untreated)

Per serving:
P: 39 g, F: 15 g, C: 12 g,
kJ: 1398, kcal: 334

1 Wash the fish fillets under cold running water, pat well dry, cut
in serving-sized pieces and sprinkle with salt and pepper.

2 Beat the egg and water together with a fork in a deep plate. Roll
the fish fillets first in flour (photograph 1), then in egg and finally
in breadcrumbs. Press the breadcrumbs firmly onto the fish and
shake off any loose crumbs.

3 Heat the oil in a pan. Fry the fillets over medium heat for about
5 minutes per side until golden brown (photograph 2), then
leave to drain on kitchen paper (photograph 3).

4 Garnish the fish fillets with lemon slices and serve.

Tip: Instead of breadcrumbs, you can also roll the fish fillets in egg and
sesame seeds.

Accompaniment: **Potato salad (page 200) or parsley potatoes (page 210)
and tomato salad (page 195).**

Steamed fish
Low in fat

1 Rinse the cod fish under cold running water, pat dry and rub with salt and pepper inside and outside.

2 Meanwhile, prepare the soup vegetables. Peel the celeriac and cut out any bad parts. Peel the carrots and cut off the green leaves and tips. Wash the celeriac and carrots and leave to drain. Remove the outer leaves of the leeks, cut off the root ends and dark green leaves. Cut in half lengthways, wash thoroughly and leave to drain. Peel the onion and cut into quarters.

3 Put the soup vegetables and onion in a large, wide saucepan with the water, a pinch of salt, bay leaf, peppercorns, cloves and allspice berries. Bring to the boil, cover and simmer gently for about 10 minutes.

4 Add the white wine and bring to the boil again. Add the fish, cover and simmer gently for 15-20 minutes over a low heat, perhaps carefully turning it once.

5 Carefully remove the fish from the saucepan and put it on a preheated dish.

Accompaniment: Boiled potatoes and melted brown butter, mustard sauce (page 140) or mushroom sauce (page 142).

Tip: Garnish the fish before serving with lemon segments and parsley.

Variation: Other fish can be used instead of cod, but some have different cooking times. Cod, pollack and rosefish have a cooking time of about 15 minutes, zander and pike (both scaled but without fins and with heads) have a cooking time of about 20 minutes.

Preparation time:
about 50 minutes

1 kg/2¼ lb prepared cod,
   in one piece or fillets
salt
freshly ground pepper
1 bunch soup vegetables
1 onion
250 ml/8 fl oz (1 cup)
   water
1 bay leaf
5 peppercorns
3 cloves
3 allspice berries
125 ml/4 fl oz (½ cup)
   white wine

Per serving:
P: 44 g, F: 2 g, C: 0 g,
kJ: 803, kcal: 193

Fish brochettes on a bed of rocket and tomato salad

A little more expensive

Preparation time:
about 60 minutes

For the brochettes:
2 courgettes, about
    200 g/7 oz each
500 ml/17 fl oz (2¼ cups)
    water
salt
4 zander fillets, about
    125 g/4½ oz each, or
    6 plaice fillets 80 g/
    3 oz each
freshly ground pepper

For the salad:
1 bunch short-stemmed
    rocket, about 125 g/
    4½ oz
400 g/14 oz beef
    tomatoes
2 tablespoons balsamic
    vinegar
1 pinch sugar
5 tablespoons olive oil

In addition:
4 thin kebab skewers

Per serving:
P: 26 g, F: 15 g, C: 5 g,
kJ: 1078, kcal: 257

1   To make the brochettes, wash the courgettes, wipe dry, cut off the ends and cut lengthways into 12 thin slices using a slicing machine. Bring the water to the boil in a large saucepan. Add ½ teaspoon salt. Put the sliced courgettes in the salted boiling water, bring back to the boil, remove from the water, dip in cold water and pat dry.

2   Rinse the fish fillets under cold running water, pat dry, cut in half lengthways and sprinkle with salt and pepper. Roll up the courgette slices and fish fillets, making sure that the side with the skin is on the inside. Thread the rolled courgettes and fish fillets on 4 thin skewers (2 rolled zander or 3 rolled plaice fillets and 3 rolled courgette slices per skewer).

3   For the salad: Remove any wilted, yellow leaves and thick stems, wash and spin dry. Wash the tomatoes, leave to drain, make a cross-shaped incision, dip briefly in boiling water, then dip in cold water. Peel the tomatoes, remove the stalks and cut into cubes.

4   For the salad dressing: Stir the salt, pepper and sugar into the balsamic vinegar. Stir in half the oil and whisk to obtain a smooth mixture.

5   Heat the rest of the oil in a non-stick pan. Add the brochettes and fry over medium heat for about 10 minutes, turning them over now and again.

6   Arrange the rocket and diced tomatoes on the plates. Place the brochettes on top and sprinkle the dressing over them.

Accompaniment: **Warm baguette or ciabatta.**

Tip: Instead of zander or plaice fillets, 12 lemon sole or sole fillets (about 40 g/1½ oz each) can be used. The fillets must not be cut in half lengthways. Deep-frozen fillets should be defrosted according to the instructions on the package.

Rolled fish fillets on a bed of leeks

For guests

Preparation time:
about 45 minutes

4 pieces of fish fillet,
   about 150 g/5 oz each,
   e.g. rosefish, pollack or
   cod fillet
salt
freshly ground pepper
8 thin slices bacon, about
   10 g/¹⁄₃ oz each
1 kg/2¼ lb leeks
50 g/2 oz (4 tablespoons)
   butter or margarine
125 ml/4 fl oz (½ cup)
   vegetable stock
125 ml/4 fl oz (½ cup)
   whipping cream
20 g/³⁄₄ oz (3 table-
   spoons) plain (all-
   purpose) flour
2 tablespoons whipping
   cream
grated nutmeg

In addition:
4 wooden cocktail sticks

Per serving:
P: 37 g, F: 27 g, C: 10 g,
kJ: 1796, kcal: 428

1   Rinse the fish fillets under cold running water, pat dry and sprinkle with salt and pepper. Place 2 slices of bacon on each fish fillet, roll up the fillets and secure with wooden cocktail sticks.

2   To prepare the leeks: Remove the outer leaves of the leeks, cut off the root ends and dark leaves. Cut into half lengthways, wash thoroughly, leave to drain and cut into pieces 2 cm/³⁄₄ in long.

3   Melt the butter or margarine in a large pan. Add the leeks and season with salt and pepper. Add the vegetable stock and cream, cover and cook for about 5 minutes.

4   Now arrange the rolled fish fillets in between the leeks, cover again and cook gently over low heat for another 10 minutes. Remove the fish fillets, cover and keep in a warm place.

5   Stir the flour into the cream, add to the leeks and bring to the boil, stirring continuously. Season the leeks with salt, pepper and nutmeg, and arrange on a preheated dish with the rolled fish fillets.

Accompaniment: Boiled potatoes (page 210) or rice.

Tip: Add white wine to the leeks.

Variation: Instead of leeks, you can serve the fish fillets on a bed of spinach. Take 1.5 kg/3¼ lb spinach and remove any yellow, wilted leaves and thick stems. Wash carefully in plenty of water. Peel 1–2 onions and 1–2 cloves of garlic and chop finely. Heat 20 g/³⁄₄ oz (1½ tablespoons) butter or 2 tablespoons olive oil in a pan. Add the chopped onions and garlic and fry while stirring. Add the wet spinach and season with salt, pepper and nutmeg. Cover and braise the spinach for about 5 minutes. Add 150 ml/5 fl oz (⁵⁄₈ cup) whipping cream and adjust the seasoning again. Put the rolled fish fillets between the spinach and cook as indicated above. Remove the cooked fish fillets and keep in a warm place. Thicken the spinach with light gravy thickener.

Truite à la meunière (photograph)

Classic

Preparation time:
about 20 minutes

4 prepared trout, 200 g/
7 oz each, salt, pepper
40 g/1½ oz (6 table-
spoons) plain (all-
purpose) flour
2 tablespoons cooking
oil, e.g. sunflower oil
40 g/1½ oz (3 table-
spoons) butter
lemon slices (untreated)

Per serving:
P: 31 g, F: 8 g, C: 4 g,
kJ: 929, kcal: 222

1 Rinse the trout under cold running water, pat dry and rub with salt inside and out. Coat in flour and shake off any excess.

2 Heat the oil in a pan, add the trout and brown on both sides over medium heat. Add the butter and melt. Fry the trout for about 10 minutes, turning them over frequently.

3 Garnish the trout with lemon slices before serving.

Accompaniment: Boiled potatoes sprinkled with parsley (page 210), mixed green salad (page 192).

Variation: Trout with almonds (photograph): add 50-75 g (2-3 oz) slivered almonds and brown in the pan with the trout. Sprinkle over before serving.

Salmon trout with leaf spinach

For guests (6 servings)

Preparation time: about 80 minutes, excluding oven cooking time

1.5 kg/3¼ lb leaf spinach
200 g/7 oz shallots
2 cloves of garlic
300 g/10 oz mushrooms
150 g/5 oz tomatoes
4 teaspoons butter or
margarine
salt
freshly ground pepper
grated nutmeg
1 large salmon trout,
1.3 kg/2¾ lb, or 2 small
salmon trout, each
about 600 g/1¼ lb
75 g/3 oz smoked,
streaky bacon
1 bunch parsley
1 lemon (untreated)

1 Remove any yellow, wilted leaves of the spinach including the thick stems. Wash carefully in plenty of water and leave to drain. Peel the shallots and cloves of garlic. Cut half the shallots into eighths and finely chop the rest with the cloves of garlic. Wipe the mushrooms clean with kitchen paper, slice off the base of the stalks or remove entirely if they are tough and woody. If necessary rinse and pat dry. Slice half the mushrooms and chop up the rest finely. Wash the tomatoes, wipe dry, remove the stalks, cut into quarters and dice.

2 Melt the butter or margarine in pan. Add the shallots, cut into eighths, the garlic and sliced mushrooms and braise briefly. Add the spinach and braise briefly, but sufficiently to make it "collapse". Season with salt, pepper and nutmeg. Stir the diced tomatoes into the spinach.

3 Preheat the oven. Rinse the sea trout under cold running water inside and out, then pat dry. Rub with salt both inside and out. Chop the bacon finely. Rinse the parsley, pat dry, remove the leaves from the stalks and chop finely. Wash the lemon in hot water, grate the zest, cut the lemon in half and squeeze. Mix together the diced bacon, chopped mushrooms and shallots,

(continued on page 122)

6 thin slices streaky bacon

Per serving:
P: 48 g, F: 10 g, C: 5 g,
kJ: 1311, kcal: 312

parsley, grated lemon zest and juice and stuff this mixture inside the abdominal cavity of the trout.

4 Arrange the spinach in a large rectangular soufflé dish or roasting pan. Place the stuffed trout on top and perhaps garnish with remaining stuffing. Arrange the slices of bacon on the trout and put the soufflé or roasting pan in the oven on the third shelf from the bottom.

Top/bottom heat: **about 200 °C/400 °F (preheated),**
Fan oven: **about 180 °C/350 °F (preheated),** Gas mark **6 (preheated),**
Cooking time: **about 35 minutes (small trout), about 55 minutes (large trout).**

Accompaniment: **Boiled potatoes (page 210) or rice.**

Plaice with bacon
For guests

Preparation time:
about 30 minutes

4 prepared plaice, about 300 g/10 oz each
salt
freshly ground pepper
40 g/1½ oz (6 table-spoons) plain (all-purpose) flour
about 150 g/5 oz lean, streaky bacon
2-3 tablespoons cooking oil, e.g. sunflower oil
lemon segments
some sprigs of dill

Per serving:
P: 36 g, F: 9 g, C: 6 g,
kJ: 1039, kcal: 248

1 Rinse the plaice under cold running water, pat dry, rub with salt and pepper and coat in flour (photograph 1). Dice the bacon. Heat the oil in a large pan and fry the diced bacon so that the fat runs out (photograph 2). Then remove from the pan and keep in a warm place.

2 Depending on the size of the pan, brown the plaice on both sides in the bacon fat for about 15 minutes, one after the other (photograph 3). Add a little more fat if necessary. Arrange the plaice on a preheated dish and keep warm until all the plaice are cooked.

3 Sprinkle the diced bacon over the plaice and garnish with the lemon segments and sprigs of dill.

Accompaniment: **Boiled potatoes (page 210) and lamb's lettuce (page 191).**

Tip: You can also brown 150-200 g/6-7 oz crabmeat in the bacon fat and sprinkle over the plaice with the bacon.

Caprese fish

Easy

Preparation time:
about 55 minutes

4 tomatoes
2 small courgettes
250 g/9 oz mozzarella
 cheese
salt
freshly ground pepper
2 teaspoons dried Italian
 herbs
2-3 tablespoons olive oil
4 pieces rosefish or
 pollack fillet,
 130 g/4½ oz each
a few basil leaves

In addition:
fat for the dish

Per serving:
P: 38 g, F: 27 g, C: 4 g,
kJ: 1717, kcal: 410

1 Wash the tomatoes, wipe dry, remove the stalks and cut into slices.

2 Wash the courgettes, wipe dry, trim off the ends and cut into slices about 5 mm/³⁄₁₆ in thick. Drain the mozzarella and cut into 12 slices.

3 Preheat the oven and arrange half the sliced tomatoes, sliced courgettes and mozzarella slices overlapping in a shallow, greased soufflé dish. Sprinkle with salt, pepper and half the herbs, and pour 2 tablespoons oil on top.

4 Rinse the fish fillets under cold running water, pat dry, sprinkle with salt and pepper and arrange on the vegetable and cheese mixture. Cover with the rest of the sliced tomatoes, courgettes and mozzarella slices, arranged to overlap.

5 Sprinkle with salt, pepper and the rest of the mixed herbs and pour the remaining oil on top. Put the dish in the oven without a lid.

Top/bottom heat: **about 200 °C/400 °F (preheated)**,
Fan oven: **about 180 °C/350 °F (preheated)**, Gas mark **6 (preheated)**,
Cooking time: **25-30 minutes**.

6 Rinse the basil, pat dry, remove the leaves from the stems, chop finely and sprinkle over the fish gratin.

Accompaniment: **Rice or potato purée (page 218).**

Rosefish casserole with shrimps
Quick

Preparation time:
about 35 minutes

600 g/1¼ lb rosefish fillets
200 g/7 oz mushrooms
2 cloves garlic
4 teaspoons cooking oil, e.g. sunflower or olive oil
300 g/10 oz prepared shrimps
30 ml/1 fl oz (2 table- spoons) brandy
salt
freshly ground pepper
150 g/5 oz crème fraîche
1-2 tablespoons chopped parsley

Per serving:
P: 44 g, F: 23 g, C: 3 g,
kJ: 1711, kcal: 410

1 Rinse the rosefish under cold running water, pat dry, remove any remaining bones and cut the fillets in cubes of about 3 cm/1¼ in.

2 Wipe the mushrooms clean with kitchen paper, rinse if necessary and pat dry. Trim the stalk ends, remove any bad parts and slice thinly. Peel the cloves of garlic and chop coarsely.

3 Heat the oil in a pan. Add the sliced mushrooms and chopped garlic and fry lightly.

4 Add the fish and fry briefly with the mushrooms and garlic. Now add the shrimps, heat up again, cover and braise for about 5 minutes.

5 Season with brandy, salt and pepper. Stir in the crème fraîche. Sprinkle with parsley and serve immediately.

Accompaniment: Rice with wild rice or noodles tossed in butter and mixed green salad (page 192).

Tip: You can also use monkfish (angler fish) or sea bass (loup de mer) instead of rosefish.
If you use deep-frozen shrimps, rinse them briefly under cold running water and pat thoroughly dry.
Instead of parsley you can use dill and add 2–3 peeled, chopped tomatoes together with the shrimps.

Herring fillets, home-made style
(photograph)
Good for preparing in advance

Preparation time: about 30
minutes, excluding marinating time

**8 pickled herring fillets
(Matjes, about 600
g/1¼ lb)
250 ml/8 fl oz (1 cup)
water, salt, 3 onions
400 g/14 oz apples
150 g/5 oz pickled
gherkins (from the jar)
375 ml/12 fl oz (1½ cups)
whipping cream
2 tablespoons lemon juice
salt, pepper, some sugar**

Per serving:
P: 30 g, F: 53 g, C: 15 g,
kJ: 2767, kcal: 660

1   Rinse the herring fillets under cold running water, pat dry, remove any bones that may still remain and cut the fillets in cubes of 2 cm/¾ in.

2   Bring water to the boil in a pan. Add some salt. Peel the onions, cut in half, slice and blanch briefly in the boiling salted water, then leave to drain.

3   Wash the apples, peel, cut into quarters and remove the cores. Drain the pickled gherkins. Slice the apples and pickled gherkins.

4   Mix the lemon juice and cream together, season with salt, pepper and sugar, and stir in the sliced onions, apples and pickled gherkins. Put the herring fillets in the sauce, cover and leave in the refrigerator for about 12 hours to marinate.

Accompaniment: **Boiled potatoes and fried onion rings, green beans with bacon (page 162) or fried potatoes (page 216).**

Smoked fish mousse
For guests

Preparation time: about 15 minutes,
excluding cooling time

**2 smoked trout fillets,
about 125 g/4½ oz each
30 g/1 oz (2 tablespoons)
soft butter
2–4 teaspoons sour cream
1–1¼ teaspoons lemon juice
salt
freshly ground pepper
some lamb's lettuce
½ teaspoon pink pepper
berries**

Per serving:
P: 14 g, F: 9 g, C: 0 g,
kJ: 591, kcal: 141

1   Chop the trout fillets coarsely, remove any bones that may be left and purée the fillets with butter, sour cream and lemon juice.

2   Season the mixture with salt and pepper and refrigerate for about 60 minutes.

3   Cut off the root ends of the lamb's lettuce in such a way that the leaves still hold together. Remove yellowing, wilted leaves, wash the lettuce thoroughly, spin dry and arrange on 4 plates.

4   Shape the smoked fish mousse into balls using 2 tablespoons, dipped in hot water, and arrange on the lamb's lettuce salad. Garnish with pink pepper berries before serving.

Accompaniment: **Ciabatta (Italian white bread), wholewheat bread or black bread.**

Tip: **The smoked fish mousse can also be served as a starter.**

Marinated salmon

Good for preparing in advance (8 servings)

Preparation time: about 25 minutes, excluding marinating time

1 kg/2¼ lb fresh salmon
3 bunches dill
40 g/1½ oz salt
30 g/1 oz (2 tablespoons) sugar

For the dill sauce:
1 bunch dill
2 tablespoons strong mustard
2 tablespoons medium mustard
3 rounded tablespoons sugar
2 tablespoons white wine vinegar
3 tablespoons cooking oil, e.g. sunflower oil

Per serving:
P: 24 g, F: 15 g, C: 12 g,
kJ: 1144, kcal: 274

1   Rinse the salmon under cold running water, pat dry, cut in half lengthways and remove the bones, using tweezers if necessary (photograph 1).

2   Rinse the dill, pat dry, pull the leaves off the stems and chop finely. Mix the salt and sugar together and sprinkle on the two salmon halves, then sprinkle the chopped dill on top.

3   Place one salmon half with the skin downwards in a large shallow dish that is larger than the fish and a chopping board that will weigh it down. Put the other salmon half on top with the skin facing upward and cover with clingfilm. Put a small chopping board (which should be larger than the fish) on top and weigh it down with 2 or 3 weights or full, unopened cans (photograph 2). Keep the salmon refrigerated for 2–3 days, turning it periodically two or three times and basting it with the marinade.

4   Cut the salmon into thin slices at an angle towards the skin side (photograph 3) and arrange on a dish.

5   For the dill sauce, rinse the dill under cold running water, pat dry, pull the leaves off the stems and chop finely. Stir the two kinds of mustard, sugar and vinegar together and little by little whisk in the oil. Stir in the dill and serve the sauce with the salmon.

Accompaniment: **Black bread or farm-baked bread with butter.**

Tip: Before marinating the salmon, sprinkle with 1–2 tablespoons crushed white peppercorns and/or 1 tablespoon crushed juniper berries.

Variation: For **marinated salmon trout**, rinse 1 prepared salmon trout (about 1 kg/2¼ lb) under cold running water, pat dry and cut in half lengthways. Remove the backbone and the rest of the bones. Then follow the instructions above from stage 2 onwards.

Scampi brochettes
A little more expensive

Preparation time: about 40 minutes, excluding defrosting time

12 large frozen prawns, shelled with heads removed
4 cocktail tomatoes
½ yellow and ½ green pepper
4 cloves garlic
8 small mushrooms

For the mixture:
2 cloves garlic
30 g/1 oz (2 tablespoons) butter or margarine
2 teaspoons lemon juice
salt
freshly ground pepper
1 pinch sugar

In addition:
8 wooden or metal kebab skewers

Per serving:
P: 4 g, F: 7 g, C: 4 g,
kJ: 385, kcal: 92

1   Defrost the scampi following the instructions on the package. Then rinse the scampi under cold running water and pat dry.

2   Wash the cherry tomatoes, pat dry, cut in half and remove the stalks. Remove the stalks, white skin and seeds of the pepper halves. Wash the peppers and cut into large pieces. Peel the cloves of garlic and cut in half. Wipe the mushrooms clean with kitchen paper, rinse if necessary and pat dry. Cut off the stalk ends, remove any bad parts and slice. Thread all the ingredients alternately on wooden or stainless steel skewers.

3   For the mixture peel the cloves of garlic and push through a garlic press. Melt the butter or margarine. Add the garlic, lemon juice, salt, pepper and sugar, stir well and coat the brochettes with this mixture.

4   Heat a non-stick pan without fat. Place the brochettes in the pan, add the scampi and cook for 2 minutes on each side.

Accompaniment: Risotto, rice or baguette and mixed green salad.

Tip: The brochettes can also be grilled. Put them on aluminium foil under the preheated oven grill for about 5 minutes.

Mussels cooked in wine

Classic

Preparation time:
about 60 minutes

2 kg/4½ lb mussels
2 onions
1 bunch soup vegetables
50 g/2 oz (4 tablespoons)
butter or margarine
500 ml/17 fl oz (2¼ cups)
dry white wine
salt
freshly ground pepper

Per serving:
P: 10 g, F: 12 g, C: 2 g,
kJ: 1027, kcal: 245

1   Wash the mussels thoroughly in plenty of cold water and brush each one individually (photograph 1) until they no longer feel sandy (any mussels that open while being washed are not edible). Remove filaments if there are any (photograph 2).

2   Peel the onions and cut in rings. Prepare the soup vegetables: peel the celeriac and remove the bad parts, peel the carrots and cut off the green leaves and the tips. Wash the celeriac and carrots and leave to drain: Remove the outer leaves of the leeks, cut off the root ends and dark leaves. Cut in half lengthways, wash thoroughly and leave to drain. Coarsely chop the vegetables.

3   Melt the butter or margarine in a pan. Add the onions and soup vegetables and fry briefly while stirring. Add the white wine, season with salt and pepper and bring to the boil. Put the mussels in, cover and heat them without boiling until they open up (about 10 minutes) stirring occasionally. (Any mussels that have not opened during cooking are not edible).

4   Remove the mussels from the cooking liquid with a skimming ladle (photograph 3) and put in a preheated bowl. Strain the cooking liquid through a sieve, season with salt and pepper and serve with the mussels.

Accompaniment: **Wholemeal bread with butter.**

Variation: For **mussels Livorno style** (main photograph), prepare the mussels as indicated in point 1. Peel 6 tomatoes and chop into cubes. Peel 2 onions and chop finely. Peel 2 cloves of garlic and push through a garlic press. Finely chop 2 preserved chillies. Heat 8 tablespoons olive oil in a large pan. Add the onions, garlic and chillies and braise, stirring continuously. Add the chopped tomatoes and 200 ml/7 fl oz (⅞ cup) vegetables stock or white wine and bring to the boil. Add the mussels and braise for about 10 minutes, stirring now and again. Season with salt and pepper and garnish with lemon quarters before serving.

Sauces

A good sauce should complete and emphasize the taste of a dish without dominating it. Many dishes produce roasting juices or stock during the cooking process which can then be used to make a sauce. On the other hand, some dishes, such as fried or grilled meat or fish or vegetables, do not produce any juices or stock that could be used as a base for a sauce. In this case you can either use deep-frozen home-made stock, for instance, brown beef stock (page 144) or white poultry stock (page 145), or bought ready-made products such as instant stock cubes or granules.

Stock

A stock is a concentrated liquid which is used when boiling, braising, frying or roasting meat, poultry, game, fish or vegetables.

To make a white stock, cook bones, meat, fish trimmings (the pieces left over after filleting), fish or soup vegetables for a long time (2-3 hours, fish about 1 hour) in water seasoned with spices and herbs. Stocks which are made from meat, bones and gristle set as jelly when they cool down. The cold set stock can then be spooned out like jelly.

To make a brown stock, add a little water, stock or wine to the roasting or braising juices of beef, veal, poultry, bones and vegetables. The liquid is boiled in order to reduce it and small amounts of liquid are then added. The more often this process is repeated the stronger and tastier the stock will be.

Types of sauces

1. Basic white sauces

A basic white sauce (page 140) is based on a roux made from flour fried until light yellow. White sauces can easily be varied by adding cheese, capers, herbs, curry powder, lemon juice, white, horseradish or mustard.

2. Brown gravy

A dark basic sauce (page 141) is based on a roux made from flour fried until light or dark brown. Brown gravy can be varied by adding red currant jelly, cranberry jelly, orange juice, sour cherries, orange marmalade, green peppercorns, red wine, Madeira, sherry, cognac, mustard or crème fraîche.

3. Beaten sauces

A beaten sauce made from very fresh egg yolk, spices and liquid (for instance wine, stock, juice) which is beaten until thick and foamy over a hot bain-marie to which melted, slightly cooled-down butter is added at the end. Here are a few guidelines you should follow:

- Preferably, use a stainless steel bain-marie bowl.
- For the bain-marie base, fill a large saucepan ¾ full with water. The water should only bubble very gently (simmering) and not boil.
- Place the bain-marie bowl with the ingredients in the saucepan with the water and beat the mixture with a whisk or hand-mixer set at the lowest power until it becomes thick and foamy.
- Now slowly add the melted, slightly cooled-down butter to the egg yolk mixture.
- Taste with a clean spoon.
- Prepare the sauce as near as possible to the time of serving because it collapses very quickly (it can be kept warm for a short time over the hot water).

Beaten sauces can be varied by adding herbs, lemon juice, white wine, crushed peppercorns, paprika, grated cheese or orange juice. Sweet beaten sauces can be enhanced by the addition of vanilla, ginger, orange juice, lemon juice or white wine.

4. Cold sauces

To make cold sauces, all the ingredients are mixed together when cold (for instance, mayonnaise, remoulade and salad dressings such as vinaigrette). When making cold sauces using raw egg it is extremely important to use only fresh eggs. Keep the finished sauce in the refrigerator and use within 24 hours.

Thickening sauces

The base of a sauce is in fact already created during the cooking process. But this base does usually not have the desired consistency, so a thickening agent will be needed. The seasoning will also need to be adjusted when the sauce is finished.

Roux

Brown the flour in melted fat (for instance butter or margarine) until light or dark brown. Add stock to the flour and fat mixture stirring constantly and cook the sauce until the right consistency has been achieved.

Flour and butter

Knead together ⅔ softened butter with ⅓ flour and add to the boiling liquid little by little until the desired consistency has been achieved. This type of sauce thickens very quickly.

Vegetables

Braise some vegetables and onions, then blend together with the cooking juices. If desired, the mixture can be passed through a sieve. This makes a light, low calorie thickening agent.

Flour, cornflour

Mix together some cold liquid (for instance water or stock) and flour or cornflour. Add this mixture to the hot liquid and cook for about 5 minutes. The aroma of more delicate sauces can often be masked with this kind of method.

Egg yolk

Mix together an egg yolk with a little milk or cream and stir slowly into the sauce which must first be removed from the heat. Now stir vigorously until the sauce thickens. Do not bring back to the boil because the egg yolk would curdle.

Whipping cream

Stir whipping cream into the sauce and cook until the sauce has the desired consistency. Cream with a 10% fat content should not be used because it will flocculate over heat.

Crème fraîche, double cream

Add crème fraîche or double cream to the sauce and stir well. The high fat content will make the sauce thicken beautifully.

Butter

Stir ice-cold flakes of butter into the sauce using a mixing spoon or whisk. The sauce must remain hot throughout but not boil. Serve immediately because this type of sauce becomes thin very quickly.

Pumpernickel, gingerbread

Stir finely crumbled pumpernickel or gingerbread into the liquid, bring to the boil and simmer briefly. Then strain the sauce through a sieve if desired. This is a traditional method for thickening dark sauces.

Gravy thickener

Stir in light or dark gravy thickener (depending on the kind of sauce you are making) into the liquid following the instruction on the package. Very quick and easy.

Frankfurt green sauce (photograph)
Classic

Preparation time:
about 30 minutes

about 150 g/5 oz fresh
herbs for Frankfurt
green sauce
150 g/5 oz crème fraîche
or sour cream
1 small onion
150 g/5 oz natural yogurt
3-4 teaspoons olive oil
1 teaspoon mustard
1 squeeze lemon juice
½ teaspoon sugar
salt, white pepper

Per serving:
P: 4 g, F: 15 g, C: 7 g,
kJ: 736, kcal: 176

1 Rinse the herbs, pat dry, remove the leaves from the stems, chop coarsely and purée with 2 tablespoons crème fraîche or sour cream. Or simply chop the herbs very finely. Peel the onion and chop finely.

2 Now stir the herbs and cream mixture or the finely chopped herbs into the rest of the crème fraîche or soured cream together with the yogurt, chopped onion, oil and mustard. Season the sauce with lemon juice, sugar, salt and pepper and refrigerate until serving.

Uses: Frankfurt green sauce can be served with new potatoes, with hard-boiled eggs or with boiled beef.

Tip: The "real" Frankfurt sauce includes 7 fresh herbs, but the herbs can be varied according to the season. You can also buy bunches of mixed herbs, specially put together for Frankfurt green sauce, each about 150 g/5 oz. If these are not available where you live, you can also buy a large bunch of mixed herbs, for instance, parsley, chives, chervil, burnet, borage, lemon balm, cress or sorrel. If you cannot find fresh herbs you can also use deep-frozen herbs (4 packs of 25 g/1 oz each).

Cheese sauce
Easy

Preparation time:
about 15 minutes

30 g/1 oz (2 tablespoons)
butter or margarine
25 g/1 oz (4 tablespoons)
flour
375 ml/12 fl oz (1½ cups)
vegetable stock
150 g/5 oz soft cheese
salt
a few squeezes of lemon
juice

1 Melt the butter or margarine in a saucepan. Add the flour and stir until the mixture turns pale yellow.

2 Add the vegetable stock and stir vigorously with a whisk, making sure that there are no lumps.

3 Bring the sauce to the boil and simmer gently for 5 minutes without a lid, stirring occasionally.

4 Add the processed cheese and stir to make it melt in the sauce. Season with salt and lemon juice.

Uses: Cheese sauce is delicious served with Brussels sprouts (page 175), or with meat such as medallions of pork.

(continued on page 140)

Tip: To reduce the calories you can use half of the cheese and replace the other half with herb or paprika quark. The sauce should not be allowed to boil after the quark has been added.

Variation: To make a **blue cheese sauce**, use only 10 g/⅓ oz flour, replace the processed cheese with 150 g/5 oz Roquefort or gorgonzola and add 5 tablespoons whipping cream. Season the sauce with 1-2 tablespoons white wine instead of lemon juice and a little pepper. Serve with noodles.

Per serving: **P: 6 g, F: 18 g, C: 5 g, kJ: 845, kcal: 202**

Basic white sauce
Q u i c k

Preparation time:
about 15 minutes

25 g/1 oz (2 tablespoons)
   butter or margarine
20 g/¾ oz (3 table-
   spoons) plain (all-
   purpose) flour
375 ml/12 fl oz (1½ cups)
   stock, e.g vegetable
   stock
salt
freshly ground pepper

Per serving:
P: 1 g, F: 5 g, C: 4 g,
kJ: 274, kcal: 65

1 Melt the butter or margarine in a pan. Add the flour and stir over heat until the mixture turns a pale yellow.

2 Add the stock and stir vigorously using a whisk, making sure that there are no lumps.

3 Bring the sauce to the boil and simmer gently for about 5 minutes without the lid on, stirring occasionally. Season with salt and pepper.

Uses: White sauce is an ideal base for herb and cheese sauces and is perfect for serving with vegetables, fish or fried meat.

Variation 1: To make **mustard sauce**, make the white sauce with 250 ml/ 8 fl oz (1 cup) milk and 125 ml/4 fl oz (½ cup) whipping cream instead of the 375 ml/12 fl oz (1½ cups) of stock. Finally, stir in 2 tablespoons medium-hot mustard and season the sauce with lemon juice, sugar and salt.

Variation 2: To make **horseradish sauce**, make the white sauce with 125 ml/ 4 fl oz (½ cup) vegetable stock, 125 ml/4 fl oz (½ cup) milk and 125 ml/4 fl oz (½ cup) whipping cream instead of the 375 ml/12 fl oz (1½ cups) of stock. Finally, stir in 2 tablespoons grated horseradish (from a jar) and season the sauce with salt, white pepper, sugar and lemon juice.

Variation 3: To make **herb sauce**, make the white sauce with 250 ml/8 fl oz (1 cup) milk and 125 ml/4 fl oz (½ cup) vegetable stock instead of the 375 ml/ 12 fl oz (1½ cups) of stock. Finally, stir in 3 tablespoons chopped herbs (for instance parsley, chervil or dill) and 2 tablespoons crème fraîche, then season the sauce with salt, pepper and grated nutmeg.

Basic brown sauce
Quick

1   Melt the butter or margarine in a pan. Add the flour and stir over heat until the mixture turns a medium to dark brown. Add the stock and stir vigorously using a whisk, making sure that there are no lumps.

2   Bring the sauce to the boil and simmer gently for about 5 minutes without the lid on, stirring occasionally. Season with salt and pepper.

Uses: Brown sauce is ideal with liver or with ragouts made from dark meat.

Variation: Clean and wash 1 bunch of soup vegetables, cut into small pieces and soften in the butter. Dust with the flour and make the sauce as described above, but cook with 1 bay leaf and 1 sprig of thyme, both rinsed. When the cooking time is completed pour the sauce through a sieve) and season to taste with salt, pepper and 2-3 tablespoons of port or sherry. This variation is excellent as a sauce for meat cut into strips.

Preparation time:
about 15 minutes

25 g/1 oz (2 tablespoons) butter or margarine
20 g/¾ oz (3 tablespoons) plain (all-purpose) flour
375 ml/12 fl oz (1½ cups) stock, e.g. vegetable stock
salt
freshly ground pepper

Per serving:
P: 1 g, F: 5 g, C: 4 g,
kJ: 274, kcal: 65

Béchamel sauce
Classic

1   Peel the onion and chop into small dice. Also finely dice the ham. Melt the butter or margarine in a pan over medium heat. Add the diced ham and cook briefly. Stir in the flour and the diced onion and cook until the flour is bright yellow.

2   Add the vegetable stock and milk or cream. Stir vigorously using a whisk, making sure that there are no lumps.

3   Bring the sauce to the boil and simmer gently uncovered over low heat, stirring it occasionally. Season the sauce to taste with salt, pepper and nutmeg.

Uses: Béchamel sauce goes well with vegetables, e.g. carrots (page 158) or kohlrabi (page 164). It is also good with steamed fish (page 115).

Preparation time:
about 15 minutes

1 onion
40 g/1½ oz uncooked ham
30 g/1 oz (2 tablespoons) butter or margarine
25 g/1 oz (4 tablespoons) plain (all-purpose) flour
125 ml/4 fl oz (½ cup) vegetable stock
250 ml/8 fl oz (1 cup) milk or whipping cream
salt, pepper
grated nutmeg

Per serving:
P: 4 g, F: 18 g, C: 8 g,
kJ: 873, kcal: 208

Mushroom sauce
Sophisticated

Preparation time:
about 20 minutes

250 g/9 oz mushrooms
50 g/2 oz streaky bacon
2 teaspoons cooking oil,
e.g. sunflower oil
250 ml/8 fl oz (1 cup)
vegetable stock
15 g/½ oz (1 tablespoon)
soft butter
15 g/½ oz (2 tablespoons)
plain (all-purpose) flour
150 g/5 oz crème fraîche
salt
freshly ground pepper
2 teaspoons chopped
parsley

Per serving:
P: 6 g, F: 18 g, C: 5 g,
kJ: 846, kcal: 204

1   Remove stalk ends of the mushrooms, cut out any bad parts and wipe clean with kitchen paper. Rinse if necessary, pat dry and slice. Dice the bacon.

2   Heat the oil in a pan. Add the diced bacon and braise briefly, stirring continuously. Now add the sliced mushrooms and the stock and bring to the boil and simmer gently uncovered for about 5 minutes.

3   Knead the butter and flour together, add to the mixture and stir with a whisk or mixing spoon to dissolve it in the sauce. Let the sauce simmer gently uncovered for about 5 minutes, stirring occasionally.

4   Stir in the crème fraîche. Season the sauce with salt and pepper and stir in the parsley.

Uses: Mushroom sauce is delicious served with beef steak, schnitzel and fried fish fillets or steak.

Variation 1: To make a **vegetarian mushroom sauce**, leave out the bacon and braise the mushrooms in 15 g/½ oz (1 tablespoon) butter or 1–2 table-spoons olive oil. In addition, season the sauce with 1 teaspoon chopped rosemary.

Variation 2: For a **mushroom sauce with ceps**, rinse about 10 g/⅓ oz dried ceps in a sieve under cold water and allow to drain. Heat up the vegetable stock, remove from the heat, add the ceps and leave to soak for about 30 minutes. Prepare the sauce as indicated above and add the stock with the ceps.

Hollandaise
Classic

Preparation time: about
15 minutes, excluding cooling time

150 g/5 oz butter
2 yolks from
  2 medium eggs
4 teaspoons white wine
squeeze of lemon juice
salt
freshly ground pepper

Per serving:
P: 2 g, F: 34, C: 0 g,
kJ: 1345, kcal: 321

1 Melt the butter, let it cool down slightly and skim off the froth.

2 Beat together the egg yolks and white wine in a bowl using a whisk. Place the bowl in hot water (the water must not boil!). Whisk the egg yolk mixture until it has thickened sufficiently (photograph 1).

3 Beat the melted butter slowly into the egg yolk mixture (photograph 2). Season the sauce with lemon juice, salt and pepper.

Note: Only use very fresh eggs for this sauce.

Uses: Hollandaise sauce is particularly good with asparagus, broccoli, cauliflower or other light vegetables.

Variation 1: To make **Béarnaise sauce** (photograph), replace the white wine with a decoction of herbs made as follows. Peel 1 onion, chop finely and put in a saucepan. Add 1 teaspoon chopped tarragon, 1 teaspoon chopped chervil, 2 teaspoons white wine vinegar and 1 tablespoon water and bring to the boil. Remove the pan from the heat and allow the herb decoction to draw with the lid on for about 5 minutes, then strain through a fine sieve. Stir 1–2 teaspoons chopped chervil and chopped tarragon into the finished sauce (photograph 3). Season the sauce with salt, pepper and lemon juice.

Variation 2: To make **Maltaise sauce**, replace the white wine with 2 tablespoons freshly squeezed blood-orange juice, 2 teaspoons warm water and 1 tablespoon lemon juice. Season the sauce with salt and sugar and sprinkle with the grated zest of ¼ untreated orange.

Tip: A beaten sauce will only keep warm in the bain-marie for a short time. If it stands too long, the sauce will separate into fat and egg yolk, in other words it will curdle. That is why a beaten sauce should be prepared very shortly before serving. A curdled sauce can be salvaged either by puréeing with a hand blender or by mixing 1 egg with 1 tablespoon cold water and little by little stirring the curdled sauce from the bain-marie.

Tomato sauce
Vegetarian

Preparation time:
about 25 minutes

1 kg/2¼ lb ripe tomatoes
1 onion
1 clove garlic
1-2 tablespoons olive oil
4 teaspoons tomato
   paste (optional)
salt
freshly ground pepper
about 1 teaspoon sugar
2 teaspoons chopped
   oregano

Per serving:
P: 2 g, F: 7 g, C: 8 g,
kJ: 442, kcal: 104

1   Wash the tomatoes, leave to drain, make cross-shaped incision, dip briefly in boiling water, then dip in cold water. Peel the tomatoes (photograph 1), remove the stalks and cut into cubes. Peel the onions and clove of garlic and chop finely.

2   Heat the oil in a pan, add the chopped onion and garlic and fry. Now add the chopped tomatoes, stir in tomato purée if used and season with salt and pepper. Bring to the boil and simmer gently covered over low heat for about 15 minutes, stirring occasionally.

3   Purée with a hand blender if desired (photograph 2), season with salt, pepper, sugar and oregano.

Uses: Tomato sauce is delicious with noodles or served hot or cold with grilled food, or cold with a fondue.

Tip: If the finished sauce is too thin you can either boil it down a little longer or thicken it with arrowroot. You can also use unpeeled tomatoes and strain the finished sauce through a sieve to remove the skins.
Instead of fresh tomatoes you can also use 1 large tin of peeled tomatoes (800 g/1¾ lb), including the juice.
The addition of tomato purée makes the sauce thicker and gives it a more intense tomato flavour.

Variation 1: To make **tomato sauce with bacon**, leave out the olive oil and replace it with 50 g/2 oz diced streaky bacon sweated in 2 tablespoons vegetable oil (photograph 3) in which you then fry the onion and garlic. Make the sauce as described above but do not purée.

Variation 2: To make **tomato and cream sauce**, prepare the sauce as described above. Then stir 1 tablespoon cornflour into 100 ml/3½ fl oz (½ cup) whipping cream, add to the boiling sauce and bring to the boil. Season with salt, pepper, sugar and oregano.

Variation 3: To make **tomato and vegetable sauce,** wash a bunch of soup vegetables, cut into small pieces and braise together with 1 peeled, chopped onion and 1 peeled, chopped clove of garlic in 2–3 tablespoons olive oil. Add 1 bay leaf and 125 ml/4 fl oz (½ cup) vegetable stock. Cover and cook the sauce over low heat for about 15 minutes. Add 1 tin (800 g/1¾ lb) peeled tomatoes with the juice and cook for a further 5 minutes. Remove the bay leaf, purée the sauce and season with salt, pepper and sugar. Sprinkle with 1 tablespoon chopped basil before serving.

Bolognese sauce
Popular

1   Peel the onion and garlic. Peel the carrots and cut off the green leaves and the tips. Peel the celeriac and remove the bad parts. Wash the carrots and celeriac and leave to drain. Finely chop up all the vegetables.

2   Heat the oil in a pan. Add all the vegetables and fry over medium heat. Next add the minced beef and continue frying while stirring, using a fork to squash any lumps of meat that might form.

3   Chop up the tinned tomatoes and add to meat and vegetables together with the juice and the tomato purée. Season with oregano, salt and pepper. Bring the sauce to the boil and simmer gently uncovered over low heat.

4   Add the red wine and adjust the seasoning with salt and pepper.

Uses: A Bolognese sauce is delicious served with pasta such as spaghetti or macaroni, potato dumplings (page 220) or bread dumplings (page 233).

Tip: Sprinkle with 1 tablespoon chopped basil and grated Parmesan or mature Gouda cheese just before serving.
If children are going to eat the Bolognese sauce you can easily leave out the red wine.

Preparation time:
about 35 minutes

1 onion
1 clove garlic
100 g/3½ oz carrots
about 50 g/2 oz celeriac
4 teaspoons cooking oil,
   e.g. sunflower or olive
   oil
250 g/9 oz minced beef
1 can (800 g/1¾ lb)
   peeled tomatoes
4 teaspoons tomato
   purée
1 teaspoon dried, chopped
   oregano
salt
freshly ground pepper
1–2 tablespoons red wine

Per serving:
P: 15 g, F: 14 g, C: 8 g,
kJ: 933, kcal: 222

Mayonnaise (photograph bottom right)
Quick

Preparation time:
about 10 minutes

1 yolk of 1 medium egg
1–2 teaspoons white wine
   vinegar or lemon juice
salt
½–1 teaspoon medium
   mustard
125 ml/4 fl oz (½ cup)
   cooking oil, e.g.
   sunflower oil

Per serving:
P: 1 g, F: 33 g, C: 0 g,
kJ: 1231, kcal: 294

1   Whisk together the egg yolk with the vinegar or lemon juice, salt and mustard in a bowl, using a whisk or hand-mixer with a whisk attachment to obtain a thick mixture.

2   Add the oil little by little, 1–2 tablespoons at a time, stirring continuously (with this method it is not necessary to dribble the oil in drop by drop because the spices added to the egg yolk will prevent the mayonnaise from curdling).

Uses: Mayonnaise is an ideal base for cold sauces and dips, and is delicious served with a fondue or in sandwiches.

Tip: All the ingredients used to make the mayonnaise should be the same temperature so that they bind together properly.
Should the mayonnaise curdle, mix together 1 egg yolk and vinegar or lemon juice and stir the mayonnaise into it little by little.

Note: Only use very fresh eggs; check the sell-by date! Store the mayonnaise in the refrigerator and consume within 24 hours.

Variation 1: For a **light mayonnaise** (top of photograph), make the mayonnaise as described above but use only 5 tablespoons oil. Then add 4 tablespoons low-fat quark and 1 tablespoon whipping cream to the mayonnaise. Optionally, ½ peeled, crushed clove of garlic may be added.

Variation 2: To make a **cold curry sauce** (bottom left of photograph), make the mayonnaise as described above, add 1–2 teaspoons curry powder and 150 g/5 oz natural yogurt (3.5% fat) or sour milk. To make a sweet curry sauce, add 1–2 tablespoons of apricot jam, rubbed through a sieve, to the curried mayonnaise described here.

Variation 3: To make a **remoulade sauce** (centre right of photograph), shell 2 hard-boiled eggs, rub the egg yolks through a sieve and chop up the egg whites. Mix the hard-boiled egg yolk with 1 raw egg yolk and make the mayonnaise as described above. Finally add 1 medium-sized, finely chopped pickled gherkin, 2 tablespoons chopped herbs (for instance, parsley, chives, dill, chervil or cress), 1 teaspoon drained, chopped capers and stir in the chopped egg white. Season the remoulade sauce with salt, pepper and sugar.

Variation 4: To make **tartare sauce** (centre left of photograph) peel 4 shallots or small onions, chop finely and add to the mayonnaise together with 2 teaspoons drained, chopped capers, 2 tablespoons chopped herbs (such as parsley, dill or chervil). Season with salt.

Vegetables

For daily nutrition, vegetables are very important. They contain a high proportion of carbohydrates and roughage, mineral salts, trace elements and vitamins. In addition, most kinds of vegetables have a low energy content and a high water content (75–95%).

Division

Tubers and root vegetables
e.g. potatoes, celeriac, carrots, turnips, black salsify

Leaf vegetables
e.g. artichokes, chicory, Swiss chard, spinach

Cabbage vegetables
e.g. cauliflower, broccoli, kale, Brussels sprouts, red cabbage, cabbage, Savoy cabbage

Onion vegetables
e.g. spring onions, garlic, leek, onions

Podded fruits
e.g. beans, peas, lentils, soya beans, chick peas

Fruit vegetables
e.g. aubergines, beans, cucumbers, pumpkin, peppers, tomatoes

Stick vegetables
e.g. fennels, rhubarb, asparagus, celery

Mushrooms
e.g. mushrooms, oyster mushrooms, Shiitake mushrooms

Buying and storage

- Many types of vegetables are offered all year round, so the customer can be confident of finding a good supply. Native vegetables that have a particular season are often preferable, since they will be especially full of flavour and inexpensive.
- It is best to buy crisp, fresh vegetables at markets or direct from the growers. Vegetables with wilted stems and leaves are no longer fresh.
- The storage time should be as short as possible, so that the minimum amount of nutritional value and flavour is lost.
- Vegetables keep best in the crisper of the refrigerator or in a cool cellar or larder.
- Frozen vegetables widen the range available throughout the year. Since vegetables are frozen as quickly as possible after being harvested, the loss of nutrients is relatively low.
- If possible, buy mushrooms loose, since if packed in plastic film they will mature too quickly. Packed mushrooms should be taken out of the packaging and stored in a paper bag in the refrigerator. Mushrooms are fresh if the stalk and cap are firmly connected together.

Preparation

A significant loss of nutrients can occur very quickly if fresh vegetables are improperly treated. They are very sensitive to the effects of air, heat, water and light. The following tips will help preserve nutrients as much as possible.
- Clean vegetables at the last possible moment before using them.
- Always wash vegetables before chopping them.
- Rinse vegetables briefly but thoroughly under cold running water and let drain.

Chopping onions

Peel the onion and cut in half in the direction of the root. With a knife make vertical cuts close together through the half onion with a knife, but leaving the root completely untouched; then make horizontal cuts up to the root. Finally, chop vertically to make dice. Repeat with the other half.

Preparing peppers by hollowing out with a spoon

Cut off the top of each pepper, then remove the white walls and seeds with a spoon.

Clean mushrooms by rubing with kitchen paper

It is not usually necessary to rinse cultivated mushrooms. Rubbing with kitchen paper is enough.

Peeling asparagus

Thinly peel white asparagus from head to end with a potato peeler or sharp knife, being careful to remove the peelings without injuring the heads. Cut off the asparagus ends and any woody part of the stems.

Peel only the bottom third of green asparagus and trim off the end.

Peeling tomatoes

Wash the tomatoes, leave to drain, make cross-shaped incisions in the top end, dip briefly in boiling water, then dip in cold water so the skins can be easily peeled off.

Preparation

Vegetables should be cooked quickly so that as few nutrients as possible are lost in the course of preparation and the flavours are preserved. Cook vegetables so that they are still crisp to the bite. With a short cooking time, vegetables preserve their minerals and fresh colour. Cook frozen vegetables in a little liquid without defrosting them, or braise them with diced onion.

Braising

Braising is the process of cooking vegetables in their own juices or in very little liquid. Put vegetables still wet from being rinsed into a saucepan with some seasoning, cover with a tight-fitting lid and cook the vegetables over a low heat, adding a little water only if necessary. In being heated, the liquid turns to steam, which condenses on the lid and drips back onto the vegetables. In this process, the vegetables are cooked at less than 100 °C/212 °F. The taste and flavour elements are preserved and the vegetable hardly needs further seasoning.

Steaming

To steam vegetables (cooking them over steam in a sieve), cover the bottom of the saucepan with water, put the vegetables in a matching sieve and cover with a tight-fitting lid. The vegetables cook in the steam.

Boiling

Some kinds of vegetables must be boiled. To boil vegetables (boiling them in a lot of liquid), almost cover them in liquid. Some vegetables, such as potatoes, are brought to the boil from cold, while others such as green beans are added to boiling water.

Little glossary

Artichokes

Firm green flower heads with tightly packed leaves that are thick and fleshy towards the base. When the heads are cooked, the leaves are pulled off but only the fleshy part is eaten, accompanied by a sauce. Before being eaten the hairy "choke" must be cut out with a knife. There are also violet artichokes, which are eaten whole.

Asparagus

A spring vegetable available from the beginning of March to the end of June. Underground stem with edible shoots with white, green or violet heads. Green asparagus

grows above the ground and has a more intense taste.

Aubergines (eggplant)

Long, oval-shaped vegetables with a smooth peel, deep purple colour and little flavour of their own. The skin can be eaten.

Beans

There are many different types (e.g. princess beans, French or green beans and broad beans). Beans should never be eaten raw since they contain phasin. This substance can cause inflammation of the stomach and intestines but it is destroyed in the course of cooking.

Beetroot

A root vegetable very rich in minerals and nutrients. It has powerful dyeing properties so rubber gloves should be worn when preparing it.

Black salsify

Long, dark-brown root vegetable. A winter vegetable rich in minerals and vitamins.

Broccoli
Green-violet heads with small florets, not quite as tight as cauliflower.

Brussels sprouts
Thick, powerful stem covered with cabbage-like buds that are the size of walnuts. A winter vegetable very rich in vitamin C.

Carrots
Sturdy root vegetable with a pointed end. Very rich in vitamin A, which is easily absorbed by the body when combined with a little fat (for instance, by adding butter to the carrots). There are many varieties on the market.

Cauliflower
A solid white to pale yellow head consisting of many small florets. Before cooking, place the cauliflower head downwards in saltwater for about 2 minutes in order to wash out any insects. Romanesco is a green cauliflower.

Celeriac
Firm, full-flavoured yellowish root. When buying celeriac, make sure it does not sound hollow when you tap it because this would mean that it is woody inside.

Chestnuts
Also called sweet or Spanish chestnuts, these are available fresh, roasted, in tins or preserved in syrup.

Chicory
Slightly bitter vegetable that is also used as a salad. The bitter stalk should be cut out.

Chinese cabbage
Large oblong heads of pale green colour. Tastes good as vegetable or salad.

Courgettes (zucchini)
Dark green or yellow, cucumber-like fruits with firm flesh. The smaller the courgette, the more delicate the taste. The flowers are also edible.

Cucumbers
There are salad cucumbers and pickled cucumbers or gherkins. Cucumbers grown in the open are often bitter at the stalk end, in which case you should cut off the ends.

Fennel
White, fleshy leaf stalks that form a solid bulb at the base. The delicate leaves can also be used. Fennel has a slight taste of aniseed.

Jerusalem artichoke
The beige-reddish brown roots of this tuberous plant, which is related to the sunflower and artichoke, have a sweet, nutty taste.

Kale
The leaves have a frizzy edge and a strong central rib. They should really only be eaten after the first frost because the starch present in the leaves will then have been converted into sugar. In addition, the cold also makes the cabbage more digestible.

Kohlrabi
Vegetable with a smooth, firm, bright green and blue-violet turnip-like stalk. Kohlrabi is very tender when young but is often quite woody when older. The tender leaves can also be eaten.

Leaf spinach
Leaf vegetable rich in vitamins and mineral elements. The leaves are cut off above the root and must be washed very thoroughly.

Leeks
Firm stem consisting of pale to dark green leaves with small roots. Leeks are rich in minerals and have a strong flavour.

Malze

Because of its high sugar content (varying between 4% and 14%) it is also known as sweetcorn. Corn on the cob can be bought fresh but when removed from the cob, sweetcorn is usually sold canned or frozen.

Mushrooms

Mushrooms available on the market are mainly cultivated. Mushrooms are white, pink or brown (ceps which have a more intense mushroom taste). Cut off the base of the stalk if there is any compost attached to it.

Okra

Plant cultivated as a vegetable and mainly used fresh. The pods produce a milky mucilage during the cooking process which is also present when okra is canned.

Onions

A large family with many varieties that vary considerably in shape, size, colour and taste. Ordinary onions are large with a relatively mild taste. Shallots are often braised whole. In the case of spring onions, the green leaves can also be used.

Parsnip

A root vegetable with a spicy taste that can be cooked like carrots.

Peas

There are sugar peas, petits pois and marrowfat peas. Before preparing, the peas are removed from the pods (shelled).

Sugar peas or mangetout are flat, bright green pods containing very small peas. They are eaten whole. You can buy ready prepared and washed sugar peas but make sure that the ends are not dry. Fresh sugar peas are crisp, not soft.

Peppers

Peppers are available in several colours (red, green, yellow and orange). They are rich in vitamin C and potassium.

Pointed cabbage

A cone-shaped cabbage variety with a loose heart, it has a more delicate flavour than white cabbage.

Pulses

Pulses are the vegetables that are highest in protein while also rich in vitamin B, folic acid, iron and fibre. Pulses can be stored for a very long time if kept in dry conditions in closed containers. Pulses must be washed before use and soaked before cooking, depending on the kind used.

Pumpkin

Bright yellow to bright orange fruit with a thick skin and numerous seeds and fibres. There are several varieties that vary greatly in size.

Red cabbage
Very firm head with smooth leaves, slightly curly at the edges. Its blue-red colouring matter turns red with the addition of acid (for instance, vinegar).

Savoy cabbage
Green curly leaves without much heart.

Stem celery
Greenish-white, crisp stems that grow from a tuber-like base. The delicate leaves can also be used.

Swede
Root vegetable with white to yellowish flesh, very rich in vitamins and minerals. Young swedes are very tender.

Swiss chard
Crisp stalks with narrow leaves with a thick central rib. Very rich in vitamins and minerals, it has a mild, nutty taste. Swiss chard can also be used instead of leaf spinach.

Tomatoes
Firm red fruits with juicy flesh that vary in size (for instance, beef tomatoes, cherry tomatoes, etc.) and in shape (for instance, plum tomatoes) depending on the variety. When used in cooked dishes they should be peeled. There are also green and yellow tomatoes. Do not store tomatoes with cucumbers because tomatoes give off ethylene, a gas that makes cucumbers turn yellow very quickly.

Turnip leaves
The leaves and shoots of particular varieties of white turnip. The leaves are very tender and should therefore be used when still very fresh.

White cabbage
A yellowish-green, firm, full-hearted cabbage variety. Season with crushed or ground caraway seeds, aniseed or fennel seeds. This gives the cabbage a sweetish taste while also making it more digestible.

White cabbage

Savoy cabbage

Curly kale

Red cabbage

Roasted vegetables (photograph)
Vegetarian

Preparation time:
about 60 minutes

1 kg/2¼ lb firm medium potatoes
salt
freshly ground pepper
5 tablespoons olive oil
400 g/14 oz red peppers
200 g/7 oz yellow peppers
400 g/14 oz courgettes
2 sprigs rosemary
4 cloves garlic

Per serving:
P: 8 g, F: 19 g, C: 46 g,
kJ: 1640, kcal: 391

1 Preheat the oven. Scrub the potatoes thoroughly under cold running water, pat dry, and cut into quarters lengthways. Put in a roasting tin, sprinkle with salt and pepper and 2 tablespoons of oil. Put the roasting tin in the oven.

Top/bottom heat: about 180 °C/350 °F (preheated),
Fan oven: about 160 °C/325 °F (preheated), Gas mark 4 (preheated),
Cooking time: about 20 minutes.

2 In the meantime, cut the peppers into quarters, remove the stalks, remove the seeds and white membranes, wash and cut into small pieces. Wash the courgettes, dry, cut off the ends and cut the courgettes into small pieces. Season the vegetables with salt and pepper, then mix with the remaining oil.

3 Rinse the rosemary sprigs and pat dry. Peel the garlic and mix the cloves with the vegetables and rosemary sprigs. Add to the precooked potatoes in the roasting tin. Mix all the ingredients together.

4 Put the roasting tin in the oven again and cook for a further 20-25 minutes at the oven temperature given above.

Tip: Serve the roasted vegetables as a vegetarian entrée on their own or with tomato sauce (page 148).
It can also be served as a dinner party dish, e.g. to accompany roasts.

Carrots
For children

Preparation time:
about 30 minutes

1 kg/2¼ lb carrots
50 g/2 oz (4 tablespoons) butter
100 ml/3½ fl oz (½ cup) vegetable stock
salt

1 Peel the carrots and cut off the green leaves and tips. Wash, leave to drain and cut in slices or batons.

2 Melt the butter in a pan. Cook the carrots briefly while stirring. Add the vegetable stock and cook the carrots covered over low heat for 10-15 minutes.

3 Season the carrots with salt and sugar, sprinkle with parsley and serve.

(continued on page 160)

1 level teaspoon sugar
3-4 teaspoons chopped
   parsley

Per serving:
P: 2 g, F: 11 g, C: 11 g,
kJ: 637, kcal: 152

Tip: Serve the carrots as an accompaniment to meat, fish and poultry dishes or as part of a dish of assorted vegetables (photograph page 163).

Variation 1: Carrots with garlic and basil. Peel 2 cloves garlic, cut into thin slices, cook with the carrots and mix in 2 tablespoons chopped basil instead of parsley.

Variation 2: Carrots with ginger and orange. Braise the carrots in the butter. Then add 1 tablespoon sugar, the grated peel of 1 untreated orange, a piece of fresh ginger root about 3 cm/1¼ in long, peeled and cut into small matchsticks, salt and pepper. Stir together, then pour in 125 ml/4 fl oz (½ cup) water instead of the vegetable stock. Cook covered for 5-6 minutes, then cook uncovered for a further 5-6 minutes, stirring from time to time.

Variation 3: Glazed carrots. Clean a 1 kg/2¼ lb bunch of young or finger carrots, leaving some green on them. Wash the carrots, braise in 50 g/2 oz dissolved butter, mix in 4 tablespoons sugar and pour in 100 ml/3½ fl oz (½ cup) vegetable stock. Cook the carrots covered over low heat for about 15 minutes, add salt and sprinkle 1 tablespoon chopped mint before serving.

Parsnip and carrot medley
Sophisticated

Preparation time:
about 25 minutes

300 g/10 oz carrots
700 g/1½ lb parsnips
50 g/2 oz (4 tablespoons)
   butter
125 ml/4 fl oz (½ cup)
   vegetable stock
salt
freshly ground pepper
2 teaspoons cut smooth
   parsley

Per serving:
P: 2 g, F: 11 g, C: 19 g,
kJ: 782, kcal: 187

1 Peel the carrots and parsnips and cut off the green leaves and tips. Wash and leave to drain. Cut the carrots into thin slices. Cut the tops of the parsnips into thin slices, quarter the lower ends and cut into thin slices lengthways.

2 Melt the butter in a saucepan. Cook the carrot slices over low heat for about 5 minutes while stirring. Add the sliced parsnips and vegetable stock. Add salt and pepper and cook the vegetables covered for a further 6-8 minutes, stirring occasionally.

3 Season the vegetables to taste with salt and pepper, sprinkle with parsley and serve.

Tip: Serve the parsnip and carrot medley with fish dishes, fried poultry and veal or poultry ragouts.

Variation: Parsley and carrot medley with kohlrabi. Use only 400 g/14 oz parsnip and in addition 300 g/10 oz kohlrabi. Prepare the 3 kinds of vegetables as described above, cutting the kohlrabi first into quarters and then into slices. Cook the kohlrabi slices and 1-2 teaspoons of thyme together with the carrot slices and proceed as described above.

Stuffed onions
G o o d   v a l u e

1 Bring the water to the boil in a saucepan. Meanwhile, peel the onions. Put the onions in the cooking water with 1 teaspoon of salt and par-boil covered over low heat for about 20 minutes.

2 Remove the onions from the water with a skimming ladle and leave to cool. Measure off 75 ml/3 fl oz (³/₈ cup) from the cooking liquid. Preheat the oven. Cut the onions in half horizontally and scoop out 3-4 layers (photograph 1). Chop the pieces of onion that have been scooped out from the inside into small pieces (photograph 2).

3 Melt the butter or margarine in a pan. Cook the onion pieces in it gently for 3-4 minutes while stirring. Stir in the cream and the measured cooking liquid, season with salt and pepper and put in a flat casserole dish.

4 Mix the minced meat with 2 tablespoons of parsley and fill the onion halves with it (photograph 3). Place the onion halves in the casserole dish. Put the dish on a shelf in the oven without covering.

Top/bottom heat: **about 200 °C/400 °F (preheated)**,
Fan oven: **about 180 °C/350 °F (preheated)**, Gas mark **6 (preheated)**,
Cooking time: **about 35 minutes.**

5 Sprinkle the onion halves with the remaining parsley and serve with the sauce.

Accompaniment: **Potato purée (page 218), or baguette.**

Variation: **Stuffed onions in vegetable sauce.** Prepare and stuff the onions as described above. Also clean and wash 1 bunch soup vegetables, cut into small dice or strips and braise gently with the chopped scooped-out onion. Then add 125 ml/4 fl oz (½ cup) of the cooking liquid and cook the vegetables for about 10 minutes. Stir in the whipping cream and 1 teaspoon drained capers, season with salt and pepper and add the vegetable sauce to the casserole dish. After cooking in the oven, purée the vegetables if desired, season to taste with salt and pepper and serve with the onion halves.

Preparation time: about 70 minutes, excluding cooling time

1 ¼-1½ litres/3½ pints (9 cups) water
2 large onions, about 750 g/1½ lb together
salt
15 g/½ oz butter or margarine
2 tablespoons whipping cream
freshly ground pepper
375 g/13 oz Thuringian mince (spiced minced pork)
2 tablespoons chopped parsley

Per serving:
P: 19 g, F: 25 g, C: 9 g,
kJ: 1403, kcal: 336

Green beans
Easy

Preparation time:
about 30 minutes

750 g/1½ lb green beans
3-4 sprigs savory
salt
1 onion
40 g/1½ oz butter or
    margarine
freshly ground pepper
grated nutmeg
2 teaspoons chopped
    parsley

Per serving:
P: 4 g, F: 9 g, C: 10 g,
kJ: 570, kcal: 136

1   Bring water to the boil in a saucepan. Meanwhile, cut the ends off the beans and pull off any strings. Wash the beans and cut or break into pieces. Rinse the savory. Add salt to the cooking water at the rate of 1 teaspoon per 1 litre/1¾ pints (4½ cups) water. Add the beans and savory, bring to the boil again and cook the beans covered for 15-20 minutes.

2   In the meantime, peel and dice the onion. Melt the butter or margarine. Lightly braise the diced onion.

3   Drain the cooked beans in a colander and remove the savory. Add the beans to the diced onion and stir. Season the beans with salt, pepper and nutmeg, sprinkle with parsley and serve.

Tip: Green beans can be part of a dish of assorted vegetables (photograph). They can be served with meat dishes, or with herrings.
Yellow wax beans can be prepared in the same way. Princess or Kenya beans are very tender, with a cooking time of 8-12 minutes. Dip the cooked beans in cold water so that they keep their green colour.

Variation: Green beans with bacon. Put 70 g/3 oz diced streaky bacon in a pan, add butter or margarine and sweat gently. Add the diced onion and lightly braise. Add the beans and toss together. Serve with lamb.

Petit pois
For children

Preparation time:
about 15 minutes

35 g/1¼ oz butter
750 g/1½ lb frozen petit
    pois, salt, 1 pinch sugar
100 ml/3½ fl oz (½ cup)
    vegetable stock
2 teaspoons chopped
    parsley

Per serving:
P: 14 g, F: 8 g, C: 24 g,
kJ: 965, kcal: 230

1   Melt the butter in a pan. Add the peas without defrosting and cook gently while stirring. Add salt, sugar and the vegetable stock, then cook covered over low heat for about 8 minutes, stirring occasionally.

2   Season the peas with salt and sugar, sprinkle with parsley and serve.

Tip: Serve the peas with meat or poultry dishes, or as part of an assorted vegetable dish (photograph).
If using fresh peas, 2 kg/4½ lb unshelled peas in their pods are needed to make 750 g/1½ lb peas. Shell the peas, wash, leave to drain and then cook as described above.

Chicory in ham (photograph)
Sophisticated

Preparation time:
about 50 minutes

4 large chicory chicons
50 g/2 oz (4 tablespoons)
   butter
2 teaspoons cooking oil,
   e.g. sunflower oil
4 slices cooked ham
150 g/5 oz crème fraîche
150 g/5 oz natural yogurt
   (3.5% fat)
200 g/7 oz soft cheese
salt, pepper
50 g/2 oz grated Gouda
   cheese

Per serving:
P: 25 g, F: 47 g, C: 7 g,
kJ: 2286, kcal: 547

1 Preheat the oven at the top and bottom. Remove the outer wilted leaves from the chicory, cut the chicory in half lengthways,
   wash, leave to dry and cut out the bitter stalk in a wedge shape
   so that the leaves are still held together.

2 Heat the butter and oil in a pan. Place the chicory halves in it
   with the cut side downwards and cook over low heat for about
   10 minutes.

3 Cut the ham slices in half, put 1 half-slice on each chicory half
   and place in a flat casserole.

4 Heat the crème fraîche and yogurt in the pan, bring to the boil
   and dissolve the soft cheese in it while stirring.

5 Season the sauce with salt and pepper, then pour it over the
   chicory halves. Scatter the grated cheese over the top. Put the
   dish uncovered onto the shelf in the oven.

Top/bottom heat: **about 180 °C/350 °F (preheated),**
Fan oven: **about 160 °C/325 °F (preheated),** Gas mark **4 (preheated),**
Cooking time: **about 20 minutes.**

Accompaniment: Small potatoes or rice.

Kohlrabi
For children

Preparation time:
about 30 minutes

1 kg/2¼ lb kohlrabi
30 g/1 oz (2 tablespoons)
   butter
100 ml/3½ fl oz (½ cup)
   vegetable stock
salt, grated nutmeg
2 teaspoons chopped
   parsley

Per serving:
P: 3 g, F: 7 g, C: 6 g,
kJ: 410, kcal: 98

1 Peel the kohlrabi, putting aside some of the soft kohlrabi leaves
   for garnishing the dish. Wash the kohlrabi, leave it to drain and
   cut it first into slices, then into strips.

2 Melt the butter in a pan. Gently cook the kohlrabi strips while
   stirring. Add the vegetable stock. Cook the kohlrabi covered over
   low heat for 10-15 minutes, stirring occasionally.

3 Season the kohlrabi with salt and nutmeg. Rinse the kohlrabi
   leaves that have been put aside, leave to drain and chop. Sprinkle the kohlrabi with the green leaves and parsley before serving.

Tip: Serve kohlrabi with meat or poultry dishes, or as part of an assorted
vegetable dish (photograph page 162).
Kohlrabi is also very delicious in a béchamel sauce (page 141).

Stuffed mushrooms
Good for preparing in advance

Preparation time: about 60
minutes, excluding cooling time

600 g/1¼ lb leaf spinach
1 small onion
60 g/2 oz butter
salt
freshly ground pepper
grated nutmeg
12 large mushrooms,
** about 600 g/1¼ lb in all**
125 g/4½ oz double cream
** herb cheese**
4 teaspoons breadcrumbs
40 g/1½ oz grated
** Emmental cheese**
vegetable stock
** (optional)**
250 ml/8 fl oz (1 cup)
** whipping cream**
gravy thickener
½ teaspoon granulated
** instant vegetable stock**

In addition:
fat for the mould

Per serving:
P: 17 g, F: 45 g, C: 8 g,
kJ: 2069, kcal: 494

1 Sort the spinach, remove any thick stems, wash the spinach thoroughly and leave to drain. Peel the onion and dice.

2 Melt 40 g/1½ oz butter in a pan. Gently cook the diced onion in it. Add the spinach, season with salt, pepper and nutmeg, and cook covered over gentle heat for about 5 minutes, stirring carefully. Put the spinach in a colander and reserve the drained cooking liquid. When the spinach has cooled a little, cut it into small pieces. Preheat the oven.

3 Cut off the ends of the mushroom stalks and remove any bad bits. Rub the mushrooms with kitchen paper, wash only if necessary and pat dry. Remove the stalks from the heads and cut them into small dice.

4 Melt the remaining butter. Cook the diced mushroom in it for 1-2 minutes and season with salt and pepper. Stir in the soft cheese, then add the breadcrumbs and the spinach and mix together. Season again with salt, pepper and nutmeg to taste.

5 Sprinkle the inside of the mushroom heads with salt and pepper, spoon a heap of the spinach mixture onto each one and put in a greased casserole. Scatter the Emmental cheese over each one.

6 Measure 125 ml/4 fl oz (½ cup) of the reserved spinach cooking liquid, making up the quantity with vegetable stock if necessary. Bring the liquid to the boil with the cream and thicken with the sauce thickener. Season the sauce to taste with salt, pepper and vegetable stock granules and pour into the casserole dish. Put the dish uncovered on a shelf in the oven.

Top/bottom heat: **about 180 °C/350 °F (preheated),**
Fan oven: **about 160 °C/325 °F (preheated),** Gas mark **4 (preheated),**
Cooking time: **45 minutes.**

Tip: Serve the stuffed mushrooms as a vegetarian entrée with baguette or ciabatta (Italian white bread).
Served as a starter with tomato slices or some green salad, the stuffed mushrooms are enough for 8-10 servings.

Variation: **Stuffed mushrooms with tomato sauce** instead of the cream sauce. Pour one 500 g/18 oz can of puréed tomatoes into the casserole dish and season with salt, pepper and paprika. After cooking, sprinkle the mushrooms with 2 tablespoons chopped basil.

Celeriac escalopes (photograph)
Vegetarian

Preparation time: about 25
minutes, excluding frying time

800 g/1¾ lb celeriac
salt
freshly ground pepper
4 teaspoons lemon juice
2 eggs
100 g/3½ oz (1 cup) plain
  (all-purpose) flour
200 g/7 oz breadcrumbs
3 tablespoons cooking oil,
  e.g. sunflower oil
50 g/2 oz (4 tablespoons)
  butter

Per serving:
P: 8 g, F: 21 g, C: 31 g,
kJ: 1439, kcal: 344

1   Peel the celeriac, cut out any bad parts, wash and leave to drain. Cut into slices 5 mm/³⁄₁₆ in thick and sprinkle with salt, pepper and lemon juice.

2   Whisk the eggs in a deep plate with a fork. Dip the celeriac slices first in flour, then in the egg and finally in the breadcrumbs. Press the breadcrumbs firmly onto the slices.

3   Heat some of the oil in a frying pan. Fry the celeriac slices a few at a time for about 4 minutes per side until golden yellow. Shortly before the end of the cooking time of each batch add some butter to the pan and melt it.

Tip: Serve the celeriac as a vegetarian entrée, e.g. with tomato sauce (page 148), herb curd cheese and salad.
Slices of radish may be served, or prepare cut red beet in slices.

Variation: The celeriac can also be made with different coatings. For these, mix 180 g/6½ oz breadcrumbs with 30 g/1 oz grated Parmesan cheese or 30 g/1 oz finely chopped sunflower seeds.

Shallots in red wine
With alcohol

Preparation time:
about 30 minutes

500 g/18 oz shallots
25 g/1 oz (2 tablespoons)
  butter
20 g/¾ oz sugar
250 ml/8 fl oz (1 cup) red
  wine
salt, pepper
2 teaspoons chopped
  smooth parsley

Per serving:
P: 2 g, F: 5 g, C: 10 g,
kJ: 562, kcal: 134

1   Peel the shallots and halve if necessary. Melt the butter and cook the shallots in it until golden yellow. Scatter the sugar over top and stir until it caramelises.

2   Add the red wine and cook shallots uncovered over low heat for about 15 minutes. Season the shallots with salt and pepper to taste and sprinkle with parsley before serving.

Tip: Serve the shallots with steaks, fried liver (page 94) or roasts.
Instead of butter, the shallots can be cooked in 3 tablespoons of olive oil.
The shallots in red wine will keep for about 1 week in the refrigerator.
Served cold, they taste good on bread, or they may be part of an appetiser plate.

Variation: Stir 100 g/3½ oz crème fraîche into the cooked shallots and season again to taste.

Stuffed peppers (cover photograph)
Popular

Preparation time: about 80 minutes, excluding cooling time

4 peppers, 150 g/5 oz each
250 g/9 oz large onions
500 g/18 oz tomatoes
4 tablespoons olive oil
400 g/14 oz minced meat, half beef, half pork
4 teaspoons tomato purée
salt
freshly ground pepper
about 375 ml/12 fl oz (1½ cups) vegetable stock
15 g/½ oz (2 tablespoons) plain (all-purpose) flour
4 tablespoons whipping cream
salt
freshly ground pepper
dried chopped oregano
some sugar

Per serving:
P: 23 g, F: 37 g, C: 14 g,
kJ: 1992, kcal: 475

1 Wash the peppers and dry them. Cut off and reserve the stalk end of each pepper to make a "lid". Remove the seeds as well as the white pith inside and rinse the peppers. Peel and chop the onions. Wash the tomatoes, dry and remove the stalks. Cut 3 tomatoes in half, remove the cores and dice.

2 Heat two tablespoons of oil in a pan. Gently cook half the chopped onions in it. Add the minced meat and brown while stirring, breaking up any lumps with a fork.

3 Mix in the diced tomatoes and half the tomato purée, season with salt and pepper and leave to cool. Then fill the prepared peppers with the mixture. Put the "lid" back on each pepper.

4 Cut the remaining tomatoes into pieces. Heat the remaining oil in a large saucepan. Add the remaining chopped onions and cook gently. Put the peppers next to each other in the pan. Add the tomato pieces and 375 ml/12 fl oz (1½ cups) vegetable stock. Cook the peppers covered over low heat for about 50 minutes. Then put the peppers on a preheated dish.

5 For the sauce, pour the cooking liquid with the tomato pieces and onions through a sieve. Measure off 375 ml/12 fl oz (1½ cups), adding vegetable stock to make up the quantity if necessary. Stir in the remaining tomato purée and bring all to the boil. Mix the flour with the cream and stir into the cooking liquid little by little. Cook gently for about 10 minutes, stirring occasionally.

6 Season the sauce with salt, pepper, oregano and sugar and serve with the stuffed peppers.

Accompaniment: Rice, boiled potatoes or potatoes boiled in their skins, and a mixed green salad (page 192).

Variation: Peppers stuffed with chicken or turkey. Replace the minced meat with 400 g/14 oz chopped chicken or turkey breast fillets. Rinse the fillets under running cold water, pat dry, cut into very fine dice (or cut into large dice and purée with the slicing attachment of the hand mixer). Then continue as described above. Season the sauce with 2 tablespoons chopped parsley instead of oregano.

Cooked peppers
Easy

1 Cut the peppers in half. Remove the stalks and seeds as well as the white pith inside. Wash the peppers and cut into thin strips or dice. Peel and finely chop the onions and garlic.

2 Heat the oil in a pan. Gently cook the chopped onion and garlic in it while stirring. Add the peppers, season with salt, sugar, pepper and vinegar and cook covered over low heat for about 15 minutes. Season the peppers again to taste.

3 If too much liquid collects in the pan, remove the vegetables with a skimming ladle and put in a preheated bowl. Cook the liquid uncovered for a few minutes more to reduce the quantity and pour over the peppers.

4 Sprinkle the peppers with parsley and serve.

Tip: The peppers are excellent with fried or steamed fish fillets, or with roast chicken or turkey.

Variation 1: **Peppers and tomatoes.** Use only about 500 g/18 oz peppers and prepare as described above. While they are cooking wash 500 g/18 oz tomatoes, leave to drain and cut them crossways. Scald briefly in boiling water and dip into cold water. Peel the tomatoes, remove the stalks and cut the tomatoes into quarters. Add them to the pepper mixture about 3 minutes before the end of the cooking time. Season the vegetables to taste and sprinkle with 1 tablespoon chopped basil instead of the parsley. Serve hot or cold with garlic curd cheese.

Variation 2: **Peppers and leeks.** Use only about 700 g/1½ lb peppers and replace the onions with 300 g/10 oz leeks. Remove the outer leaves of the leeks and cut off the root ends and dark green leaves. Cut the leeks in half lengthways and wash thoroughly. Let dry and cut crossways to make strips. Gently cook the leek and then continue as described above.

Variation 3: **Peppers and mushrooms.** Use only about 500 g/18 oz peppers. Take 500 g/18 oz mushrooms, cut off the stalks and remove any bad parts, wipe clean with kitchen paper, rinse if necessary, pat dry and cut into slices. Heat 2 tablespoons of the oil, add the mushroom slices and brown briefly over high heat, season with salt and remove from the pan. Cook the peppers as described above, stir in the mushrooms at the end of the cooking time and heat through.

Preparation time:
about 35 minutes

1 kg/2¼ lb peppers (red, green and yellow)
2 onions
3 cloves garlic
4 tablespoons olive oil
salt
1 pinch sugar
freshly ground pepper
2 tablespoons white wine vinegar
4 teaspoons chopped parsley

Per serving:
P: 3 g, F: 15 g, C: 8 g,
kJ: 757, kcal: 181

Hunter's cabbage (photograph)
Good for preparing in advance

Preparation time:
about 45 minutes

1 kg/2¼ lb cabbage
1 small onion
100 g/3½ oz streaky
    bacon
4 teaspoons cooking oil,
    e.g. sunflower oil
250 ml/8 fl oz (1 cup)
    vegetable stock
salt, pepper
herb vinegar
1 pinch sugar

Per serving:

P: 7 g, F: 7 g, C: 9 g,
kJ: 560, kcal: 134

1 Remove the outer wilted leaves from the cabbage, cut the cabbage into quarters, rinse, leave to dry, cut out the stalk and cut the cabbage into fine strips. Peel and chop the onion. Cut the bacon into dice.

2 Heat the oil in a pan and add the diced bacon. Then add the chopped onion and cook gently while stirring. Then add the cabbage strips and continue cooking gently, stirring from time to time.

3 Add the vegetable stock, season the cabbage with salt and pepper and cook covered over low heat for about 25 minutes. Season to taste with salt, pepper, vinegar and sugar.

Tip: Hunter's cabbage is an excellent accompaniment for braised pork (page 63) with boiled potatoes.
Instead of ordinary cabbage, hunter's cabbage may be made with Savoy cabbage, pointed cabbage or Chinese cabbage. With pointed or Chinese cabbage, reduce the cooking time to 10–15 minutes.

Sauerkraut
Classic

Preparation time:
about 60 minutes

4 onions, 1 apple
2 tablespoons cooking
    oil, e.g. sunflower oil
750 g/1½ lb sauerkraut
125 ml/4 fl oz (½ cup)
    water or white wine
1 bay leaf
4 juniper berries
6 peppercorns
salt, sugar, pepper

Per serving:

P: 3 g, F: 8 g, C: 7 g,
kJ: 514, kcal: 123

1 Peel and chop the onions. Wash the apple, peel, quarter, core and cut into slices.

2 Heat the oil in a pan. Gently cook the chopped onion. Pull the sauerkraut loosely apart and add the water or white wine. Put the apple slices on the sauerkraut.

3 Add the bay leaf, juniper berries and peppercorns, season with salt and cook the sauerkraut covered over low heat for 25–30 minutes, stirring occasionally. Add some liquid at intervals if necessary. Season the sauerkraut with salt, sugar and pepper.

Tip: Serve the sauerkraut with cured rib of pork Kassel style (page 72) and potato purée (page218).
Sauerkraut becomes thicker if a grated raw potato is added in the last 10 minutes of cooking.
If desired, replace the apple with 150 g/5 oz pineapple pieces (from the can, drained from the juice). Add some pineapple juice to the sauerkraut to taste.

Ceps (photograph)
A little more expensive

Preparation time:
about 30 minutes

500 g/18 oz ceps
1 clove garlic
150 g/5 oz tomatoes
3 tablespoons olive oil
salt, pepper
2 teaspoons chopped
    parsley

Per serving:
P: 6 g, F: 13 g, C: 2 g,
kJ: 576, kcal: 137

1   Cut the stalks off the ceps and remove any bad parts, wipe clean with kitchen paper, rinse if necessary, pat dry and cut into slices lengthways. Peel and finely chop the garlic. Cut out the stalks from the tomatoes, peel and dice.

2   Heat half the oil in a pan. Cook half the sliced ceps over medium heat for 5-7 minutes. Season with salt and pepper, remove, put on preheated plates and keep in a warm place. Cook the remaining sliced ceps in the same way.

3   Sweat the garlic in the remaining cooking oil. Add the diced tomato and heat through. Stir in the parsley. Season with salt and pepper and pour over the ceps.

Mushroom in cream sauce
Classic

Preparation time:
about 35 minutes

800 g/1¾ lb mushrooms
    or oyster mushrooms
2 onions
1 bunch spring onions
30 g/1 oz (2 tablespoons)
    butter, salt, pepper
100 ml/3½ fl oz (½ cup)
    vegetable stock
150 g/5 oz crème fraîche
1 pinch cayenne pepper
Worcestershire sauce
about 1 teaspoon lemon
    juice, some sugar
4 teaspoons chopped
    flat-leaved parsley

Per serving:
P: 9 g, F: 18 g, C: 8 g,
kJ: 937, kcal: 226

1   Cut the stalks off the mushrooms and remove any bad parts, wipe clean with kitchen paper, rinse if necessary and pat dry. Cut the mushrooms into slices or the oyster mushrooms into strips. Peel and chop the onion. Cut off the root ends from the spring onions, remove the dark green parts, wash the spring onions, leave to drain and cut into rings.

2   Heat the butter in a wide pan. Gently cook the chopped onion while stirring. Add the mushrooms and cook them gently as well. Add the vegetable stock and the mushrooms. Cook covered over low heat for 6-8 minutes, stirring occasionally. Season with salt and pepper.

3   Add the spring onion rings and cook for 1-2 minutes. Stir in the crème fraîche and heat through. Season to taste with cayenne pepper, Worcestershire sauce, lemon juice and sugar and sprinkle with parsley.

Tip: Serve mushrooms in cream-sauce with steaks, escalopes or breadcrumb dumplings (page 233).
White wine may be used instead of vegetable stock.

Mixed vegetables with sesame seeds
(photograph)

Vegetarian

Preparation time:
about 40 minutes

50 g/2 oz hulled sesame
  seeds
400 g/14 oz carrots
700 g/1½ lb broccoli
300 g/10 oz leeks
4 sticks celery
salt
2 tablespoons cooking
  oil, e.g. olive oil
freshly ground pepper

Per serving:
P: 9 g, F: 14 g, C: 12 g,
kJ: 885, kcal: 211

1   Toast the sesame seeds in a pan without fat over low heat until golden brown, shaking it to turn them occasionally.

2   Peel the carrots and cut off the green leaves and tips. Wash the carrots, leave to drain and cut into batons. Remove the leaves from the broccoli, cut into rosettes, peel the stems and cut into pieces. Wash the broccoli and leave to drain.

3   Remove the outer leaves of the leeks, cut off the root ends and dark green leaves. Cut in half lengthways, wash thoroughly and leave to drain. Remove the root ends and withered leaves from the sticks of celery, pull off the outside threads, wash the sticks, leave to drain and cut into thin slices.

4   Bring water to the boil in a saucepan, add salt at the rate of 1 teaspoon salt to 1 litre/1¾ pints (4½ cups) of water. Blanch the carrot batons, celery slices and broccoli in the boiling salted water for about 3 minutes. Empty them into a colander, dip into cold water and leave to drain well.

5   Heat the oil in a large pan or a wok. Add all the vegetables and cook over medium heat for about 5 minutes. Season with salt and pepper and sprinkle with sesame seeds before serving.

Tip: Serve the mixed vegetables as a vegetarian entree with whole grain rice and tomato sauce (page 148) or mushroom sauce (page 142). They may also be served with fried meat or fish.

Savoy cabbage
Good value

Preparation time:
about 55 minutes

1 kg/2¼ lb Savoy cabbage
1 onion
40 g/1½ oz butter or
  margarine
125 ml/4 fl oz (½ cup)
  vegetable stock

1   Remove the outer wilted leaves from the Savoy cabbage, cut the cabbage into eight segments, rinse and leave to drain. Cut off the stalks and chop the Savoy cabbage into fine strips. Peel and chop the onion.

2   Melt the butter or margarine in a pan. Gently cook the chopped onion. Add the cabbage strips and gently cook. Add the vegetable stock and salt and pepper. Cook the cabbage strips covered over low heat for 20–30 minutes.

(continued on page 180)

salt, pepper
1 pinch sugar
1 pinch grated lemon peel
    (untreated)
3-4 teaspoons lemon
    juice or white wine

Per serving:
P: 5 g, F: 9 g, C: 6 g,
kJ: 536, kcal: 128

3   Season the Savoy cabbage to taste with salt, pepper, sugar, lemon peel, lemon juice or wine.

Tip: Serve the Savoy cabbage with meat dishes.
Season the cabbage with pounded or ground caraway, anise or fennel seeds. This will make the cabbage easier to digest.

Variation 1: Instead of Savoy cabbage, Chinese cabbage or pointed cabbage may also be used. Cooking time for both kinds of cabbage: 10-15 minutes.

Variation 2: **Savoy cabbage and carrots.** Use only 800 g/1¾ lb Savoy cabbage prepared as described above. In addition, prepare 250 g/9 oz carrots, peel and wash, leave to drain and cut into strips. Peel 1-2 cloves garlic and cut in slices. Cook the carrots and garlic together with the Savoy cabbage as described above.

Cheese courgettes
Sophisticated

Preparation time: about 30 minutes

400 g/14 oz courgettes
salt
freshly ground pepper
1 egg
2 tablespoons water
100 g/3½ oz freshly
    grated Parmesan
    cheese
75 g/3 oz breadcrumbs
75 g/3 oz (¾ cup) plain
    (all-purpose) flour
125 ml/4 fl oz (½ cup)
    cooking oil, e.g.
    sunflower oil

Per serving:
P: 12 g, F: 23 g, C: 20 g,
kJ: 1401, kcal: 335

1   Wash the courgettes, dry them and cut off the ends. Cut the courgettes diagonally into slices 5 mm/³⁄₁₆ in thick (photograph 1) and sprinkle with salt and pepper.

2   Using a fork, mix the egg with the water in a deep plate. Mix the Parmesan with the breadcrumbs. Dip the courgette slices first in the flour, then in the egg and finally in the Parmesan and breadcrumb mixture (photograph 2).

3   Heat some of the oil in a pan. Fry the courgette slices a few at a time over medium heat for about 5 minutes until golden yellow (photograph 3), turning them occasionally. Leave them to drain on kitchen paper or a wire rack.

Tip: Serve the cheese courgettes as a light meal or as a starter with herbal curd cheese or tomato sauce (page 148). As an entrée, the quantity is enough for 2 servings, perhaps served with a mixed green salad (page 192). Pumpkin or aubergine slices may be prepared in the same way.

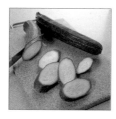  

Red lentils with peppers
Vegetarian

Preparation time:
about 30 minutes

2 onions
2 cloves garlic
350 g/12 oz red or yellow
   peppers
4 teaspoons olive oil
250 g/9 oz dried red
   lentils
1 teaspoon dried, chopped
   thyme
400 ml/14 fl oz (1¾ cups)
   vegetable stock
1 bunch spring onions
salt
freshly ground pepper
1 pinch cayenne pepper
2-3 teaspoons lemon
   juice
1 teaspoon honey or
   ½ teaspoon sugar

Per serving:
P: 16 g, F: 6 g, C: 36 g,
kJ: 1131, kcal: 270

1   Peel and chop the onions. Peel the garlic and cut into slices. Cut
    the peppers in half. Remove the stalks and seeds as well as the
    white pith inside. Wash the peppers and cut into strips.

2   Heat the oil in a pan. Gently cook the chopped onion and garlic
    slices while stirring. Add the lentils, strips of pepper and thyme
    together with the vegetable stock. Bring to the boil and cook
    covered over low heat for about 8 minutes.

3   Meanwhile, cut the root ends off the spring onions and remove
    the dark green parts. Wash the spring onions and cut into rings.
    Stir the spring onion rings into the lentils and cook covered for
    about 3 minutes. Season with salt, pepper, cayenne pepper,
    lemon juice and honey or sugar.

Tip: Serve the red lentils with bread and roast chicken or turkey breasts or
poached eggs.

Variation: **Green lentils.** Put 250 g/9 oz dried green lentils into a sieve and
rinse. Add to 600 ml/21 oz (2½ cups) vegetable stock and 1 bay leaf in a
saucepan, bring to the boil and cook covered over medium heat for
20-25 minutes. In the meantime, prepare 200 g/7 oz celeriac and 200 g/7 oz
carrots, peel, wash and cut into small dice. Clean 200 g/7 oz leeks cut in half
lengthways, wash and cut into strips. Melt 40 g/1½ oz butter or margarine and
gently cook the vegetables in it for about 2 minutes while stirring. Add the
vegetables and 125 ml/4 fl oz (½ cup) vegetable stock to the lentils. Cook
covered for about 10 more minutes. Season to taste with salt, pepper, sugar
and about 2 tablespoons of vinegar, e.g. balsamic vinegar. Sprinkle with
1 tablespoon chopped parsley. Serve as an accompaniment to fried meat loaf,
cured rib of pork, Kassel style (page 72) or Viennese sausages and spätzle
(page 226).

Rocket with Parmesan (photograph)
A little more expensive

Preparation time: about 25
minutes, excluding cooling time

30 g/1 oz pine kernels
125 g/4½ oz rocket
**200 g/7 oz cocktail
tomatoes**
30 g/1 oz Parmesan

For the sauce:
**1-2 tablespoons balsamic
vinegar**
½ teaspoon liquid honey
salt, pepper
3 tablespoons olive oil

Per serving:
**P: 6 g, F: 19 g, C: 3 g,
kJ: 852, kcal: 203**

1   Fry the pine nuts in a pan without fat until golden-brown and
leave to cool.

2   Sort the rocket and remove all the yellowing, wilted leaves. Cut
off the thicker stems, wash the rocket, spin dry and cut the larger leaves in half. Wash the cocktail tomatoes, dry and cut in half
or quarters. Grate the Parmesan.

3   To make the sauce, mix together the vinegar and honey, season
with salt and pepper and whisk in the oil. Arrange the rocket in a
dish and garnish with cocktail tomatoes. Drizzle the dressing
over it and sprinkle the pine nuts and Parmesan on top.

Tip: This salad is ideal as a starter or with grilled dishes or fried meat.
Instead of pine nuts you can use peeled, flaked almonds or coarsely chopped
walnuts.

Chinese cabbage with fromage frais
For children

Preparation time:
about 25 minutes

**600 g/1¼ lb Chinese
cabbage**
**1 can tangerines, drained
weight 175 g/6 oz**
100 g/3½ oz cooked ham

For the sauce:
**100 g/3½ oz fresh herb
cheese**
**3 tablespoons each whip-
ping cream and tanger-
ine juice, from the can**
3-4 teaspoons vinegar
salt, sugar, pepper
**2 teaspoons assorted,
chopped herbs, e.g.
basil, parsley, chives**

1   Remove the outer, wilted leaves of the Chinese cabbage and cut
in half. Remove the hard inner stalk, rinse, drain thoroughly and
cut in narrow strips.

2   Drain the tangerines in a sieve, reserve the juice and put 4 tablespoons aside. Cut the ham into strips.

3   To make the sauce, mix together the fromage frais, cream and
tangerine juice and season with vinegar, salt, sugar and pepper.
Stir in the herbs. Put all salad ingredients in a bowl and stir in
the dressing just before serving.

Tip: This salad can also be served as a light meal with bread or rice. It also
makes an ideal party salad, but in this case the salad and the dressing should
be served separately. You can also use iceberg lettuce instead of Chinese
cabbage.

Per serving: **P: 10 g, F: 9 g, C: 12 g, kJ: 723, kcal: 173**

Mixed green salad
Classic

Preparation time:
about 20 minutes

¼ **head Lollo Rossa or**
   Lollo Bionda
¼ **head oak leaf salad**
200 g/7 oz chicory

For the sauce:
1 small onion
1–2 tablespoons herb
   vinegar
salt
1 pinch sugar
crushed, dried green
   peppercorns
4 tablespoons olive oil
2 teaspoons chopped
   herbs, e.g. parsley,
   chive, chervil

Per serving:
P: 1 g, F: 15 g, C: 3 g,
kJ: 635, kcal: 152

1   Remove the outer, yellowing leaves of the two kinds of lettuce. Wash, spin dry and tear into smaller pieces (photograph 1).

2   Remove the outer, wilted leaves of the chicory, cut in half length-ways, wash, leave to drain and cut out the bitter, wedge-shaped inner stalks (photograph 2). Cut the chicory into strips and mix together in a bowl with the two kinds of lettuce.

3   To make the sauce, peel the onion and chop finely. Mix together the vinegar, salt, sugar and peppercorns. Whisk in the oil and stir in the chopped onion and herbs (photograph 3). Pour the dressing over the salad, mix carefully and serve immediately.

Tip: This mixed green salad can be served as a starter and is also delicious served with meat and fish dishes, pasta and gratins.
Store fresh green salad in a large plastic bag, fill it with a little air and close carefully. Place the bag in the vegetable compartment where the lettuce cannot be crushed and will remain fresh for longer because of the air inside the bag.

Variation 1: The possibilities for variations on this recipe are endless. For instance, you can replace the round lettuce with curly endive, fresh spinach or lamb's lettuce, use hazelnut or walnut oil instead of olive oil, and raspberry vinegar instead of herb vinegar.

Variation 2: For a **mixed green salad with escalopes**, rinse 500 g/18 oz chicken, turkey or pork escalope under cold running water, pat dry, cut into thick slices and marinate in a mixture of 3 tablespoons soya sauce, seasoned with pepper. Then drain the meat slices and fry on both sides in 3 tablespoons of hot oil (for instance, sunflower oil) for about 4–6 minutes. Arrange the slices of meat, hot or cold, on the salad and serve immediately.

Bean sprout and avocado salad
Vegetarian

Preparation time:
about 30 minutes

150 g/5 oz lamb's lettuce
150 g/5 oz soy or mung
   bean sprouts
250 g/9 oz tomatoes
1 avocado

For the sauce:
1-2 tablespoons vinegar,
   e.g. herb vinegar
4 teaspoons water
salt
freshly ground pepper
1 pinch sugar
1 teaspoon medium
   mustard
3 tablespoons cooking oil,
   e.g. walnut oil

Per serving:
P: 4 g, F: 24 g, C: 4 g,
kJ: 1030, kcal: 246

1   Remove the root ends of the lamb's lettuce in such a way that the florets still hold together. Remove any yellowing leaves, wash thoroughly and spin dry. Put the bean sprouts in a sieve, rinse under cold running water and drain thoroughly. Put them on a tea towel if necessary.

2   Wash the tomatoes, wipe dry, remove the stalks and cut into slices. Cut the avocado in half lengthways, remove the stone, peel and cut into slices lengthways.

3   To make the sauce, mix together the water and vinegar, add the salt, pepper, sugar and mustard and whisk in the oil. Arrange the prepared salad ingredients in a dish and pour the sauce over them.

Tip: Serve the bean sprout and avocado salad as a light meal with bread or as an accompaniment to white meat or fish.
You can also sprinkle 50 g/2 oz chopped walnuts over the salad and the bean sprouts may be replaced with lentil sprouts.

Variation: To make a colourful bean sprout salad, remove all yellowing outer leaves of 1 round or Lollo Bionda lettuce, wash the salad, spin dry and shred into pieces. Peel 2 red onions and cut into strips. Peel 2 carrots and cut off the green leaves and tips. Wash the carrots, drain and chop coarsely. Prepare 150 g/5 oz soya or mung bean sprouts as indicated above. To make the salad dressing, mix together 2–3 tablespoons herb vinegar with 1–2 tablespoons water, add salt, pepper and sugar, whisk in 5 tablespoons vegetable oil (e.g. sunflower oil) and pour over the salad; mix well. Sprinkle 2 tablespoons sesame seeds over the salad.

Pork sausage and cheese salad
(photograph)

Easy

Preparation time: about 35
minutes, excluding soaking time

250 g/9 oz onions
250 g/9 oz Emmental
cheese, 350 g/12 oz
cooked pork sausages,
75 g/3 oz pickles

For the sauce:
4 teaspoons wine vinegar
4 teaspoons water
1 teaspoon mustard
salt, pepper, sugar
3 tablespoons cooking oil
2 teaspoons chopped
chives

Per serving:
P: 28 g, F: 51 g, C: 4 g,
kJ: 2481, kcal: 539

1 Peel the onions, cut into rings, put in boiling water and cook for 2 minutes. Pour into a sieve and leave to drain.

2 Remove the rind from the Emmental cheese and cut into strips. Remove the skin from the sausage and cut the meat in half lengthways if necessary. Cut the sausage meat and pickled gherkins into slices.

3 To make the sauce, mix together the vinegar with the water, add the mustard, salt, pepper and sugar and whisk in the oil. Pour the dressing over the salad ingredients and mix well. Leave the salad to stand for 1 hour for the sauce to impregnate the ingredients. Sprinkle with chopped chives before serving.

Tip: The pork sausage and cheese salad can be served as a light meal with pretzels or rolls or as part of a party buffet.
This salad can also be prepared with chicken meat sausage.

Variation: To make a **smoked loin of pork and cheese salad**, use smoked loin of pork instead of pork sausage, cut into strips and add to the salad.

Egg salad with leeks
For guests

Preparation time:
about 40 minutes

300 g/10 oz leeks
300 g/10 oz carrots
½ head iceberg lettuce
(about 150 g/5 oz)
6 hard-boiled eggs

For the sauce:
100 g/3½ oz salad
mayonnaise
150 g/5 oz natural yogurt
4 teaspoons lemon juice
salt, pepper, sugar
2 teaspoons chopped
chives

1 Remove the outer leaves of the leeks, cut off the root ends and dark leaves. Cut in half lengthways, wash thoroughly, leave to drain and cut into very fine strips. Peel the carrots and cut off the green leaves and tips. Wash the carrots, leave to drain and grate coarsely.

2 Remove the outer, yellowing leaves of the iceberg lettuce, cut into very fine strips, wash and spin dry. Shell the eggs and cut into six segments (perhaps with an egg slicer).

3 To make the mayonnaise, mix together the yogurt and lemon juice and season with salt, pepper and sugar. Stir the dressing into the prepared salad ingredients (except for the eggs) and mix well. Check the seasoning and adjust if necessary. Garnish with the egg segments and sprinkle the chopped chives on top.

Tip: Serve the egg and leek salad with bread or boiled potatoes as a light meal. It is also ideal as part of a party buffet.

Per serving: **P: 14 g, F: 24 g, C: 9 g, kJ: 1287, kcal: 307**

Potato salad with mayonnaise
Traditional

Preparation time: about 45
minutes, excluding cooling and
soaking time

**800 g/1³⁄₄ lb firm cooking
potatoes**
2 onions
**250 ml/8 fl oz (1 cup)
vegetable stock**
**100 g/3¹⁄₂ oz pickled
gherkins (from the jar)**
3 hard-boiled eggs

For the sauce:
**3 tablespoons
mayonnaise**
**2 tablespoons gherkin
liquid**
salt
freshly ground pepper

Per serving:
P: 10 g, F: 10 g, C: 29 g,
kJ: 1044, kcal: 249

1 Wash the potatoes, put in a saucepan filled with water, bring to the boil, cover and cook over medium heat for about 20-25 minutes.

2 Drain the potatoes when cooked, rinse briefly under cold running water and leave to drain. Peel while still hot and leave to cool down. Then cut the potatoes into slices and put in a large bowl.

3 Peel the onions, cut into very small cubes and bring to the boil in the vegetable stock. Cover and cook for 1 minute. Pour the hot onion and stock mixture over the sliced potatoes and leave to soak for at least 30 minutes. Cut the pickled gherkins into slices or cubes. Shell the eggs and cut into cubes.

4 For the sauce, stir the liquid from the gherkins into the mayonnaise. Then mix together all the ingredients with the cooled potato slices in the onion stock mixture. Season with salt and pepper and leave to stand for at least 30 minutes.

Tip: Potato salad is delicious served with grilled dishes, sausages, meat loaf made of liver, ham and pork, roast gammon or meat balls (page 78).

Variation 1: To make **potato salad with pork sausage**, take 1 peeled, cored and diced apple and 250 g/9 oz cooked pork sausage, removed from its skin and cut into cubes. Add to the salad and mix well.

Variation 2: To make **potato salad with radishes**, cut off the root tips and the leaves of a bunch of radishes, wash, cut into slices and stir into the salad. Rinse the radish leaves, pat dry, cut into strips and stir into the sauce together with 50 g/2 oz natural yogurt (3.5% fat).

Variation 3: To make **potato salad with pumpkin**, use a jar of pickled pumpkin (drained weight 200 g/7 oz) instead of gherkins. Drain in a colander, reserve the liquid and use 3 tablespoons of this liquid for the sauce instead of the gherkin liquid. Cut the pumpkin pieces smaller if necessary.

Variation 4: To make **potato salad with tomatoes**, leave out the gherkins and eggs. Take 4 tomatoes, wash, wipe dry and remove the stalks. Cut the tomatoes into four, remove the seeds and cut into cubes. Wash 1 small courgette, wipe dry, cut off the ends and slice thinly. Add these two ingredients to the salad. To make the sauce, stir together 300 g/10 oz natural yogurt (3.5% fat) with 1-2 tablespoons vinegar, 2 tablespoons olive oil and season with salt, pepper and sugar. Pour over the salad and mix well. Sprinkle 2 tablespoons of chopped chives on top.

Warm potato salad
Good for preparing in advance

1   Wash the potatoes, put in a pan and cover with water. Bring to
the boil, cover and cook over low heat for about 20-25 minutes.

2   In the meantime, peel the onions for the sauce and cut into
cubes. Dice the bacon, put in a frying pan without fat and cook
over medium heat so that the fat is released. Strain the fat
through a sieve into a small bowl and reserve the fried diced
bacon.

3   Add the diced onions to the stock and bring to the boil. Cover
and cook for about 5 minutes. Add the vinegar, salt, pepper and
sugar and stir in the bacon fat.

4   Drain the potatoes when cooked and rinse briefly in cold water.
Drain again and peel while still hot. Cut into slices and arrange in
a heat-resistant dish. Pour the salad dressing over the sliced
potatoes and mix well. Leave to stand for a few hours so that the
flavours can soak in.

5   Preheat the oven. Check the seasoning and add salt, pepper and
vinegar to taste. Put the dish in the oven and stir occasionally.

Top/bottom heat: **about 150 °C/300 °F (preheated),**
Fan oven: **about 130 °C/250 °F (not preheated),** Gas mark ½ (preheated),
Cooking time: **15-20 minutes.**

6   Stir in the chives, scatter the fried diced bacon on top and serve
warm.

Tip: Serve the hot potato salad with gammon, Vienna sausages, small
frankfurters or meat loaf made of liver, ham and pork.

Variation 1: Streaky bacon can be used instead of fatty bacon. In this case
fry the diced bacon in 2 tablespoons hot vegetable oil (e.g. sunflower oil) to
release the fat.

Variation 2: To turn this dish into a vegetarian dish, leave out the bacon and
stir in 4 tablespoons olive or walnut oil into the sauce.

Variation 3: To make a **warm potato salad with pumpkin seeds**, fry 70 g/
3 oz pumpkin seeds in a pan without fat and make the sauce without bacon
fat. Instead, use 4 tablespoons vegetable oil (e.g. sunflower oil). Stir the
pumpkin seeds into the salad and sprinkle some pumpkin seed oil over the
salad according to taste.

Preparation time: about 50
minutes, excluding soaking time

**1 kg/2¼ lb firm cooking
  potatoes**

For the sauce:
2 onions
75 g/3 oz fatty bacon
**125 ml/4 fl oz (½ cup)
  vegetable stock**
**2-3 tablespoons herb
  vinegar**
salt
freshly ground pepper
1 pinch sugar

**4 teaspoons chopped
  chives**

Per serving:
**P: 6 g, F: 15 g, C: 35 g,
kJ: 1263, kcal: 301**

Rice salad
Sophisticated (4-6 servings)

Preparation time: about 30
minutes, excluding cooling and
soaking time

about 600 ml/21 oz
 (2½ cups) water
1 lightly rounded
 teaspoon salt
200 g/7 oz long grain or
 brown rice
200 g/7 oz slices of
 cooked ham
150 g/5 oz black grapes
150 g/5 oz celery stalks
1 banana

For the sauce:
150 g/5 oz natural yogurt
 (3.5% fat)
4 teaspoons mayonnaise
2 tablespoons whipping
 cream
4 teaspoons lemon juice
salt
freshly ground pepper
some sugar

Per serving:
P: 14 g, F: 9 g, C: 41 g,
kJ: 1261, kcal: 301

1   Bring the water to the boil in a covered pan. Then add the salt
    and rice, stir and bring to the boil again. Cover and cook over low
    heat for 12-15 minutes (brown rice about 20 minutes). Drain the
    rice in a sieve and allow to cool down, stirring occasionally.

2   Cut the ham slices into strips. Wash the grapes, drain, remove
    the stalks, cut the grapes in half and remove the seeds if any.

3   Remove the root ends, yellowing leaves and tough stringy fibres
    from the celery. Wash the stalks, drain and cut into thin slices.
    Peel the banana and slice.

4   To make the sauce, mix together the mayonnaise, cream and
    lemon juice, then season with salt, pepper and sugar. Stir the
    dressing into the salad ingredients, let soak in and check the
    seasoning again, adding more salt, pepper and sugar if neces-
    sary.

Variation 1: Instead of long grain rice or brown rice you can also make this
salad with a mixture of rice and wild rice. Cook this mixture following the
instructions on the packet and add 50 g/2 oz raisins about 10 minutes before
the end of the cooking time. Drain the rice and raisins and rinse quickly with
cold water.

Variation 2: To make **curried rice salad**, heat 3 tablespoons vegetable oil,
add the rice, fry briefly and stir in 1-2 teaspoons curry powder. Add 750 ml/
1¼ pints (3½ cups) vegetable or chicken stock, cover and simmer gently over
low heat for about 20 minutes. Mix the cooked rice with the other ingredients
listed above.

Potatoes, rice & pasta

Pasta

Cooking pasta

Pasta should always be cooked in plenty of water so that it has enough space to expand and does not stick together. You need 1 litre water per 100 g pasta (2 pints or 5 cups per 4 oz). If the quantity exceeds 400–500 g/14–18 oz it should be cooked in 2 saucepans. Add 1 teaspoon salt for each litre/ 2 pints (5 cups) of water. The salt and pasta should only be added to the water when it is boiling. Cook the pasta uncovered over medium heat following the instructions on the packet (home-made pasta only needs a few minutes) until al dente, stirring occasionally. Strain the cooked pasta in a colander, rinse under hot water (or cold water for pasta salad) and drain.

Pasta is a popular and very versatile food that can be served as a side dish, in soups or on its own as a main dish. It comes in many forms and colours; it may be stuffed or plain, dried or fresh, the latter being be found in refrigerated compartments in shops. Pasta is easy to store (especially dried pasta which keeps for a very long time) and also to prepare. There are two kinds of pasta: pasta made from flour, water, salt and egg, and pasta made from semolina,

flour, water and salt, but without egg.

Those who prefer can also make the pasta themselves (for instance, spätzle, page 226). The pasta dough can be coloured according to taste, for instance with tomato purée, puréed spinach, very finely chopped herbs, saffron or beetroot juice.

Potatoes

Potatoes contain important vitamins, minerals, nutrients and fibre. They have excellent physiologically nutritional properties that are best preserved when prepared without fat and care is taken not to destroy the nutrients they contain. Different potato varieties have different properties. This is why the choice of potato is very important. Based on their cooking properties potatoes are classed as follows:

- Varieties with waxy, firm flesh. These varieties are particularly suitable for salads, boiling and fried potatoes.
- Varieties with fairly firm flesh. These are very suitable for boiling, as jacket potatoes, for frying and baking (en papillote) or as a roast vegetable.
- Floury varieties. These are ideal for making dumplings, potato fritters, pancakes, potato cakes, or for use in soups and stews.

Storing

Potatoes should be stored in a dark, well ventilated, cool space (4–6 °C/39–43 °F). If there is any light and the temperature is too high the potatoes will begin to germinate and sometimes turn green in places. Potatoes may be covered with paper. If you do not have good storage facilities it is best to buy smaller amounts which will only be stored for a short time.

Tips

- For jacket potatoes, always choose potatoes of the same size so that they will take the same time to cook (prick with a fork or knife to check whether the potatoes are cooked).

- For boiled potatoes, cut the potatoes in pieces of roughly the same size so that they will take the same time to cook.
- Only peel the potatoes just before you are going to prepare them. Put them in cold water so that they do not discolour.
- Early potatoes (the earliest can be harvested at the beginning of June) have such a thin skin that they do not need peeling. In this case, wash and brush the potatoes very carefully to remove all soil. Early potatoes contain very little starch so they are not suitable for many dishes such as dumplings, potato dough or roast vegetables.
- To boil potatoes, barely cover them in water or cook with very little water, in a potato steamer.
- After pouring away the cooking liquid, return the potatoes to the pan and leave uncovered to let the steam evaporates, while shaking the pan slightly. You can also put a tea towel or kitchen paper between the saucepan and the lid to absorb the steam.

Dumplings

Dumplings are made from various basic doughs. These are usually made from raw or cooked potatoes or bread rolls, but yeast dough, semolina and spelt are also used. Depending on the recipe, different flavours can be added to the dough, which is normally savoury but may also be sweet.

People who prefer to spare themselves the trouble of making dumplings themselves can also buy them ready-made.

Tips:

- Mix the ingredients very thoroughly so that they form a homogenous mass.
- Cut out the dumplings with a spoon and shape them with your hands, previously moistened or lightly coated in flour.
- To fill dumplings, first shape into a ball, then make a hole large enough to be filled with the stuffing. Then carefully press the dough back over the stuffing and smooth out the surface.
- Oblong dumplings are made with two spoons, previously moistened. Press the mass from one spoon onto the other until an oblong dumpling is formed.

- When they have been made, put the dumplings on a plate moistened with water or lightly coated with flour to prevent sticking.
- Dumplings need a lot of room to cook, so a large pan is needed.
- Test one dumpling to check whether the dough is the right consistency. If the dumpling disintegrates, add a little more semolina, potato or flour. But if the dumpling is too firm, add a little more stock, milk, curd cheese or egg to the dough.
- Put the dumplings in boiling water, lower the heat and cook the dumplings with the lid on, except for yeast-based dumplings. Do not boil: the water should only be "moving" very gently.
- Shake the pan lightly now and again to make the dumplings rise to the surface.
- Towards the end of the cooking time, take one dumpling out of the water and open using two forks. If the inside is dry, the dumplings are ready. If the inside is moist, the dumplings must cook a little longer.
- When the dumplings are done, remove from the water with a skimming ladle and leave to drain thoroughly.

Rice

Rice is rich in vitamins and minerals, low in calories and very easy to digest.

Basmati rice
An aromatic variety of rice which develops a delicate fragrance when cooked.

Brown rice
The brownish grains still have the soft, silvery inner membrane and the seedling that contains important vitamins and minerals.

Because this variety goes rancid rather quickly it also should be used soon after purchase and not stored for too long. It takes longer to cook than polished rice varieties. Polished rice is produced when the silvery membrane of the brown rice is removed. This involves the grains being cleaned, polished and glazed. Polished rice contains fewer vitamins than brown rice. The fatty elements are removed and it can be stored for longer.

Easy-cook rice
This type of rice is pre-cooked after polishing, so it only needs to be cooked for 3–5 minutes.

Long grain rice (Patna rice)
This is a widely used variety of rice. The grains are long and narrow and appear slightly transparent when uncooked. This variety is ideally suited for spicy rice-based dishes.

Parboiled rice
In the case of parboiled rice, the vitamins and minerals are transferred from the silvery membrane to the inner core of the grain. This means that the rice retains its vitamins and minerals when it is cleaned and polished. Parboiled rice is slightly yellowish before cooking and turns white when

cooked. The grains remain separate even when the rice is cooked again.

Risotto rice

This has a medium-sized grain (i.e. between short grain and long grain) and originates from Italy. It produces a lot of starch during the cooking process which gives risotto its creamy consistency.

Short grain rice

This variety has short grains as the name suggests. It produces a lot of starch when it swells up, while also becoming very soft and mushy. This variety is almost exclusively used for making rice puddings.

Wild rice

Strictly speaking, wild rice is not rice but the seed of a variety of aquatic grasses. The grains are thin, almost black and have a nutty flavour. It is very expensive and is usually only available mixed with long-grain rice.

Preparation

Rice trebles in volume during the cooking process. This means that 1 cup of raw rice produces 3 cups of cooked rice. The cooking time depends on the type of rice. Unhusked rice needs to be cooked for 35–40 minutes, while husked rice only needs

from 15-20 minutes (follow the instructions on the packet). You can cook rice either in plenty of boiling salted water, or first fry it in a little oil and then cook in less liquid to enable it to swell (ratio of rice to liquid = 1 to 2). Many vitamins and minerals are lost when the cooking liquid is poured away. But when rice swells up it absorbs all the liquid so that it retains all the nutrients.

Tip

- Cooked rice will not stick together if you place a tea towel between the saucepan and the lid. The steam produced by the rice will then be absorbed by the towel, thus preventing condensation. A further advantage is that the rice does not continue to cook.
- Arrange the cooked rice in a soup tureen, greased mould or cup, press down lightly and turn over on a preheated dish.
- To heat up large quantities of rice, put in a greased, heat-resistant dish, cover and heat in the oven preheated to 150 °C/300 °F (Gas mark 2).
- Leftover rice will keep in the refrigerator for up to 3 days but it should be covered. It is even better to freeze leftover rice, then defrost it in a

sieve over hot steam before reheating it.
- Rice which will be added to soup should be slightly undercooked and only added to the soup just before serving because it continues to cook in the hot liquid.

Cereal

The term cereal refers to cereal grains such as rice, rye, wheat, barley, oats, millet, buckwheat and maize. Cereals also include pearl barley, starch, sago and custard powder. Cereals are very important in the diet because they contain important vitamins, minerals, trace elements and fibre. Cereals come in a variety of forms including whole grain, crushed flakes and finely or coarsely ground.

Potatoes baked in foil (photograph)
Easy

Preparation time:
about 60 minutes

**8 floury cooking
potatoes, about
1 kg/2¼ lb
salt**

For the sauce:
**150 g/5 oz crème fraîche
2 teaspoons chopped
parsley
salt
freshly ground pepper
some ground caraway
seed (optional)**

In addition:
aluminium foil

Per serving:
P: 6 g, F: 12 g, C: 39 g,
kJ: 1207, kcal: 290

1 Preheat the oven at the top and bottom. Brush the potatoes thoroughly clean under cold running water, pat dry and make a lengthways incision 1 cm/³⁄₈ in deep (photograph 1). Wrap each potato separately in foil (photograph 2) and put on a shelf in the bottom third of the oven.

Top/bottom heat: about 200 °C/400 °F (preheated),
Fan oven: about 180 °C/350 °F (not preheated), Gas mark 6 (preheated),
Cooking time: 45–60 minutes.

2 In the meantime, make the sauce. Stir the chopped parsley into the crème fraîche and season with salt and pepper. Add a little caraway if desired.

3 When the potatoes are cooked, open up the aluminium foil, split the potato open using two forks (photograph 3) and pour in the sauce.

Tip: Serve baked potatoes with grilled fish or vegetables, with steak or as a snack.
Very large potatoes (250 g/9 oz) are sold as baking potatoes, and usually 1 potato per person will be enough.

Variation 1: **Potatoes baked in foil with salmon** (photograph). Cut 100 g/3½ oz smoked salmon or gravad lax into very fine strips. Stuff the hot baked potatoes with the crème fraîche and garnish with the strips of salmon.

Variation 2: **Potatoes baked in foil with horseradish curd cheese.** Instead of crème fraîche, mix 200 g/7 oz curd cheese (20% fat) with 1–2 tablespoons milk and stir in 1–2 tablespoons grated horseradish (from a jar) and season with salt. Finely chop 100 g/3½ oz ham and stir into the sauce. Fill the hot potatoes with the curd cheese and ham mixture.

Variation 3: **Potatoes baked in foil with Bolognese sauce.** Prepare half the amount of the Bolognese sauce following the recipe on page 149, reduce until thick, fill the hot potatoes with the Bolognese sauce and sprinkle 1 tablespoon chopped basil on top.

Boiled potatoes
Easy

Preparation time:
about 30 minutes

750 g/1½ lb potatoes
1 teaspoon salt

Per serving:
P: 3 g, F: 0 g, C: 22 g,
kJ: 447, kcal: 106

1 Wash the potatoes, thinly peel with a knife or potato peeler and remove any eyes.

2 Rinse the potatoes again, cut the larger potatoes into two or three pieces and put in a pan. Sprinkle with salt, barely cover with water and bring to the boil. Cook the potatoes covered for 20-25 minutes.

3 Drain the cooking water. Leave the potatoes in the open pan, shaking occasionally so that the steam escapes, or put a tea towel or kitchen paper between the lid and the pan to absorb the steam.

Tip: Boiled potatoes go well with most meat, fish or vegetable dishes with sauce.

Variation: For **parsley potatoes,** prepare the potatoes as above and toss in 20-30 g/¾-1 oz melted butter and 2 tablespoons of chopped parsley.

Potatoes boiled in their skins
Easy

Preparation time:
about 30 minutes

about 1 kg/2¼ lb
potatoes

Per serving:
P: 5 g, F: 0 g, C: 33 g,
kJ: 670, kcal: 160

1 Thoroughly wash the potatoes, cover with water and bring to the boil, then cook covered for 20-25 minutes.

2 Drain the potatoes, quench with cold water, drain and peel immediately.

Tip: These potatoes can be served as a side dish or with herb curd cheese and salad as an entrée.
The potatoes can be used in a salad or for making sauté potatoes. A firm potato is preferable for this purpose.

Variation: **Béchamel potatoes.** Cook 750 g/1½ lb firm-fleshed potatoes as above, quench with cold water, peel immediately and leave to cool a little. Make a béchamel sauce (page 141), slice the still warm potatoes into the sauce and heat through, stirring occasionally so that the sauce does not burn. Season to taste with salt, pepper and nutmeg and with 2-3 tablespoons grated horseradish (from the jar). Sprinkle with 2 tablespoons chopped parsley. Béchamel potatoes may be served as a side dish with rissoles (page 78), steamed vegetables or fried fish.

Potato pancakes
Classic

1   Wash the potatoes, peel and rinse. Peel the onions. Grate the
    potatoes (photograph 1) and onion finely over a bowl. Add the
    eggs, salt and flour and mix well (photograph 2).

2   Heat a little oil in a pan. Spoon small quantities of the potato and
    onion mixture in the pan using a gravy ladle or tablespoon (pho-
    tograph 3), press flat immediately and cook the potato pancakes
    on both sides over medium heat until the edge turns crispy
    brown.

3   Take the pancakes out of the pan, remove excess fat by dabbing
    them dry with kitchen paper and serve immediately, or keep in a
    warm place.

4   Make the rest of the pancakes in the same way.

Tip: Potato pancakes can be served with apple sauce or plum compote
(page 281), herb or horseradish curd cheese or with smoked salmon with
herb-flavoured crème fraîche and a green salad.
The potato pancakes will be even crisper if half the flour is replaced with
2–3 tablespoons rolled oats.

Variation 1: Put the fried pancakes on a baking sheet lined with greaseproof
paper. Put 1–2 slices of tomatoes and 1 slice of mozzarella on top of each
pancake, sprinkle some pepper on top and cook briefly in the preheated oven
(top/bottom heat: about 220 °C/425 °F, fan oven: about 200 °C/400 °F,
gas mark 7) until the cheese melts. Garnish with small basil leaves before
serving.

Variation 2: To make **potato pancakes with ham,** cut 50 g/2 oz ham on the
bone into thin strips and add to the potato and onion mixture together with
1–2 teaspoons marjoram. Alternatively, strips of ham may be added to crème
fraîche and served with the potato pancakes.

Preparation time:
about 45 minutes

**1 kg/2¼ lb floury
  potatoes
1 onion
3 medium eggs
1 heaped teaspoon salt
40 g/1½ oz (6 table-
  spoons) plain (all-
  purpose) flour
100 ml/3½ fl oz (½ cup)
  cooking oil, e.g.
  sunflower oil**

Per serving:
P: 11 g, F: 20 g, C: 37 g,
kJ: 1566, kcal: 373

Rösti (photograph background)
Classic

Preparation time: about 45
minutes, excluding cooling time

**500 g/18 oz firm cooking
potatoes**
salt
**4 tablespoons cooking oil,
e.g. sunflower oil**
freshly ground pepper

Per serving:
P: 2 g, F: 13 g, C: 17 g,
kJ: 797, kcal: 190

1 Wash the potatoes carefully, put in a pan filled with water, cover and bring to the boil. Cook for 20 minutes, drain, then rinse in cold water and peel. Put them in a covered container and refrigerate for at least 4 hours or overnight.

2 Grate the potatoes coarsely (photograph 1) and season with salt. Heat some of the oil in a non-stick pan (24 cm/9½ in in diameter). Put the grated potatoes in the pan, press flat (photograph 2) and fry on both sides over low heat for about 10 minutes until brown and crisp, turning once.

3 Cut the rösti into 4 pieces before serving.

Tip: Rösti are delicious served with Züricher Geschnetzeltes (thin strips of meat cooked in sauce, page 68) and fried meat.
To turn the rösti over you can slide it from the pan onto a saucepan lid and then slide it back into the pan.
You can also make several small rösti instead of one large one.

Variation 1: **Courgettes and herb rösti** (photograph foreground). Wash 100 g/3½ oz courgettes, wipe dry, cut off the ends and slice. Peel 1 onion, chop finely and stir into the grated potatoes together with 1 tablespoon dried herbs of Provence. Season with salt. Fry the rösti as indicated above. Put a few courgette slices in the pan and cover with the rösti mixture. Before returning the rösti to the pan after turning them, add a few more courgette slices to the pan and fry until brown and crisp. Serve as a snack with crème fraîche or yogurt and green salad.

Variation 2: **Mini-apple rösti.** Wash, dry and peel 2 apples, remove the cores, cut the apples in rings and sprinkle 1 tablespoon lemon juice over them. Divide the grated potato mass into 12 portions and fry the rösti as indicated above. After turning, cover each rösti with 1 apple ring and fry until they are brown and crisp. Mix together 1 tablespoon chopped chives and 200 g/7 oz sour cream, add a little salt and pour over the apple rösti. Sprinkle with coarsely ground pepper. Serve hot as a snack.

Potato gratin
For guests

Preparation time:
about 60 minutes

1 clove garlic
800 g/1¾ lb floury
  potatoes
salt
freshly ground pepper
grated nutmeg
125 ml/4 fl oz (½ cup)
  milk
125 ml/4 fl oz (½ cup)
  whipping cream
4 teaspoons grated
  Parmesan cheese

In addition:
fat for the mould

Per serving:
P: 6 g, F: 13 g, C: 26 g,
kJ: 1051, kcal: 251

1 Preheat the oven top and bottom. Peel the clove of garlic, cut in half and rub a well-greased, shallow gratin dish with it.

2 Wash the potatoes, peel, rinse and pat dry. Then cut into thin slices and arrange these in the gratin dish sloping downward like roof tiles (photograph 1). Sprinkle with salt, pepper and nutmeg (photograph 2).

3 Stir the milk and the cream together and pour over the potato slices (photograph 3). Sprinkle Parmesan on top. Put the gratin dish uncovered in the oven on the middle shelf and bake until golden brown.

Top/bottom heat: about 180 °C/350 °F (preheated),
Fan oven: about 160 °C/325 °F (not preheated), Gas mark 4 (not preheated),
Cooking time: 45 minutes.

Tip: Serve the potato gratin with meat, fish or vegetable-based dishes that have no sauce.

Variation 1: Instead of milk and cream, use 250 ml/8 fl oz (1 cup) vegetable stock flavoured with 2 tablespoons white wine or crème fraîche to pour over the potato slices. Sprinkle with Parmesan and bake as indicated above.

Variation 2: **Potato gratin with ceps.** Put 20 g/¾ oz dried ceps in a sieve and rinse with cold water. Add them to 250 ml/8 fl oz (1 cup) vegetable stock, bring to the boil and leave covered to cool down. Pour the stock with the ceps over the potatoes instead of the milk and cream. Sprinkle Parmesan on top, add a few knobs of butter and bake as indicated above.

Variation 3: **Potato and carrot gratin.** Replace 300 g/10 oz of the potatoes with thinly sliced carrots. Arrange the sliced carrots and sliced potatoes as described above in layers and sprinkle with 1 tablespoon thyme.

Potato chips (French fries)
For children

1 Wash the potatoes, peel, rinse and cut into pencil-thick sticks of equal length. Wipe dry with kitchen paper.

2 Heat the oil in a pan to about 180 °C/350 °F. Put the potato sticks in the hot oil in small amounts, using a skimming ladle and fry for about 2 minutes until half-cooked. Important: do not put too many potato sticks in the oil at once because they should not touch each other in the hot oil and in addition the oil would cool down too quickly.

3 As soon as the potato sticks turn yellow at the ends, remove them from the oil with the skimming ladle. Spread them on a baking sheet lined with kitchen paper and leave to drain. Pre-cook all the potato sticks in this way.

4 When the potato sticks have cooled down, return them to the hot oil and fry for another 4–5 minutes until brown and crisp. Remove from the oil with the skimming ladle, drain, sprinkle with salt and serve immediately.

Tip: You can check the temperature of the oil by dipping a wooden spoon in the oil. If small bubbles rise up along the handle the oil is hot enough. Lower the heat to a medium setting while frying the chips. If the oil is not hot enough the potato chips will become saturated with oil, but if the oil is too hot, the potatoes will burn without being cooked through.
If chips are made in a deep-fat fryer, a larger amount of oil will be needed (follow the manufacturer's instructions).

Variation: **Potato crisps.** Choose 500 g/18 oz potatoes with firm flesh, wash, peel, rinse and cut into thin slices with a sharp knife or vegetable slicer (photograph 1) and pat dry. Pre-cook the potato slices in small quantities in the hot oil, remove them from the oil, spread them on a wire tray and leave to drain (photograph 2). Return the crisps to the hot oil and fry again until pale brown (photograph 3). Sprinkle with salt and paprika and serve as a snack.

Preparation time:
about 60 minutes

1 kg/2¼ lb floury potatoes
salt

For cooking:
about 750 ml/1¼ pints
(3½ cups) cooking oil,
e.g. sunflower oil

Per serving:
P: 4 g, F: 10 g, C: 30 g,
kJ: 940, kcal: 224

Baked potato halves with curd cheese
(photograph)
Easy

Preparation time:
about 60 minutes

**1.2 kg/4½ lb floury
  potatoes
3 tablespoons cooking oil
40 g/1½ oz (3 table-
  spoons) butter
4 teaspoons caraway seeds
salt**

For the herb curd cheese:
**500 g/18 oz curd cheese
4 teaspoons sour cream
about 4 tablespoons milk
2 teaspoons chervil,
  parsley, dill, chives,
  salt, coarse coloured
  pepper**

In addition:
fat for the griddle

1 Preheat the oven top and bottom. Brush the potatoes until thoroughly clean under cold running water and wipe dry. Heat the oil with the butter.

2 Cut the unpeeled potatoes in half lengthways, brush the cut surfaces with the oil and butter mixture, sprinkle caraway seeds on top and arrange on a greased baking sheet with the cut surfaces facing upward. Pour the rest of the oil and butter mixture over the potatoes and sprinkle with salt.

Top/bottom heat: about 200 °C/400 °F (preheated),
Fan oven: about 180 °C/350 °F (not preheated), Gas mark 6 (preheated),
Cooking time: about 40 minutes.

3 Meanwhile, make the herb curd cheese by mixing the curd cheese with sour cream, milk and herbs. Season with salt and pepper. Serve the herb curd cheese with the baked potato halves.

Tip: Serve the baked potato halves with vegetables or a green salad, or as part of a party buffet.

Per serving: P: 5 g, F: 15 g, C: 35 g, kJ: 1256, kcal: 300

Fried potatoes
Good value

Preparation time: about 60 minutes,
excluding cooling time

**1 kg/2¼ lb floury
  potatoes
50-70 g/2-3 oz butter or
  3-4 tablespoons
  cooking oil, e.g.
  sunflower oil
salt, pepper, 2 onions**

Per serving:
P: 5 g, F: 15 g, C: 35 g,
kJ: 1256, kcal: 300

1 Wash the potatoes thoroughly and put in a saucepan filled with water. Bring to the boil, cover and cook for 20-25 minutes. Drain the potatoes, then dip briefly in cold water and peel immediately. Leave to cool, then cut into slices.

2 Heat the clarified butter or oil in a large pan, add the sliced potatoes, season with salt and pepper and fry over low heat for about 15 minutes until golden brown, turning occasionally.

3 Meanwhile, peel the onions and dice. Add the diced onions to the potatoes and fry for a further 5-10 minutes, stirring occasionally. Check the seasoning and add salt and pepper if necessary.

(continued on page 218)

Raw potato dumplings (photograph)
Classic (12 dumplings)

Preparation time:
about 60 minutes

**1.5 kg/3¼ lb firm cooking
potatoes**
250 ml/8 fl oz (1 cup) milk
**70 g/3 oz (4 tablespoons)
butter or margarine**
salt
**150 g/5 oz hard wheat
semolina flour**
1 bread roll
**salted water – 1 litre/1¾
pints (4½ cups) water
with 1 teaspoon salt**

Per serving:
P: 13 g, F: 18 g, C: 79 g,
kJ: 2242, kcal: 535

1   Wash the potatoes, peel, rinse and grate them into a bowl filled with cold water. Drain the grated potatoes in a sieve and press in a tea towel to squeeze out all the water.

2   Add 40 g/1½ oz (3 tablespoons) butter or margarine and 2 teaspoons salt to the milk and bring to the boil. Next stir in the semolina and briefly bring back to the boil. Then immediately add to the squeezed grated potatoes and form into a homogenous mass using a hand-held mixer with a kneading attachment. Check the seasoning and add salt if necessary.

3   Cut the roll into small cubes. Melt the remaining butter or margarine in a pan, add the diced roll and fry until brown, stirring occasionally.

4   Fill a saucepan with enough water for the dumplings to be able to "swim" in the liquid, add salt and bring to the boil. Make 12 dumplings from the grated potato mass, using your hands which you first moisten. Press a few fried bread croutons into each dumpling. Place the dumplings into the boiling salted water, bring back to the boil and cook covered for about 20 minutes with a lid (the water should bubble gently). Use a skimming ladle to remove the dumplings from the water when they are done. Drain them thoroughly.

Tip: Serve raw potato dumplings with roasts and meat dishes with a sauce. Leftover dumplings can be cut into slices and fried in clarified butter or vegetable oil until golden-brown on both sides.

Half-and-half potato dumplings
Classic (about 12 dumplings)

Preparation time: about 75
minutes, excluding cooling time

**1.25 g/2¾ lb firm cooking
potatoes**
1 medium egg
**65 g/2 oz (5 tablespoons)
plain (all-purpose) flour**
1 teaspoon salt

1   Wash 750 g/1½ lb of the potatoes thoroughly and bring to the boil in a saucepan of water. Cover and cook for about 20-25 minutes. Drain the potatoes, rinse with cold water and peel. Then immediately push them through a potato ricer or mash with a potato masher. Leave to cool down, cover and refrigerate until the following day.

2   Wash the rest of the potatoes, peel, rinse and grate into a bowl of cold water. Put in a sieve to drain and press in a tea towel to

(continued on page 222)

salted water – 1 litre/1¾
   pints (4½ cups) water
   with 1 teaspoon salt

Per serving:
P: 9 g, F: 2 g, C: 51 g,
kJ: 1116, kcal: 266

squeeze out all the water. Add to the cooked potato. Add the egg, flour and salt, and knead until the mixture forms a smooth consistency.

3   Shape 12 dumplings using your hands lightly coated with flour. Fill a large saucepan with enough water for the dumplings to be able to "swim" in the liquid. Add salt and bring to the boil. Put the dumplings in the boiling salted water, bring back to the boil and poach uncovered over low heat for about 20 minutes (the water should only move very slightly). When the dumplings are cooked, remove from the water with a skimming ladle and drain well.

Tip: Serve the potato dumplings with meat dishes accompanied by a sauce, e.g. roast pork or beef roulade.

Boiled potato dumplings
Classic (12 dumplings)

Preparation time: about 60 minutes, excluding cooling time

750 g/1½ lb firm cooking
   potatoes
50 g/2 oz breadcrumbs
20 g/¾ oz (3 table-
   spoons) plain (all-
   purpose) flour
2 medium eggs
salt
grated nutmeg
salted water – 1 litre/1¾
   pints (4½ cups) water
   with 1 teaspoon salt

Per serving:
P: 9 g, F: 4 g, C: 38 g,
kJ: 938, kcal: 224

1   Cover and cook for 20–25 minutes. Drain the potatoes, rinse in cold water, drain and peel. Push them through the potato ricer or mash with a potato masher. Leave to cool down, cover and refrigerate until the following day.

2   Knead the breadcrumbs, flour and eggs into the potato mixture using a hand-held mixer with kneading attachment, or using a mixing spoon. Season with salt and nutmeg. Shape 12 dumplings using your hands lightly coated with flour.

3   Fill a large saucepan with enough water for the dumplings to be able to "swim" in the liquid. Put the dumplings in the boiling salted water, bring to the boil again and cook uncovered for about 20 minutes (the water should only move very slightly). When the dumplings are cooked, remove from the water with a skimming ladle and drain thoroughly.

Tip: Serve potato dumplings with Sauerbraten (braised beef marinated in vinegar and herbs – page 60) or roast pork with red cabbage (page 175).

Variation 1: **Potato dumplings with bacon and parsley.** Chop up 100 g/ 3½ oz lean, streaky bacon and fry over medium heat to release the fat out. Add 1 tablespoon of chopped parsley, leave to cool down and add to the potato mixture. Then make the dumplings as described above.

Variation 2: **Sweet stuffed potato dumplings**. Wash 8–12 small apricots or plums (the amount depends on the size of the fruit), pat dry, halve, remove the stones and fill each with a cube of sugar. Prepare the potato purée without nutmeg and divide into 8–12 pieces of equal size. Stuff each piece with a fruit, shape into a dumpling and cook as indicated above. Melt 70 g/ 3 oz butter, then add 1–2 tablespoons breadcrumbs and 1 tablespoon sugar. Fry the mixture until golden-brown and pour over the drained dumplings.

Schupfnudeln (potato noodles)
For guests (36 dumplings)

1   Wash the potatoes, peel thinly, rinse and put in a saucepan. Add 1/2 teaspoon salt, add just enough water to cover the potatoes and bring to the boil. Cover and cook for about 20 minutes. Drain and dry the potatoes and put immediately through the potato ricer (photograph 1) or mash with a potato masher, then leave to cool down.

2   Stir the egg and flour into the potato purée and season with salt, pepper and nutmeg. Shape into finger-thick cylindrical rolls about 5 cm/2 in long, using your hands lightly coated with flour. Make the rolls slightly thinner at the ends (photograph 2).

3   Fill a large saucepan with enough water for the dumplings to be able to "swim" in the liquid and bring back to the boil. Put the dumplings in the boiling water, bring back to the boil and cook uncovered over low heat for 3–4 minutes (photograph 3). The water should only move very slightly.

4   Remove the dumplings from the water with a skimming ladle and leave to drain thoroughly. Melt the butter, add the dumplings and fry for 3–4 minutes, stirring occasionally.

Tip: Serve these dumplings with braised beef, goulash (page 59), Geschnetzeltes (small, thin slices of meat cooked in sauce, page 68) or sauerkraut (page 172).

Preparation time: about 60 minutes, excluding cooling time

300 g/10 oz floury cooking potatoes
salt
1 medium egg
100 g/3½ oz (1 cup) plain (all-purpose) flour
freshly ground pepper
grated nutmeg
salted water – 1 litre/1¾ pints (4½ cups) water with 1 teaspoon salt
30 g/1 oz (2 tablespoons) butter

Per serving:
P: 6 g, F: 8 g, C: 27 g,
kJ: 852, kcal: 203

Kastenpickert (yeast potato bread)
For guests (8 servings)

Preparation time: about 45
minutes, excluding rising, baking
and cooling time

**1 kg/2¼ lb floury
  potatoes
3 medium eggs
1 heaped teaspoon salt
125 ml/4 fl oz (½ cup)
  milk
500 g/18 oz (5 cups) plain
  (all-purpose) flour
1 packet dried yeast
250 g/9 oz raisins**

In addition:
**fat for the mould
200 ml/7 fl oz (⅞ cup)
  cooking oil, e.g.
  sunflower oil**

Per serving:
**P: 13 g, F: 29 g, C: 81 g,
kJ: 2685, kcal: 641**

1 Wash the potatoes, peel thinly, rinse and grate finely (photo-graph 1). Leave to drain in a sieve, transfer to a mixing bowl, add the eggs and salt, and mix well.

2 Heat the milk in a small saucepan. Sieve the flour in a bowl, add the dried yeast and mix very well. Mix together the warm milk and flour and yeast mixture in two stages. Knead to make a smooth, homogenous consistency, using a hand-held mixer with kneading attachment.

3 Continue kneading the dough for about 5 minutes. Then cover and put in a warm place to rise (about 60 minutes).

4 Stir the raisins into the dough and put in a well-greased bread tin (35 x 11 cm/14 x 4½ in, photograph 2), cover and leave in a warm place to rise again for about 30 minutes. Preheat the oven at top and bottom and put the tin in the oven.

Top/bottom heat: about 180 °C/350 °F (preheated),
Fan oven: about 160 °C/325 °F (not preheated), Gas mark 4 (not preheated),
Cooking time: about 60 minutes.

5 Remove the pickert from the tin and leave to cool down on a wire tray. When cool cut into 24 slices.

6 Heat a little oil in a pan and fry the pickert slices on both sides until golden brown (photograph 3).

Tip: Serve the pickert with syrup, jam or apple sauce (page 280). It is also delicious with butter and it can be served with coffee.

Variation: **Yeast pancakes** (makes about 20). Make the dough as described above but use only 2 eggs. Finally, stir in the raisins. Fry in a pan, a few at a time. Spoon the dough mixture into the frying pan, press flat and fry the pancakes on both sides until golden brown. Drain briefly on kitchen paper. Serve the pancakes in the same way as pickert.

Spätzle
Good value

Preparation time:
about 35 minutes

**250 g/9 oz (2½ cups)
plain (all-purpose) flour
2 medium eggs
scant ½ teaspoon salt
about 3 tablespoons
water
3 litres/5 pints (13 cups)
water
3 teaspoons salt
40 g/1½ oz (3 table-
spoons) butter**

Per serving:
P: 10 g, F: 12 g, C: 45 g,
kJ: 1361, kcal: 325

1 Sieve the flour into a bowl. Add the eggs, salt and 5 tablespoons water. Knead all the ingredients together using a hand-held mixer with a kneading attachment (photograph 1) or wooden spoon, making sure that there are no lumps. Continue kneading until the dough begins to form air bubbles.

2 Bring 3 litres/5 pints (13 cups) water to the boil and add salt. Push the dough through a spätzle ricer or spätzle press (photograph 2) into the boiling water and poach for 3–5 minutes; the spätzle are done when they float to the surface.

3 Remove the spätzle from the water using a skimming ladle, transfer to a sieve or colander, rinse under cold water and drain. Brown the butter in a pan and toss the spätzle in it (photograph 3).

Tip: Serve spätzle as an accompaniment to braised beef (page 62), goulash (page 59) or escalopes (page 68).

Variation 1: To make **spätzle coated with breadcrumbs**, melt 30 g/1 oz (2 tablespoons) butter in a pan, stir in 2 tablespoons breadcrumbs and pour over the spätzle.

Variation 2: To make **spätzle with fried onions** (photograph), peel 3 onions, cut into rings, brown in melted butter or margarine and pour over the spätzle just before serving.

Variation 3: To make **cheese spätzle**, make the spätzle as described above but using 400 g/14 oz wheat flour, 4 medium eggs, 1 level teaspoon salt and 150 ml/5 fl oz (5/8 cup) water. Arrange the drained spätzle and 200 g/7 oz grated Emmental cheese in layers in a greased gratin dish (the top layer should be cheese). Put the dish in the preheated oven (top and bottom heat) at a temperature of about 200 °C/400 °F, fan oven about 180 °C/350 °F, gas mark 6 and bake the cheese spätzle for about 20 minutes. Sprinkle the cheese spätzle with fried onion rings (made from 4 onions) and serve with a mixed salad as a main dish.

Maultaschen (stuffed Swabian pockets)
Suitable for freezing (24 pieces)

Preparation time:
about 75 minutes, without baking
and cooling time

Preparation for the
spinach filling:
**600 g/1¼ lb frozen leaf
 spinach**

For the dough:
**300 g/12 oz (3 cups) plain
 (all-purpose) flour
2 medium eggs
3 tablespoons water
some salt**

For the spinach filling:
**2 onions
2 cloves garlic
4 teaspoons cooking oil,
 e.g. sunflower or olive
 oil
salt
freshly ground pepper
grated nutmeg
1 yolk of 1 medium egg**

**1 white of 1 medium egg
1.5 litres/2¾ pints
 (7 cups) vegetable or
 meat stock**

Per serving:
P: 18 g, F: 11 g, C: 57 g,
kJ: 1686, kcal: 402

1 Defrost the spinach following the instructions on the packet to make the spinach stuffing.

2 To make the dough, sieve the flour into a bowl, then add the eggs, water and salt. Knead all the ingredients together to make a smooth dough, using a hand-held mixer with kneading attachment. Cover and leave to rest for about 40 minutes.

3 Meanwhile, squeeze the defrosted spinach to remove all the water and coarsely chop. Peel and chop the onions and garlic.

4 Heat the oil in a pan, add the chopped onions and garlic and fry while stirring. Then add the spinach, stir, cover and braise over low heat for about 3 minutes. Season with salt, pepper and nutmeg and leave to cool a little. Finally stir in the egg yolk.

5 Roll out the dough thinly on a floured work surface and cut out squares 10 x 10 cm/4 x 4 in from the dough. Put a little stuffing on each square. Beat the egg white with a fork and brush along the edges of each square. Fold the squares into triangles and press the edges together.

6 Heat the vegetable or meat stock in a pan. Put half the stuffed pockets in the liquid and poach uncovered over medium heat for about 15 minutes. Remove the stuffed pockets from the water with a skimming ladle and keep in a warm place. Repeat the same operation with the rest of the stuffed pockets.

7 Serve the stuffed pockets with a little stock in soup bowls.

Tip: Drain the cooked stuffed pockets and fry on both sides in melted butter. Then serve with breadcrumbs browned in butter and onion rings (from 6–8 onions) fried in clarified butter or vegetable oil (photograph).

Variation: **Pockets stuffed with minced meat.** Peel and chop 1 onion. Heat 1 tablespoon vegetable oil in a pan. Add the chopped onion and fry over medium heat. Add the fried onion to 300 g/10 oz minced meat (half beef, half pork), 1 medium egg, yolk of 1 medium egg and 2 tablespoons chopped parsley, mix well and season with salt and pepper. Stuff the dough squares and poach as described above.

Colourful meat risotto
Sophisticated

Preparation time:
about 65 minutes

1 red and 1 green pepper,
  175 g/6 oz each
250 g/9 oz onions
500 g/18 oz pork without
  bones, e.g. from the
  neck
60 g/2 oz streaky bacon
4 teaspoons cooking oil,
  e.g. sunflower oil
4 teaspoons tomato
  purée
1-2 teaspoon paprika
salt
freshly ground pepper
1 pinch cayenne pepper
1 teaspoon chopped
  lovage leaves
500 ml/17 fl oz (2¼ cups)
  vegetable stock
250 g/9 oz long-grain
  rice
500 g/18 oz tomatoes
2 teaspoons chopped
  small-leaved basil

Per serving:
P: 35 g, F: 24 g, C: 60 g,
kJ: 2505, kcal: 598

1 Cut the peppers in half, remove the stalks and seeds, including the white membrane inside. Wash the peppers and cut into pieces. Peel the onions and cut into four or eight segments.

2 Rinse the pork under cold running water, pat dry and cut into cubes of 1.5 cm/⅝ in. Chop the bacon finely.

3 Heat the oil in a pan, add the bacon and fry to release the fat. Now add the cubed pork and fry while stirring. Finally, add the onions and fry with the rest of the ingredients.

4 Stir in the tomato purée and season with paprika, salt, pepper, cayenne pepper and lovage. Add 250 ml/8 fl oz (1 cup) of the vegetable stock, cover and braise the meat and onions over low heat for about 10-15 minutes.

5 Now add the cut peppers and rice to the meat and onion, add the rest of the vegetable stock, cover and braise for a further 15-20 minutes.

6 Meanwhile, wash the tomatoes, drain, make cross-shaped cuts in the ends, dip briefly in boiling water and then dip in cold water. Peel the tomatoes, remove the stalks and cut the tomatoes into quarters.

7 Add the tomatoes and braise for another 3-5 minutes. Season with salt and cayenne pepper and sprinkle with a few basil leaves just before serving.

Tip: Serve with a mixed green salad (page 192).

Variation: **You can also add a can of drained sweet corn (drained weight 285 g/10 oz) to the risotto (photograph).**

Spinach and sheep's cheese lasagne

Vegetarian

Preparation time:
about 50 minutes

3 cloves garlic
3 onions
3 tablespoons olive oil
600 g/1¼ lb frozen leaf
   spinach
about 2 tablespoons
   water
salt
freshly ground pepper
grated nutmeg

For the béchamel sauce:
50 g/2 oz (4 tablespoons)
   butter or margarine
50 g/2 oz (½ cup) plain
   (all-purpose) flour
500 ml/17 fl oz (2¼ cups)
   milk
500 ml/17 fl oz (2¼ cups)
   vegetable stock
salt
freshly ground pepper
grated nutmeg

300 g/10 oz sheep's
   cheese
225 g/8 oz sheets
   lasagne, not pre-cooked
100 g/3½ oz grated
   gratin cheese

Per serving:
P: 37 g, F: 47g, C: 57 g,
kJ: 3384, kcal: 808

1   Peel the garlic and onions and chop finely. Heat the oil in a
    saucepan or frying pan. Add the chopped onions and garlic and
    fry until transparent. Add the frozen spinach and water, cover
    and defrost the spinach over low heat. Season with salt, pepper
    and nutmeg. Preheat the oven.

2   To make the béchamel sauce, melt the butter or margarine in a
    pan and stir in the flour until the mixture turns pale yellow. Add
    the milk and vegetable stock and beat with a whisk, making sure
    that there are no lumps in the mixture. Bring the sauce to the
    boil and cook uncovered over low heat for about 5 minutes, stir-
    ring occasionally. Season generously with salt, pepper and nut-
    meg.

3   Crumble the sheep's cheese. Pour a little sauce in a rectangular
    gratin dish, then line the bottom with a sheet of lasagne, fol-
    lowed by a layer of spinach and some sheep's cheese on top and
    cover with more béchamel sauce.

4   Continue with alternate layers of lasagne, spinach, sheep's
    cheese and béchamel until you have four layers of lasagne. Now
    pour the rest of the béchamel sauce over the lasagne and sprin-
    kle gratin cheese on top. Bake in the oven uncovered .

Top/bottom heat: about 200 °C/400 °F (preheated),
Fan oven: about 180 °C/350 °F (preheated), Gas mark 6 (preheated),
Cooking time: 35 minutes.

Potato bake

Good value

Preparation time: about 75 minutes, excluding cooling time

1 kg/2¼ lb firm cooking potatoes
5 hard-boiled eggs
3 smoked sausages,
100 g/3½ oz each
salt
freshly ground pepper
300 g/10 oz sour cream
30 g/1 oz breadcrumbs
50 g/2 oz (4 tablespoons) butter

Per serving:
P: 29 g, F: 53 g, C: 42 g,
kJ: 3192, kcal: 762

1 Wash the potatoes thoroughly, put in a pan filled with water and bring to the boil. Cover and cook for about 20-25 minutes. Drain the potatoes, then place them in cold water and drain. Peel immediately and leave to cool down. Meanwhile, preheat the oven.

2 Shell the eggs and slice them. Then slice the potatoes and the smoked sausages. Arrange these ingredients in alternate layers in a shallow gratin dish. Sprinkle salt and pepper on layers of sliced potatoes and sliced eggs. Finish with a layer of potatoes.

3 Season the soured cream with salt and pepper, mix well and pour over the potatoes. Sprinkle the breadcrumbs on top and dot with knobs of butter. Bake the potato gratin uncovered in the oven.

Top/bottom heat: **about 200 °C/400 °F (preheated),**
Fan oven: **about 180 °C/350 °F (not preheated),** Gas mark **6 (preheated),**
Cooking time: **about 35 minutes.**

Tip: **Serve potato bake with a carrot and apple salad (page 194).**
If you use thick soured cream you can make it less thick by adding 5 tablespoons milk.

Variation: **Potato and courgette bake with cabanossi** (photograph).
Instead of hard-boiled eggs use 300 g/10 oz courgettes. Wash the courgettes, wipe dry, cut both ends and slice. Sprinkle with salt and leave for about 10 minutes. Use 300 g/10 oz cabanossi (garlic sausage) instead of the smoked sausages and cut into slices. Pat the courgettes dry and arrange with the sliced potatoes and cabanossi so that they overlap. Sprinkle pepper on the potato and courgette slices. Beat together the sour cream and 2 medium eggs, season with salt and pepper and pour over the gratin. Sprinkle breadcrumbs on top, dot with knobs of butter and bake as above.

Pancake gratin

Vegetarian

Preparation time: about 100 minutes, excluding batter resting and cooling time

For the pancakes:
185 g/6½ oz (1½ cups)
  plain (all-purpose) flour
3 medium eggs
1 pinch sugar
1 pinch salt
225 ml/7½ fl oz (1 cup)
  milk
150 ml/5 fl oz (⅝ cup)
  mineral water
40 g/1½ oz margarine or
  3 tablespoons cooking
  oil, e.g. sunflower oil

For the filling:
2 onions, 2 cloves garlic
250 g/9 oz carrots
30 g/1 oz (2 tablespoons)
  margarine or 2 table-
  spoons cooking oil, e.g.
  sunflower oil
450 g/1 lb frozen leaf
  spinach
salt, pepper
grated nutmeg

For the sauce:
200 g/7 oz fromage frais
1 medium egg
salt, pepper

In addition:
fat for the mould
125 g/4½ oz mozzarella
  cheese
some small-leaved basil

Per serving:
P: 29 g, F: 52 g, C: 43 g,
kJ: 3151, kcal: 752

1 Sieve the flour for the pancakes into a mixing bowl and make a well in the centre. Whisk together the eggs, sugar, salt, milk and mineral water and pour a little of this mixture into the well. Starting from the middle, mix together a little of the egg mixture and the flour, adding the rest of the egg mixture little by little, making sure that there are no lumps. Leave the batter to stand for 20–30 minutes.

2 Heat some of the margarine or oil in a pan and pour a thin layer of batter into the pan. As soon as the edges turn golden yellow, carefully turn over the pancake using a wooden spatula. Alternatively, slide the pancake onto a plate and return to the pan on the other side. Fry the second side until it is golden yellow, too. Add a little more oil or margarine before turning the pancake. Make sure the pancake is golden brown on both sides. Make 6–8 pancakes (depending on the size of the frying pan), stacking the pancakes on top of each other and let them cool down.

3 To make the stuffing, peel and chop the onions and garlic. Peel the carrots and cut off the green leaves and tips, then wash, drain and cut into small dice.

4 Heat the oil or margarine in a pan. Add the chopped onions and garlic and fry while stirring. Add the carrots and frozen spinach, cover and cook over low heat for about 10–15 minutes until the spinach is defrosted, stirring occasionally. Preheat the oven. Boil way any excess liquid in the vegetable mixture. Season with salt, pepper and nutmeg and leave to cool.

5 Meanwhile mix together the fromage frais, milk and egg and season with salt and pepper.

6 Put the pancakes next to each other on the worktop and spoon the stuffing onto each pancake. Roll them up and arrange next to each other in a shallow, greased gratin dish (about 30 x 24 cm/ 12 x 10 in). Pour the sauce over each one. Cut the mozzarella into thin strips and scatter on top. Bake uncovered in the oven.

Top/bottom heat: **about 200 °C/400 °F (preheated),**
Fan oven: **about 180 °C/350 °F (preheated),** Gas mark **6 (preheated),**
Cooking time: **about 35 minutes.**

7 Garnish with basil leaves just before serving.

(continued on page 240)

Variation: **Pancake gratin with sheep's cheese and raisins.** Add 50 g/2 oz raisins and fry with the vegetables. Season the vegetables with salt, pepper, ground cumin and ground coriander seeds. Prepare the sauce with puréed sheep's or goat's cheese instead of fromage frais. Make the gratin as described in the recipe and bake.

Rice and vegetable gratin

For children

Preparation time:
about 50 minutes

300 g/10 oz carrots
4 teaspoons cooking oil,
    e.g. sunflower oil
250 g/9 oz long-grain
    rice
4 teaspoons curry powder
500 ml/17 fl oz (2¼ cups)
    vegetable stock
40 g/1½ oz butter or
    margarine
300 g/10 oz frozen peas
salt
freshly ground pepper
1 pinch sugar
2 medium eggs
200 ml/7 fl oz (⅞ cup)
    whipping cream
grated nutmeg
125 g/4½ oz grated,
    medium mature Gouda
    cheese

Per serving:
P: 23 g, F: 41 g, C: 64 g,
kJ: 3042, kcal: 726

1 Peel the carrots and cut off the green leaves and tips. Wash the carrots, drain and cut into small dice.

2 Heat the oil in a pan. Add the rice and fry until transparent. Sprinkle the curry powder over the rice and fry briefly. Add the vegetable stock, bring to the boil, cover and cook over low heat for about 10 minutes. Preheat the oven.

3 Meanwhile melt the butter or margarine. Add the diced carrots and fry. Stir in the peas and season with salt, pepper and sugar. Mix the rice and vegetables together and put in a shallow gratin dish.

4 Whisk the eggs into the cream, season with salt, pepper and nutmeg and stir in the cheese. Pour the egg and cream mixture over the rice and vegetables in the gratin dish. Bake in the oven without out a lid.

Top/bottom heat: about 180 °C/350 °F (preheated),
Fan oven: about 160 °C/325 °F (preheated), Gas mark 4 (not preheated),
Cooking time: about 25 minutes.

Tip: Serve the rice and vegetable gratin with green salad, cold roast or ham. You can use a similar amount of brown rice, but in this case the cooking time for the rice will be about 20 minutes.

Variation: **Rice and vegetable gratin with chicken fillets** (photograph). Rinse 300 g/10 oz chicken fillets under cold running water, pat dry, cut into strips and brown on all sides in the oil. Season with salt and pepper and remove from the pan. Fry the rice in the remaining cooking fat until transparent and continue as indicated above. Stir the chicken into the rice and vegetable mixture, put in a gratin dish and bake as indicated above.

Cereal and vegetable gratin

Vegetarian

Preparation time:
about 60 minutes

800 g/1¾ lb cauliflower
1 bunch spring onions
150 g/5 oz celeriac
200 g/7 oz carrots
2 onions
40 g/1½ oz butter or
margarine
200 g/7 oz mixed cereal
grains
½ teaspoon dried,
chopped thyme
1 teaspoon mustard seeds
salt
freshly ground pepper
400 ml/14 fl oz (1¾ cups)
vegetable stock
500 ml/17 fl oz (2¼ cups)
water
4 teaspoons chopped
parsley or chervil
200 g/7 oz sour cream
3 tablespoons milk
50 g/2 oz grated medium
mature Gouda cheese
30 g/1 oz grated
Parmesan cheese

Per serving:
P: 18 g, F: 27 g, C: 49 g,
kJ: 2154, kcal: 512

1   Remove the leaves from the cauliflower and trim off any black spots on the florets. Cut off the stump and divide into florets. Cut off the root ends of the spring onions and remove the dark green leaves. Wash the spring onions, drain them and cut into pieces 3 cm/1¼ in long.

2   Peel the celeriac and cut out any bad parts. Peel the carrots and cut off the green leaves and tips. Wash the celeriac and carrots, drain and cut into small dice. Peel and chop the onions.

3   Melt the butter or margarine in a pan. Add the mixed cereals and fry while stirring continuously. Add the thyme, mustard seeds, diced carrots, celeriac and onions and season with salt and pepper. Pour in the vegetable stock, bring to the boil, cover and cook over low heat for about 20 minutes. Preheat the oven.

4   Meanwhile bring the water to the boil. Add ½ teaspoon salt and the cauliflower florets, cover and cook for about 5 minutes. Transfer to a sieve, run under cold running water and drain.

5   Stir the parsley or chervil into the cereal mixture and put in a shallow gratin dish. Arrange the cauliflower florets and cut spring onions on top.

6   Mix together the sour cream and milk and pour over the vegetables in the gratin dish. Sprinkle the two cheeses on top. Bake uncovered in the oven.

Top/bottom heat: **about 200 °C/400 °F (preheated),**
Fan oven: **about 180 °C/350 °F (preheated),** Gas mark **6 (preheated),**
Cooking time: **about 25 minutes.**

Tip: **Serve the gratin with a green salad. It is also delicious served with fried meat or fish, in which case it will serve 6–8.**

Variation 1: **The same amount of brown rice can be used instead of mixed cereals, making the gratin as described above.**

Variation 2: **The spring onions may be replaced with 200 g/7 oz green beans. Top and tail the beans, remove any strings, and break or cut into two or three pieces. Precook the beans with the cauliflower florets and make the gratin as described above.**

Omelette with mushroom filling

Good value (2 servings)

Preparation time:
about 60 minutes

For the filling:
400 g/14 oz mushrooms
1 onion
50 g/2 oz streaky bacon
4 teaspoons cooking oil,
 e.g. sunflower oil or
 20 g/³/₄ oz (1½ table-
 spoons) clarified butter
salt
freshly ground pepper
50 ml /1½ fl oz (3 table-
 spoons) whipping cream
4 teaspoons chopped
 parsley

For the omelette:
6 medium eggs
1 pinch salt
1 pinch paprika
2 tablespoons cooking
 oil, e.g. sunflower oil or
 30 g/1 oz (2 table-
 spoons) clarified butter

Per serving:
P: 35 g, F: 54 g, C: 5 g,
kJ: 2623, kcal: 626

1 For the mushroom filling, cut off the stalk ends and any bad parts, rub the mushrooms with kitchen paper, rinse if necessary, pat dry and cut into slices. Peel and chop the onion. Dice the bacon.

2 Heat the oil or clarified butter in a pan. Cook the diced bacon to release the fat. Add the chopped onion and mushroom slices and cook briefly. Season with salt and pepper and cook for about 8 minutes over medium heat, stirring occasionally.

3 Mix in the cream, season again to taste with salt and pepper, mix in the parsley and keep the filling warm.

4 Mix the eggs for the omelette with salt and paprika.

5 Heat half the oil or clarified butter in a non-stick pan, 22-24 cm/8½-9½ in diameter. Add half the egg mixture and cook covered over low heat for 4-5 minutes. The underside of the omelette should be slightly browned.

6 Slide the omelette onto a preheated plate, add half the mushroom filling, fold the omelette over and keep warm. Prepare the other omelette in the same way.

Tip: Serve the omelette as an entree with a mixed green salad (page 192) or lamb's lettuce salad (page 191), made without the egg.
The omelette should be prepared immediately before it is served.
If you want to make the omelette light and airy, beat the egg white until it is stiff and fold into the yolk mixture.

Variation: Instead of the mushroom filling, make an **omelette with mozzarella and tomatoes** (photograph). Drain 125 g/4½ oz mozzarella cheese and cut into thin slices. Wash and dry 2 tomatoes, remove the stalks and cut into slices. Use half the omelette mixture for each omelette. Put half the slices of cheese and tomato on each omelette, sprinkle with salt and pepper and fold the omelette over. The omelettes may be garnished with small-leafed basil.

Stuffed eggs

Good value

Preparation time:
about 25 minutes

**4 hard-boiled medium
  eggs**
1 tablespoon mayonnaise
**1 slightly heaped
  teaspoon mustard**
salt
freshly ground pepper
1 pinch sugar
some salad leaves
**8 preserved anchovy
  fillets**
about 3 pickled gherkins
some cocktail tomatoes
chopped parsley

Per serving:
P: 9 g, F: 9 g, C: 2 g,
kJ: 523, kcal: 125

1   Shell the eggs, cut in half lengthways and remove the yolks
    (photograph 1). Rub the egg yolks through a sieve (photograph 2),
    add the mayonnaise and mustard and stir into a smooth mass
    (photograph 3). Season with salt, pepper and sugar. Put the mix-
    ture in a piping bag with a large star-shaped nozzle and squeeze
    into the hollows of the egg halves.

2   Wash the lettuce leaves and spin dry. Pat the sardine fillets dry.
    Drain the gherkins and cut into strips. Wash the cherry toma-
    toes, wipe dry and cut in half. Arrange the egg halves on the let-
    tuce leaves. Garnish with the anchovy fillets, strips of gherkin
    and cherry tomatoes. Sprinkle with parsley before serving.

Tip: Serve stuffed eggs with salad dishes, as part of a buffet or as a starter
with toast or baguette.

Variation 1: **Eggs stuffed with curried curd cheese.** Take 50 g/2 oz fromage
frais, 1 teaspoon crème fraîche and ½ teaspoon curry powder and stir into the
egg yolks rubbed through a sieve. Season with salt, pepper and sugar and fill
the egg halves with this mixture. Garnish with 1–2 tablespoons crab or
shrimps, some dill and slices of lemon.

Variation 2: **Eggs with Parmesan stuffing.** Stir 1 tablespoon crème fraîche,
1 tablespoon finely grated Parmesan and a few chopped pink pepper berries
into the egg yolks rubbed through a sieve. Season with salt and pepper and
fill the egg halves with the mixture. Garnish with 1 tablespoon roasted pine
nuts and 1 tablespoon chopped rocket.

Variation 3: **Eggs with herb curd cheese stuffing.** Stir 1 tablespoon each
crème fraîche and herb curd cheese into the egg yolk rubbed through a sieve.
Season with salt and sugar. Spoon into the egg halves and garnish with about
100 g/3½ oz coloured peppers, cut into strips.

Variation 4: **Eggs with tomato flavoured curd cheese.** Mix together
2 tablespoons curd cheese, 1–2 teaspoons tomato purée and 1 teaspoon
drained, finely chopped capers and stir into the egg yolk rubbed through a
sieve. Season with salt and sugar, fill the egg halves with this mixture and
garnish with 50 g/2 oz ham cut into thin strips.

Egg fricassée
Mit Alkohol

Preparation time:
about 45 minutes

300 g/10 oz mushrooms
1 can or jar of asparagus
    pieces, drained weight
    175 g/6 oz
about 250 ml/8 fl oz
    (1 cup) vegetable stock
6 hard-boiled eggs
20 g/³⁄₄ oz (1½ table-
    spoons) butter or
    margarine
25 g/1 oz (4 tablespoons)
    plain (all-purpose) flour
1 egg yolk
2 tablespoons white wine
salt
freshly ground white
    pepper
1 pinch sugar
about 2 teaspoons lemon
    juice
2 teaspoons chopped
    parsley

Per serving:
P: 16 g, F: 15 g, C: 7 g,
kJ: 972, kcal: 232

1   Cut off the ends of the mushroom stalks. Remove any bad parts from the mushrooms and wipe clean with kitchen paper. If necessary, rinse and pat dry. Cut the mushrooms into slices.

2   Drain the asparagus in a colander, reserving the liquid. Top up with vegetable stock to make 375 ml/12 fl oz (1½ cups) liquid. Shell the eggs and cut into six, using an egg slicer or knife.

3   Melt the butter or margarine in a pan. Add the sliced mushrooms and fry briefly while stirring. Season with salt and pepper, sprinkle the flour on the mushrooms and continue cooking until the flour turns pale yellow, stirring continuously. Now add the asparagus and stock liquid, stirring vigorously with a whisk and making sure that there are no lumps. Bring the sauce to the boil and cook uncovered over low heat for about 5 minutes, stirring occasionally.

4   Add the sliced eggs and asparagus to the sauce and cook for a further 5 minutes over low heat, stirring very gently now and again. Whisk together the egg yolk and white wine, and stir 3 tablespoons of sauce into this mixture; do not allow it to boil at this point. Season with salt, pepper, sugar and lemon juice and sprinkle with parsley.

Tip: An egg fricassée is an ideal way of using up leftover hard-boiled eggs, for instance, Easter eggs.

Variation 1: Add 2 teaspoons drained capers to the fricassée towards the end of the cooking process.

Variation 2: Add 100 g/3½ oz peas (deep-frozen or from a can) to the asparagus and the eggs, and heat up.

Variation 3: Instead of fresh mushrooms you could use 200 g/7 oz drained, tinned mushrooms. In this case do not fry the mushrooms but heat them in the sauce together with the asparagus and eggs.

Eggs with mustard sauce

Good value

1 Preheat the oven. Put 2 eggs each in 4 well-greased heat-resistant ramekins. Dice the bacon and scatter over the eggs. Sprinkle with pepper and chopped chives and put in the oven to bake.

Top/bottom heat: **about 200 °C/400 °F (preheated)**,
Fan oven: **about 180 °C/350 °F (preheated)**, Gas mark **6 (preheated)**,
Cooking time: **about 25 minutes**.

2 Meanwhile, add salt and mustard to the crème fraîche to make the mustard sauce. When the eggs are done, remove from the oven, ease out of the ramekins by loosening them along the edges and arrange on a dish. Garnish with parsley. Serve with the mustard sauce.

Tip: Eggs with mustard sauce make an ideal main course for 4 people, served with potatoes sprinkled with parsley (page 210) and salad. As a snack, there is enough for 8 people.
The sauce can also be made with crème fraîche flavoured with herbs.

Per serving: P: 19 g, F: 27 g, C: 3 g, kJ: 1374, kcal: 329

Preparation time:
about 35 minutes

8 medium eggs
75 g/3 oz streaky bacon
freshly ground pepper
4 teaspoons chopped
chives

For the mustard sauce:
150 g/5 oz (1 cup) crème
fraîche, salt
2 teaspoons granulated
mustard

some small parsley leaves

In addition:
fat for the ramekins

Boiled eggs

Easy

1 Pierce the eggs at the blunt end with a needle or egg-pricker so that they do not crack when they boil. Bring some water to the boil in a small saucepan.

2 Place the eggs on a spoon or skimming ladle and lower them carefully into the boiling water (the eggs should be covered by the water). Bring the water to the boil again and boil the eggs uncovered over low heat. For soft-boiled medium eggs, the cooking time is 5 minutes. For medium-boiled eggs, the cooking time is 8 minutes. For hard-boiled eggs, the cooking time is 10 minutes. Add 1 minute to the cooking time if the eggs are large.

3 Remove the eggs from the water with a spoon or skimming ladle and dip in cold water so that they easier to shell.

Tip: If the eggs have come straight from the refrigerator, add 1 more minute to the cooking time. Very cold eggs should be pre-warmed in lukewarm water to prevent the shells from cracking.

Preparation time:
about 10 minutes

4 fresh medium eggs

Per serving:
P: 7 g, F: 6 g, C: 0 g,
kJ: 355, kcal: 85

Pancakes
For children (about 7 pancakes)

Preparation time:
about 40 minutes, excluding
resting time

250 g/9 oz plain (all-purpose) flour
4 medium eggs
2 teaspoons sugar
1 pinch salt
375 ml/12 fl oz (1½ cups) milk
125 ml/4 fl oz (½ cup) mineral water
5 tablespoons cooking oil, e.g. sunflower oil or 80 g/3 oz (6 tablespoons) clarified butter

Per serving:
P: 10 g, F: 17 g, C: 29 g,
kJ: 1290, kcal: 308

1 Sieve the flour in a bowl and make a well in the centre. Beat together the eggs, milk and mineral water using a whisk and stir in the sugar and salt. Pour a little of this mixture in the well and mix with the flour around. Now add the rest of the egg-mixture little by little to the flour, making sure that there are no lumps. Let the batter rest for 20–30 minutes.

2 Heat the oil or clarified butter in a non-stick frying pan (diameter about 24 cm/9½ in) and pour a thin layer of batter to coat the base of the pan. As soon as the edges turn golden yellow, turn the pancakes very gently with a wide spatula or slide the pancake onto plate and return to the pan on the other side. Cook until the second side is golden yellow. Add a little more fat before cooking the second side.

3 Continue making the rest of the pancakes in the same way, stirring the batter each time before making each pancake.

Tip: You can serve pancakes with stewed fruit, cinnamon sugar, maple syrup or fruit. The pancakes will be more delicate and lighter if you separate the eggs and only use the yolks in the batter. Shortly before making the pancakes beat the egg whites stiff and fold into the batter.
Keep the pancakes you have already made in a warm oven, heated top and bottom to 80 °C/180 °F or 60 °C/14 °F if it is a fan oven. Sprinkle each pancake with a little sugar before stacking them. This will prevent them from sticking together.

Variation 1: **Apple pancakes.** Make the batter as described above. Wash 1 kg/2¼ lb of slightly sharp apples (for instance Bramleys), peel, cut into quarters, remove the cores and cut lengthways into thin slices. Divide into 7 portions. Heat a small amount of the oil or clarified butter in the pan, add 1 portion of the sliced apples and fry for 2–3 minutes. Then pour a thin layer of batter on top and cook over medium heat, now and again lifting the pancake from the bottom of the pan to cook as described above. Make the rest of the pancakes as indicated above. Serve the pancakes with cinnamon sugar.

Variation 2: **Bacon pancakes.** Make the batter as described above, but only with 1 pinch of sugar. Cut 200 g/7 oz bacon into slices, and for each pancake fry a portion in the hot oil or clarified butter until golden brown. Pour the batter on top and cook as indicated above. Proceed with the rest of the batter and bacon in the same way. Serve the bacon pancakes with a green salad.

Kaiserschmarrn (pancakes Austrian style)
Quick (2 pancakes)

1 Sieve the flour into a bowl and make a well in the centre. Separate the eggs. Whisk together the egg yolk, milk or cream and add 1 pinch of salt, then pour a little of this mixture in the well. Starting from the middle, mix together the egg yolk mixture and flour, then add the rest of the egg yolk mixture little by little, making sure that there are no lumps. Beat the egg whites stiff and fold in with the raisins.

2 Heat a little of the oil or clarified butter in a frying pan (diameter 28 cm/11 in). Pour half the batter into the pan and cook over medium until pale yellow underneath. Using a spatula, cut the pancake (which will still be a little liquid on top) into quarters. Turn them, adding a little oil or butter if necessary, and cook until golden yellow.

3 Then pull the pancakes into small pieces using 2 spatulas, put on a plate and keep in a warm place. Cook the rest of the batter in the same way. Sprinkle with icing sugar before serving.

Tip: Kaiserschmarrn can be served as a sweet main course for 2 or as a dessert for 4. Serve with stewed plums or apricots.

Variation: Soak the raisins in 1–2 tablespoons warm brown rum for 30 minutes. Then add the raisins with the rum to the batter as indicated above.

Preparation time:
about 30 minutes

100 g/3½ oz (1 cup) plain (all-purpose) flour
4 medium eggs
1 pinch salt
200 ml/7 fl oz (⅞ cup) whipping cream or milk
50 g/2 oz raisins
3 tablespoons cooking oil, e.g. sunflower oil or 50 g/2 oz (4 tablespoons) clarified butter
icing sugar

Per serving:
P: 22 g, F: 70 g, C: 61 g,
kJ: 4011, kcal: 958

Curd cheese pancakes
Easy (2 servings)

1 Mix together the curd cheese, flour, egg, lemon juice and sugar.

2 Heat some of the oil or clarified butter in a frying pan. Put a tablespoon of batter in the pan, press lightly to flatten and fry over low heat until golden brown on both sides.

Tip: Serve the curd cheese pancakes with a medley of strawberries, raspberries and blackberries, sprinkled with sugar.
As a sweet main course, they will serve 2 people (double the amounts for 4 people), while as a pudding they will serve 4 people.

Per serving: P: 25 g, F: 19 g, C: 23 g, kJ: 1540, kcal: 368

Preparation time:
about 25 minutes

250 g/9 oz curd cheese
2 heaped tablespoons plain (all-purpose) flour,
2 medium eggs
4 teaspoons lemon juice
4 teaspoons sugar
2 tablespoons cooking oil, e.g. sunflower oil or 25 g/1 oz (2 tablespoons) clarified butter

French toast (photograph left)
Good value (6 servings)

Preparation time:
about 40 minutes

300 ml/10 fl oz (1¼ cups)
  milk
2 medium eggs
50 g/2 oz sugar
6 slices white bread
  (2–5 days old) about
  1.5 cm/⅝ in thick
3 tablespoons cooking oil,
  e.g. sunflower oil or
  50 g/2 oz (4 table-
  spoons) clarified butter

Per serving:
P: 6 g, F: 13 g, C: 25 g,
kJ: 996, kcal: 238

1 Mix the milk, eggs and sugar together. Put the slices of white bread in a shallow dish, pour the egg and milk mixture over the top. Let the mixture become absorbed by the bread (turning once or twice) but make sure the bread does not become too soggy.

2 Heat a little oil or clarified butter in a non-stick frying pan. Add the slices of bread and fry on both sides over medium heat for about 8 minutes until crisp and brown. Serve hot.

Tip: Serve French toast as a sweet main meal with stewed plums (page 281), apple sauce (page 280) or vanilla sauce (page 287).

Variation 1: **Almond or vanilla-flavoured French toast**. Add 3 tablespoons almond liqueur or 3 drops of vanilla essence to the milk and egg mixture. Instead of an ordinary white loaf, you can use 12 thin slices of baguette. After soaking the slices of baguette in the egg and milk mixture, coat in about 75 g/3 oz peeled, ground almonds and fry as indicated above.

Variation 2: **Savoury French toast** (right of photograph). Instead of adding sugar to the egg and milk mixture, add a level teaspoon salt, a little pepper and grated nutmeg. Coat the slices of bread previously soaked in the egg and milk mixture with about 100 g/3½ oz ground sunflower seeds or about 75 g/3 oz peeled, ground almonds and fry as indicated above. After turning the slices of bread, put 1 slice of salami, tomato and cheese on each slice, sprinkle with dried oregano and fry covered until the cheese begins to melt. Serve with a green salad or a vegetable salad.

Tip: Savoury French toast (see variation 2) can also be served as a side dish with soups. For a garlic flavour, peel and crush 1–2 cloves garlic in a garlic press, add to the milk and stand for 20 minutes. Pour the milk through a sieve and stir into the eggs together with the seasoning. Soak the slices of bread in this mixture and fry as described above.

Pork fillet toast with cheese
(photograph top)

A little more expensive

Preparation time:
about 30 minutes

300 g/10 oz pork fillet
4 teaspoons cooking oil,
  e.g. sunflower oil
salt
freshly ground pepper
4 slices bacon, 60 g/2 oz
  each
4 slices white bread
30 g/1 oz (2 tablespoons)
  butter
200 g/7 oz Camembert
some salad leaves,
  e.g. lettuce, endive
  salad
coarsely ground pepper
  (optional)

In addition:
baking parchment

Per serving:
P: 32 g, F: 22 g, C: 10 g,
kJ: 1536, kcal: 367

1 Preheat the oven. Rinse the pork fillet under cold running water, pat dry and cut into 8 slices. Heat the oil in a pan. Add the pork slices and fry on each side for about 2 minutes, season with salt and pepper, remove from the pan and keep in a warm place.

2 Fry the bacon briefly in the remaining fat and remove from the pan. Toast the slices of bread and spread with butter. Cut the Camembert into slices.

3 Rinse the lettuce leaves, pat dry and arrange on the toasted bread. Then garnish with the slices of bacon, pork fillet and camembert.

4 Put the pieces of toast on a baking sheet lined with greaseproof paper. Put the baking sheet with the toast under the oven grill until the cheese begins to melt. Sprinkle with pepper if desired.

Variation 1: **Cheese on toast with spring onions** (photograph bottom right). Wash 2 tomatoes, pat dry, remove the stalks and cut the tomatoes into slices. Cut off the root ends and dark green leaves of the spring onions, wash and drain. Then cut to the length of the 4 slices of bread and cut in half. Toast the slices of bread, spread with 60 g/2 oz peanut butter. Then arrange 1 slice of roast meat (20 g/³⁄₄ oz each), 2-3 slices of tomatoes, ¹⁄₂ spring onion and 1 slice of Danish butter cheese (30 g/1 oz each) on top. Put the garnished toast on a baking sheet lined with baking parchment and place under the preheated oven grill until the cheese begins to melt.

Variation 2: **Hawaiian toast** (photograph bottom left). Toast 4 slices of bread and spread with 30 g/1 oz (2 tablespoons) butter. Garnish each piece of toast with 1 slice cooked ham (40 g/1¹⁄₂ oz each), 1 slice pineapple from a can (80 g/3 oz each) and 1 slice of cheese, for instance young Gouda (60 g/2 oz each). Put the garnished pieces of toast on a baking sheet lined with baking parchment and put in the oven preheated top and bottom to about 200 °C/ 400 °F, fan oven about 180 °C/350 °F, gas mark 6, for about 8 minutes.

Tip: Serve with a mixed green salad (page 192) or iceberg salad (page 190). If you do not have an oven grill, put the pieces of toast in a preheated oven until the cheese begins to melt (see variations for the temperatures).

Unleavened bread pizza
Easy

Preparation time:
about 40 minutes

1 unleavened bread
4 tomatoes
½ bunch spring onions
125 g/4½ oz feta or
    sheep's cheese
50 g/2 oz black olives
250 g/9 oz spiced minced
    pork
100 g/3½ oz tzatziki
some chopped Greek
    herbs and spices

In addition:
baking parchment

Per serving:
P: 19 g, F: 23 g, C: 6 g,
kJ: 1298, kcal: 310

1   Put the unleavened bread on a baking sheet lined with baking parchment. Preheat the oven.

2   Wash the tomatoes, wipe dry, remove the stalks and cut the tomatoes into thin slices. Cut off the root ends and remove the dark green leaves of the spring onions. Wash the spring onions, drain and chop into fine rings.

3   Drain the feta or sheep's cheese and cut into small dice. Stone the olives, cut up coarsely and mix with the diced cheese.

4   Spread a thin layer of minced pork on the unleavened bread and dot with knobs of tzatziki. Arrange the sliced tomatoes and spring onions on top and sprinkle with chopped herbs.

5   Sprinkle the olive and cheese mixture on top and put in the oven.

Top/bottom heat: about 180 °C/350 °F (preheated),
Fan oven: about 160 °C/325 °F (preheated), Gas mark 4 (preheated),
Cooking time: about 20 minutes.

6   Cut the unleavened bread into pieces before serving.

Tip: Serve the unleavened bread pizza with, for instance, green salad or sliced pickled pumpkins.

Variation: **Unleavened bread pizza with strips of chicken breast.** Replace the spicy minced pork with 250 g/9 oz chicken breast fillet. First rinse it under cold running water, pat dry and cut into short, thin strips before frying in 2 tablespoons hot olive oil. Then season with salt, pepper and sweet paprika, leave to cool and arrange on the unleavened bread instead of the minced pork. Now garnish with the remaining ingredients and bake.

Stuffed baguette sandwiches
For children (4 pieces)

1 Wash the tomatoes, wipe dry and remove the stalks. Wash the cucumbers, wipe dry and cut the ends. Cut the tomatoes and cucumbers into slices. Cut the ham into strips and the Camembert into slices. Wash the lettuce and herbs and pat dry.

2 Cut the baguette in half horizontally and spread with butter. Then arrange the lettuce leaves, sliced tomatoes, sliced cucumber, strips of ham, slices of Camembert and herbs on top. Then place the other half on top.

Tip: Season the sliced cucumber and tomatoes with salt and pepper.

Variation: **Stuffed unleavened bread.** Clean, peel and wash 150 g/5 oz carrots and chop up coarsely. Wash 70 g/3 oz iceberg salad and cut into thin strips. Cut 100 g/3½ oz smoked loin of pork into strips. Season 1–2 teaspoons balsamic vinegar with salt and pepper. Whisk in 2 tablespoons olive oil. Pour the sauce over the rest of the ingredients and add 1 tablespoon chopped chives. Crisp up 1 round unleavened bread, cut into four and cut open horizontally but do not cut through completely along the edges. Open up and fill with the salad mixture.

Preparation time:
about 15 minutes

2 tomatoes
150 g/5 oz cucumber
100 g/3½ oz cooked ham
200 g/7 oz Camembert
some salad leaves
herbs, e.g. basil, parsley
4 baguette rolls (about
80 g/3 oz each)
40 g butter

Per piece:
P: 23 g, F: 22 g, C: 42 g,
kJ: 1933, kcal: 462

Tomatoes with mozzarella
Classic

1 Wash the tomatoes, wipe dry, remove the stalks and cut into slices. Drain the mozzarella and cut into slices as well. Arrange the sliced tomatoes and mozzarella alternately on a dish.

2 Stir together the vinegar, salt, pepper and sugar. Whisk in the oil. Pour the sauce over the ingredients and garnish with basil leaves.

Tip: Serve with ciabatta (Italian white bread).

Variation: **Tomatoes and courgettes with mozzarella.** Wash 200 g/7 oz courgettes, wipe dry, cut off the ends and slice. Fry the sliced courgettes briefly in olive oil, sprinkle with salt and allow to cool down. Arrange the sliced courgettes, tomatoes and mozzarella so that they alternate.

Preparation time:
about 15 minutes

7 tomatoes
250 g/9 oz mozzarella
cheese

For the sauce:
about 4 teaspoons
balsamic vinegar
salt, pepper, sugar
4 tablespoons olive oil
basil leaves

Per serving:
P: 14 g, F: 20 g, C: 4 g,
kJ: 1073, kcal: 256

Spiced fruity cheese snacks
For guestse (8 servings)

Preparation time:
about 50 minutes

For the dough:
400 g/14 oz plain (all-
purpose) flour
2 teaspoons baking
powder
150 g/5 oz natural
yogurt, 3.5% fat
100 ml/3½ fl oz (½ cup)
sunflower oil
½ teaspoon salt
1 medium egg

For the topping:
75 g/3 oz crème fraîche
1 small can apricots,
drained weight 225 g/
8 oz
1 small can pears, drained
weight 225 g/8 oz
100 g/3½ oz walnut
kernels
150 g/5 oz soft cheeses
(blue and white mould)

In addition:
fat for the griddle
lemon balm or oregano
(optional)

Per serving:
P: 13 g, F: 34 g, C: 50 g,
kJ: 2316, kcal: 555

1 Preheat the oven. To make the dough, stir the baking powder into the flour and sieve into a mixing bowl. Add the yogurt, oil, salt and egg. Mix together all these ingredients and knead into a smooth dough using a hand-held mixer with a kneading attachment.

2 Roll out the dough on a well-greased baking sheet (40 x 30 cm) and cover with a layer of crème fraîche.

3 Drain the apricots and pears separately in a sieve and cut into small cubes. Chop up the walnuts and dice the cheese.

4 Arrange the diced apricots on one half of the rolled-out dough and the diced pears on the other. Sprinkle the chopped walnuts and diced cheese over the whole baking sheet. Bake in the oven on the middle shelf.

Top/bottom heat: about 200 °C/400 °F (preheated),
Fan oven: about 180 °C/350 °F (preheated), Gas mark 6 (preheated),
Cooking time: about 25 minutes.

5 Cut the pastry into small pieces. If desired, wash some lemon balm or basil, pat dry and remove the leaves from the stems, then cut into strips and sprinkle over the cheese snacks. Serve the snacks hot or cold.

Tip: Serve the cheese snacks with wine or beer.

Celery with dips
For guests

Preparation time:
about 50 minutes

800 g/1¾ lb celery

For the egg dip:
3 hard-boiled eggs
100 g/3½ oz fromage frais
3 tablespoons whipping
cream or milk
2 teaspoons chopped
tarragon
salt, pepper

For the garlic dip:
2 cloves garlic
2 teaspoons capers
4 teaspoons each
chopped parsley and
chives
100 g/3½ oz fromage frais
3 tablespoons natural
yogurt, 3.5% fat
salt, pepper

For the orange and
horseradish dip:
½ orange (untreated)
100 g/3½ oz fromage
frais
2 teaspoons grated
horseradish (from the
jar), salt, pepper

For the crème-fraîche dip:
150 g/5 oz crème fraîche
2 heaped teaspoons
tomato ketchup
4 teaspoons chopped
herbs, e.g. parsley,
chives, dill, cress
salt, pepper, sugar

1 Cut off the root ends of the celery and remove any yellowing leaves and stringy fibres. Wash the stems, drain and put in a tall glass.

2 To make the egg dip (photograph, top), shell the eggs and cut in half. Take out the egg yolks, mash with a fork and mix together with the fromage frais, cream or milk and tarragon. Season with salt and pepper. Chop the egg white finely and stir in.

3 To make the garlic dip (photograph, bottom), peel the garlic and push through a garlic press. Drain the capers and chop finely. Mix together the garlic and capers with parsley, chives, fromage frais and yogurt and season with salt and pepper.

4 To make the orange-horseradish dip (photograph, centre left), wash the orange in hot water, wipe dry, cut into halves, peel one half very thinly using a sharp knife and cut the peel into thin strips or peel with a lemon zester. Then press this half orange, producing 1½-2 tablespoons of juice. Stir the orange juice into the fromage frais and horseradish. Season with salt and pepper and garnish with the strips of orange peel.

5 To make the crème fraîche dip (photograph, right), mix together the crème fraîche, tomato ketchup and herbs, and season with salt, pepper and sugar.

6 Serve the celery with these dips.

Tip: You can also use these dips with other raw vegetables cut into strips (e.g. carrots, cucumbers, peppers or kohlrabi). To make the crème fraîche dip, you can also use 1 pack (25 g/1 oz) deep-frozen mixed herbs instead of fresh ones.

Per serving: **P: 17 g, F: 43 g, C: 11 g, kJ: 2065, kcal: 495**

Little glossary

Cactus fig

The cactus fig is a reddish-green fruit with very fine prickles and inedible skin. The reddish-yellow flesh contains numerous edible seeds and has a fresh, aromatic taste. Green cactus figs are not yet ripe. Peel the fruit very carefully or cut in half and eat with a spoon.

Cape gooseberry

Cape gooseberries have a paper-thin hull that contains a round, light-yellow to yellow-orange fruit. The flesh is light coloured with a slightly sour taste, reminiscent of pineapple. Both the seeds and skin are edible. Cape gooseberries can be eaten raw and are best when they are yellow and fully ripe.

Dates

The oblong-oval fruit are reddish brown on the outside and white inside with a hard, inedible stone in the middle. Dates have a sweet, honey-like taste.

Figs

Figs are very delicate fruit which are found in various colours. The reddish flesh contains numerous small edible seeds. Only ripe figs are aromatic. Figs cannot be stored for a long time and most figs available on the market are dried.

Grapefruit

Grapefruit has a yellow to orange-coloured skin and yellow to pinkish flesh. It is very juicy with a slightly sour-bitter taste. Cut the fruit in half and eat with a spoon, press, or cut into peeled segments like an orange in fruit salads.

Guava

The guava is a round, oval or pear-shaped fruit with yellowish skin. It has a sweet-sour taste and is very rich in vitamin C.

Kiwi

Kiwi fruits have a slightly hairy, inedible olive-brown or golden yellow skin. The light green or yellow flesh that contains edible seeds has a slightly sharp taste. Peel the fruit or cut in half and scoop out the flesh using a spoon. Kiwis will keep for up to 1 week in the fridge.

Kumquat

The kumquat is a very small citrus fruit that is eaten with the skin. It is a highly aromatic fruit rich in calcium and vitamin C.

Lime

The lime is a citrus fruit with greenish fruit that is very juicy, highly aromatic and usually seedless. It is slightly less sour than a lemon but just as versatile.

Lychee

Lychees are the same size as plums with a wrinkled, red-brown inedible skin. The flesh is pale coloured and juicy with an inedible brown-black stone in the middle. They have a sweetish-sour, slightly nutty taste. The skin is easily crushed and removed when the fruit is ripe. Lychees are available in shops during the winter months.

Mango

The mango has an inedible, smooth, greenish-red to yellow skin and yellow, juicy flesh with a inedible stone in the middle. Ripe mangoes have a very intense aroma and a skin which gives slightly when pressed. The flesh is sweet and tangy.

Melon

There are many varieties of melons with various sizes and colours. The skin is inedible. The flesh is very juicy and aromatic, the taste ranging from slightly sweet (watermelon) to very sweet (Honeydew and Galia melons). The seeds and fibres inside are not edible. Melons are ripe when the area around the stalk end is slightly soft. Ripe melons are intensely fragrant.

Papayas

Papayas have a greenish-red or greenish-yellow leathery skin which is inedible. The yellow flesh is sweet with small inedible seeds. Papayas are an ideal fruit for fruit salad. They are ripe when the skin has become yellow and gives slightly when pressed with a finger.

Passion fruit

Passion fruit is greenish-yellow or greenish-red with shrivelled, inedible skin. The reddish-orange flesh which contains a large amount of seeds has a sweet aromatic taste. The skin becomes very shrivelled when the fruit is ripe.

Persimmon

The persimmon is a tomato-like, round fruit with smooth, shiny orange-coloured skin that is not edible. The slightly transparent flesh has only a few seeds. When ripe it is juicy and sweet, but when unripe it is terribly woody and stringy. It is ideally suited to purée, and as an ingredient in curd cheese-based dishes. Persimmons are slightly squarish in shape and can be eaten in the hand like an apple.

Pineapple

Pineapple is covered with inedible brown scales. The more developed the scales, the more fragrant the fruit. Ripe pineapple is very aromatic and juicy. When a pineapple is ripe the green leaves at the top are easily pulled off.

Pomegranate

This round fruit weighing up to 500 g/18 oz has a leathery skin and jelly-like flesh containing numerous edible seeds, separated into compartments by white membranes (which are bitter and not edible).

Star fruit or carambola

The star fruit or carambola is a yellow fruit that has a star-shaped appearance when cut in half. It is usually eaten fresh and often used as decoration because of its attractive shape.

Bavarian pudding (photograph bottom)
Classic (4-5 servings)

Preparation time: about 40
minutes, excluding cooling time

1 vanilla pod
250 ml/8 fl oz (1 cup) milk
6 leaves white gelatine
yolks of 3 medium eggs
75 g/3 oz sugar
250 ml/8 fl oz (1 cup)
   chilled whipping cream

Per serving:
P: 8 g, F: 24 g, C: 21 g,
kJ: 1383, kcal: 330

1 Cut open the vanilla pod. Scoop out the flesh with the back of a knife, put in the pan together with the milk and bring to the boil. Soak the gelatine in cold water, following the instructions on the packet.

2 Beat together the egg yolk and sugar in a stainless steel bowl or saucepan using a whisk. Now stir the hot milk into the egg and sugar mixture. Put the bowl or saucepan in a bain-marie and heat while whisking continuously until the mixture thickens and turns white (neither the water nor mixture should be allowed to boil or the mixture may curdle). Remove the mixture from the bain-marie.

3 Squeeze the gelatine to remove as much water as possible and dissolve in the mixture while it is still hot. Then strain the mixture through a fine sieve and allow to cool, stirring occasionally.

4 As soon as the mixture begins to set, whip the cream until stiff and fold into the setting mixture. Take 4-5 ramekins or cups, each with a capacity of 150-200 ml/5-7 fl oz (⁵⁄₈-⁷⁄₈ cup). Rinse them in cold water, fill with the mixture and refrigerate for about 3 hours until set.

5 Carefully loosen the pudding along the edges with the point of a knife. Place the ramekins or cups briefly in hot water and turn the puddings out onto the plates. Garnish to taste.

Tip: Serve Bavarian pudding with whipped cream and fruit, fruit purée or chocolate sauce (page 287).

Variation 1: **Bavarian cappuccino cream pudding** (photograph top). Dissolve 5 teaspoons instant espresso powder with the gelatine in the egg yolk and milk mixture and continue as described above. Fill cappuccino cups with this mixture and refrigerate. Before serving, beat 125 ml/4 fl oz (½ cup) whipping cream, put on top of the pudding to imitate the froth of a cappuccino and sprinkle with cocoa powder.

Variation 2: **Bavarian orange cream.** Add 3 teaspoons orange liqueur to the strained egg yolk and milk mixture and proceed as indicated above. Put the mixture in glass bowls or glasses, garnish with strips of orange peel (from 2-3 oranges) and refrigerate.

Variation 3: **Bavarian chocolate cream.** Chop up 150 g/5 oz plain chocolate, add to the egg yolk and milk mixture before adding the gelatine and dissolve into the mixture while stirring. Then dissolve the gelatine (use only 4 leaves because the pudding would set too firmly otherwise) and proceed as described above. The quantities make 6 servings of 150 ml/5 fl oz (⁵⁄₈ cup) each.

Semolina pudding
For children

Preparation time:
about 15 minutes, excluding
cooling time

½ **vanilla pod**
500 ml/17 fl oz (2¼ cups)
  milk
75 g/3 oz sugar
grated peel of
  ½ untreated lemon
50 g/2 oz soft wheat
  semolina flour
1 medium egg

Per serving:
P: 7 g, F: 6 g, C: 34 g,
kJ: 925, kcal: 221

1 Cut open the vanilla pod lengthways (photograph 1) and scoop out the flesh with the back of a knife. Add the sugar, lemon peel, vanilla pod and flesh to the milk in a pan and bring to the boil. Add the semolina to the milk, stirring continuously (photograph 2). Bring to the boil and cook for about 1 minute while stirring.

2 Take the pan from the heat and remove the vanilla pod. Separate the egg and stir the egg yolk into the milk and semolina mixture. Beat the egg white stiff and fold carefully into the hot pudding.

3 Rinse the mould, bowl or ramekins in cold water and fill with the semolina pudding. Leave to cool and then refrigerate for about 3 hours.

4 Carefully loosen the pudding around the edges and turn out onto a plate (photograph 3).

Note: Only use very fresh eggs; check the sell-by date! Keep the pudding refrigerated and eat within 24 hours.

Tip: Serve semolina pudding with fresh fruit and whipping cream, stewed plums (page 281) or puréed apricots.
Because the semolina mixture can spatter while cooking, it is advisable to use a spoon or whisk with a long handle for stirring.

Variation 1: **Polenta pudding.** Add sugar, lemon zest, vanilla pod and flesh to the milk together with 20 g/¾ oz (1½ tablespoons) butter and bring to the boil. Use polenta flour instead of semolina and proceed as described above.

Variation 2: **Semolina curd cheese pudding.** After you have added the stiffly beaten egg white, fold in 125 g/4½ oz curd cheese into the lukewarm pudding; add more sugar if desired.

Variation 3: **Semolina pudding with cinnamon.** Use 1 cinnamon stick instead of the vanilla pod.

Vanilla blancmange
Classic (4-5 servings)

1 Mix together the cornflour and half the sugar. Add the egg yolks and at least 6 tablespoons of the milk little by little, and stir to make a smooth consistency. Cut open the vanilla pod and scoop out the flesh with the back of a knife.

2 Add the salt, vanilla pod and flesh to the rest of the milk and bring to the boil. Take the pan from the heat and remove the vanilla pod. Stir in the cornflour and milk mixture. Cook for at least 1 more minute while stirring, then remove from the heat.

3 Beat the egg white stiff together with the rest of the sugar, fold into the hot cornflour and milk mixture, cover and leave to stand for 10 minutes. Rinse 4-5 cups or ramekins, size about 200 ml/ 7 fl oz (⅞ cup) each, in cold water and fill with the mixture. Refrigerate for at least 4 hours.

4 Carefully loosen the pudding around the edges with the tip of a knife. Place the cups or ramekins briefly in hot water and turn out of the mould onto dessert plates.

Tip: Only prepare in a glass bowl if you do not want to turn it out. To prevent a skin from forming, sprinkle with a little sugar or place clingfilm directly on the blancmange.
Serve the blancmange with whipped cream and fresh or stewed fruit.

Variation 1: **Almond blancmange.** Fry 70 g/3 oz chopped peeled almonds in a pan without fat over low heat until golden brown. Leave to cool down and stir into the mixture before folding the stiffly beaten egg white into it.

Variation 2: **Pistachio and orange blancmange.** Add 1 small (25 g/1 oz) pack of shelled, chopped pistachio nuts and 1 teaspoon grated orange zest from an untreated orange. Stir in 1-2 tablespoons orange liqueur if desired before folding the stiffly beaten egg white into the blancmange.

Variation 3: **Caramel blancmange.** Mix together the cornflour, egg yolk and milk and stir until you obtain a smooth consistency. Prepare the vanilla milk as indicated above and remove from the heat. To make the caramel, melt 100 g/3½ oz sugar in a small pan over medium heat, stirring continuously, until it turns light brown. Remove from the heat. Stir in 15 g/½ oz butter into the caramel mixture, then add the vanilla milk and bring to the boil while stirring. Now add the cornflour mixture and bring to the boil again. Fold in the stiffly beaten egg white and proceed as described above.

Preparation time: about 15 minutes, excluding cooling time

40 g/1½ oz cornflour (cornstarch)
60 g/2 oz sugar
500 ml/17 fl oz (2¼ cups) milk
yolks of 2 medium eggs
½ vanilla pod
1 pinch salt
white of 1 medium egg

Per serving:
P: 6 g, F: 7 g, C: 30 g, kJ: 858, kcal: 205

(continued on page 272)

Variation 4: **Chocolate blancmange.** Mix together the cornflour, egg yolk and milk and stir to make a smooth consistency. Chop up 70 g/3 oz plain chocolate and add to the rest of the milk together with 5 tablespoons whipping cream, 1 pinch of salt and 30–40 g/1–1½ oz sugar (without the vanilla pod). Stir until the chocolate melts. Now stir in the cornflour mixture and bring to the boil again. Fold in the stiffly beaten egg white and continue as described above.

Tiramisu
Popular (6 servings)

Preparation time:
about 30 minutes, without
soaking time

**500 g/18 oz mascarpone
cheese**
**100 ml/3½ fl oz (½ cup)
milk**
75 g/3 oz sugar
**2–3 drops vanilla essence
in 1 tablespoon sugar**
**40 ml/1½ fl oz (3 table-
spoons) Amaretto
almond liqueur**
**200 ml/7 fl oz (⅞ cup)
cold espresso or strong
coffee**
**200 g/7 oz sponge
fingers**
**4 teaspoons cocoa
powder**

Per serving:
**P. 8 g, F: 39 g, C: 44 g,
kJ: 2443, kcal: 583**

1   Mix together the mascarpone, milk, sugar, vanilla sugar and half the amaretto in a bowl and stir until the mixture becomes smooth and homogenous.

2   Mix together the rest of the amaretto and the espresso or coffee. Arrange half the sponge fingers in a shallow rectangular dish (of about 30 x 18 cm/12 x 7 in), pour half the coffee and amaretto mixture on top and cover with half the mascarpone mixture. Arrange the rest of the ingredients in layers following the same sequence.

3   Put the tiramisu in the refrigerator and leave for a few hours for the flavours to mingle. Sprinkle with cocoa powder just before serving.

Tip: Tiramisu is an ideal pudding for parties.

Variation 1: Replace half the mascarpone with 250 g/9 oz curd cheese (20% fat, dry weight) and thus reduce the calories.

Variation 2: **Tiramisu with peaches.** Drain 1 can of peach halves (drained weight 450 g/1 lb) and slice thinly. Prepare the mascarpone mixture as described above. Arrange half the sponge biscuits in the bowl and pour half the coffee-amaretto mixture over them. Arrange half the sliced peaches on top. Arrange the peaches and the rest of the ingredients in layers following the same sequence. Continue as described in paragraph 3 above.

Chocolate mousse
For guests

Preparation time:
about 30 minutes, excluding
cooling time

**100 g/3½ oz plain
chocolate
50 g/2 oz full milk
chocolate
yolks from 3 medium eggs
2 teaspoons sugar
2 teaspoons Cognac or
rum
egg whites from
3 medium eggs
125 ml/4 fl oz (½ cup)
chilled whipping cream**

Per serving:
P: 9 g, F: 27 g, C: 22 g,
kJ: 1548, kcal: 370

1 Chop both kinds of chocolate (photograph 1), melt in a bain-marie over low heat, stirring continuously and leave to cool a little.

2 Whisk together the egg yolks, sugar, Cognac or rum in a bowl, using a hand-held mixer with whisk attachment, until the mixture has thickened. Now stir in the melted chocolate while it is still warm.

3 Beat the egg whites so stiff that you can cut them with a knife (photograph 2). Whip the cream until stiff and carefully fold into the egg whites. Transfer the mousse into a large shallow bowl and refrigerate for at least 2 hours.

4 Arrange the mousse in spoonfuls on a plate, using an ice cream scoop or tablespoon (photograph 3), and serve.

Note: **Use only very fresh eggs that are not more than 5 days old (check the sell-by date!). Store the mousse in the refrigerator and eat within 24 hours.**

Tip: Sprinkle the chocolate with icing sugar or cocoa powder just before serving.

Variation 1: **Chocolate mousse with amaretti.** Finely chop 40 g/1½ oz amaretti (Italian almond macaroons) and carefully fold into the mousse. Then garnish with whipped cream and chopped amaretti.

Variation 2: You can serve the chocolate mousse with a **white chocolate sauce.** To make the white chocolate sauce, melt 100 g/3½ oz white chocolate in 125 ml/4 fl oz (½ cup) whipping cream in a small pan over low heat while stirring until it forms a smooth, homogenous mixture. Leave to cool down. Serve the sauce with the mousse.

Variation 3: **Vanilla chocolate mousse.** Use 150 g/5 oz white chocolate instead of the plain and milk chocolate and add 2–3 drops vanilla essence in 1 tablespoon sugar.

Swiss rice
For children (4-6 servings)

1 To make the creamed rice, add the salt, sugar and vanilla sugar to the milk in a saucepan and bring to the boil. Add the rice and bring to the boil again while stirring. Cover and cook over low heat for 20 minutes, stirring occasionally; the rice should still have a kernel firm to the bite. Leave to cool down a little, cover and refrigerate.

2 Whip the cream and fold into the cold rice. Put the creamed rice in a bowl and refrigerate until served.

3 To make the strawberry sauce, wash the strawberries, drain and remove the stalks. Purée 400 g/14 oz of the strawberries and stir in the vanilla sugar and sugar. Slice the rest of the strawberries. Serve the creamed rice with the strawberry sauce and sliced strawberries.

Tip: This dish will feed 3 as a sweet meal.

Per serving: P: 6 g, F: 17 g, C: 46 g, kJ: 1528, kcal: 365

Preparation time:
about 40 minutes, excluding cooling time

For the rice cream:
500 ml/17 fl oz (2¼ cups) milk, 1 pinch salt
50 g/2 oz sugar
2-3 drops vanilla essence in 1 tablespoon sugar
pudding rice (round grain rice)
200 ml/7 fl oz (⅞ cup) chilled whipping cream

For the strawberry sauce:
500 g/18 oz strawberries
2-3 drops vanilla essence in 1 tablespoon sugar
25 g/1 oz sugar

Frothy wine sauce
Quick

1 Whisk together the egg and egg yolk and white wine in a stainless steel bowl or stainless steel saucepan.

2 Put the bowl with this mixture in a hot bain-marie over medium heat. Whisk with a hand-held mixer with whisk attachment, set at the lowest setting, until the mixture becomes thick and frothy. The mixture should almost double in volume. Do not let the water or the mixture boil because this may make the sauce curdle. Serve the sauce immediately.

Note: Use only very fresh eggs which are not more than 5 days old; check the sell-by date! Store the sauce in the refrigerator and eat within 24 hours.

Tip: Delicious with fruit salad (page 281) or ice cream (page 286).

Variation 1: Alcohol-free frothy sauce. Use 125 ml/4 fl oz (½ cup) apple juice and 2 tablespoons lemon juice instead of wine.

Variation 2: Zabaglione. Take yolks of 3 medium eggs, 60 g/2 oz sugar and 125 ml/4 fl oz (1/2 cup) Marsala (Italian dessert wine) and make the sauce as indicated above.

Preparation time:
about 10 minutes

1 medium egg
yolk from 1 medium egg
60 g/2 oz sugar
125 ml/4 fl oz (½ cup) dry white wine

Per serving:
P: 3 g, F: 3 g, C: 15 g, kJ: 507, kcal: 121

Curd cheese with fruit
For children

Preparation time:
about 20 minutes, excluding
cooling time

**1 can of peach halves,
drained weight 450 g/
1 lb
grated zest of ½ untreated
lime or lemon
4 teaspoons lime or
lemon juice
500 g/18 oz curd cheese
150 g/5 oz natural
yogurt, 3.5% fat
2–3 tablespoons sugar
2–3 drops vanilla essence
in 1 tablespoon sugar**

Per serving:
P: 18 g, F: 5 g, C: 38 g,
kJ: 1162, kcal: 277

1 Drain the peach halves in a colander, cut into small dice and mix together with the lime or lemon zest and juice.

2 Now whisk together curd cheese, yoghurt, sugar and vanilla sugar. Pour half of this mixture into a bowl. Arrange the diced peach halves on top, then cover with the rest of the curd cheese mixture. Refrigerate for at least 30 minutes before serving.

Tip: Garnish with lemon balm leaves before serving. This is a very reasonably-priced dessert for parties. 50 g/2 oz roast grated coconut may also be added: sprinkle half over the peach mixture and the rest on top of the curd cheese.

Variation: **Chocolate curd cheese with bananas** (photograph). Break 100 g/3½ oz plain chocolate into small pieces and melt in a bowl placed in a bain-marie over low heat. Add 4–6 tablespoons milk or whipping cream to 500 g/18 oz low fat curd cheese and stir until the mixture is smooth and homogenous. Stir in 2–3 drops natural vanilla essence in 1 tablespoon sugar, the melted chocolate and 1½ tablespoons sugar. Peel 4 small ripe bananas and put 1 banana on each plate. Put the curd cheese in a pastry bag with a large star-shaped nozzle and squeeze in whorls along the banana. If desired, garnish with praliné, roasted, peeled and flaked almonds or chocolate crumbs before serving.

Baked apples
With alcohol (8 servings)

Preparation time:
about 60 minutes, excluding
soaking time

**2 teaspoons raisins
about 100 ml/3½ fl oz
(½ cup) rum
8 apples, e.g. Cox
20 g/¾ oz soft butter
20 g/¾ oz sugar
2–3 drops vanilla essence
in 1 tablespoon sugar**

1 Soak the raisins overnight in 2 tablespoons of rum.

2 Preheat the oven at the top and bottom. Wash the apples, wipe dry, remove the stalks and cores without pushing through. Arrange the apples in a well-greased gratin dish or on small heat-resistant plates.

3 Using a spoon, mix together the butter, vanilla sugar, ground almonds and soaked raisins. Fill the cored apples with this mixture using a teaspoon. Sprinkle the flaked almonds on top and press in slightly. Pour the rest of the rum over the apples. Put the dish or individual plates on a shelf in the oven.

(continued on page 278)

4 teaspoons peeled
    ground almonds
4 teaspoons peeled
    coarsely dropped
    almonds
icing sugar

In addition:
fat for the form

Per serving:
P: 1 g, F: 4 g, C: 20 g,
kJ: 644, kcal: 154

Top/bottom heat: about 200 °C/400 °F (preheated),
Fan oven: about 180° C/350 °F (not preheated), Gas mark 6 (not preheated),
Cooking time: about 40 minutes.

4 Serve the baked apples hot and sprinkle with icing sugar just
  before serving.

Tip: Serve the baked apples with vanilla sauce (page 287) or lightly whipping
cream. Ideal for pudding or at tea time.

Variation: Baked apples without alcohol. Soak the raisins in orange or apple
juice, drain and proceed as indicated above. Instead of pouring rum over the
apples, use orange or apple juice.

Red fruit pudding
Classic (6 servings)

Preparation time:
about 20 minutes, excluding
cooling time

250 g/9 oz blackberries
250 g/9 oz red currants
250 g/9 oz raspberries
250 g/9 oz strawberries
(all fruits weighed after
    being prepared)
35 g/1¼ oz cornflour
    (cornstarch)
100 g/3½ oz sugar
500 ml/17 fl oz (2¼ cups)
    fruit juice, e.g. sour
    cherry or red currant
    juice

Per serving:
P: 3 g, F: 1 g, C: 40 g,
kJ: 813, kcal: 194

1 Sort out the blackberries, wash carefully and drain thoroughly.
  Wash the red currants, drain well and remove from the stalks.
  Sort out the raspberries but do not wash. Wash the strawberries,
  drain, remove the stalks and cut into halves or quarters depending on the size.

2 Mix the cornflour with the sugar, add 4 tablespoons of the juice
  and stir well. Bring the rest of the juice to the boil in a saucepan.
  Stir in the juice and cornflour mixture, bring to the boil and
  remove the saucepan from the heat. Add the fruit and stir well.
  Put the red fruit pudding in a glass bowl or in pudding bowls and
  refrigerate.

Tip: Serve red fruit pudding with vanilla sauce (page 287) or cream. When
served as a pudding or as a sweet meal with milk (in which case it will feed
4 people). It is an ideal party dessert.
You can also make this red fruit pudding with deep-frozen fruit. In this case,
stir the deep-frozen fruit in the hot, thickened sauce.

Variation: **Green fruit pudding.** Wash 500 g/18 oz gooseberries, drain
thoroughly and remove the stalks and any leaves. Peel 250 g/9 oz kiwi fruits,
halve and cut into small pieces. Wash 250 g/9 oz seedless white grapes, drain
well, remove the stalks and cut the larger grapes in half. Mix 20 g/¾ oz
cornflour with 150 g/5 oz sugar. From 375 ml/12 fl oz (1½ cups) white grape
juice, take 4 tablespoons and add to the cornflour and sugar mixture, then
stir well. Bring the rest of the juice to the boil, stir in the cornflour and juice
mixture and bring to the boil. Stir in the gooseberries and grapes, bring
briefly to the boil, remove the pan from the heat and stir in the kiwi fruit. Put
in a bowl and refrigerate.

Fruit juice jelly with fruit
Sophisticated

1 Soak the gelatine in cold water following the instructions on the packet. Heat half the juice or nectar in a pan. Add the sugar and stir to dissolve. Squeeze out the gelatine, add to the hot juice and stir to dissolve. Then stir in the rest of the juice and leave the mixture to cool down a little.

2 Meanwhile, wash the strawberries, drain, remove the stalks and cut into slices. Wash the red currants, drain well and remove the currants from the stalks.

3 Pour a small amount of the liquid (photograph 1) into a large bowl or 4 individual bowls and refrigerate until set. Keep the rest of the liquid at room temperature so that it does not set.

4 As soon as the jelly at the bottom has set, cover with part of the fruit (photograph 2) and pour some of the remaining liquid on top. Put the bowl back in the fridge so that this liquid can set.

5 Arrange 2 more layers of fruit and jelly in the same way. The top layer should be jelly (photograph 3). Return the bowl to the fridge and leave for at least 2 hours to set.

Tip: Serve the fruit juice jelly with vanilla sauce (page 287) or cream. If the remaining liquid begins to set while you are still making the layers, put the bowl in warm water.

Variation: **Apple jelly.** Prepare the liquid as indicated above using 6 leaves of white gelatine, 500 ml/ 16 fl oz (2 cups) apple juice, 2 tablespoons lemon juice, 50 g/2 oz sugar and 2 large pinches of vanilla sugar and refrigerate. Wash 300 g/10 oz sharp apples (e.g. Granny Smith), wash, peel, cut into eighths and remove the cores. Cut the pieces into thin slices and mix with 1 tablespoon lemon juice and 250 ml/8 fl oz (1 cup) water. Arrange the liquid and the thin slices of apple in alternate layers as indicated above, but remove the sliced apples from the lemon and water mixture and pat dry before arranging them in layers in the bowl.

Preparation time:
about 30 minutes, excluding
cooling time

6 leaves gelatine
500 ml/17 fl oz (2¼ cups)
   red currant juice or
   nectar
120 g/4 oz sugar
250 g/9 oz strawberries
100 g/3½ oz red currants

Per serving:
P: 4 g, F: 0 g, C: 62 g,
kJ: 1196, kcal: 285

Apple snow
Classic

Preparation time:
about 25 minutes

750 g/1½ lb sharp apples,
  e.g. Russets or
  Bramleys
3 tablespoons water
about 50 g/2 oz sugar

Per serving:
P: 0 g, F: 1 g, C: 30 g,
kJ: 537, kcal: 129

1   Wash the apples, peel, cut into quarters and then into small pieces. Add the apples to the water in a pan and bring to the boil. Cover and cook over low heat for about 15 minutes.

2   If desired, you can purée the apples and sweeten with sugar.

Tip: Serve the Apple snow as a pudding either on its own or with whipped cream, or with potato pancakes (page 211) or with potato and Kastenpickert (page 224).
You can also use apples that have not been peeled. In this case, wash the apples, remove the stalks and any leaves, cut the apples into pieces and cook as indicated above. Then rub the stewed apples through a sieve.

Variation 1: **Apple compote**, a "lumpier" variation of stewed apples. Coarsely chop the peeled, cored apples, cook with a little water for about 10 minutes as indicated above, do not purée and add sugar to sweeten.

Variation 2: **Layered stewed apples and curd cheese pudding.** Make half the amount of stewed apples as described above and leave to cool. Fry 50 g/ 2 oz sunflower seeds in a pan without fat over low heat until golden brown and leave to cool down. Mix together 500 g/18 oz curd cheese, 2–3 tablespoons sugar and 2–3 drops natural vanilla essence in 1 tablespoon sugar. Arrange half the curd cheese mixture, stewed apples and sunflower seeds in layers in a glass bowl, then cover with the rest of the curd cheese, stewed apples and sunflower seeds, arranged again in layers. Refrigerate for about 30 minutes.

Pear compote
Easy

Preparation time: about
20 minutes, excluding cooling time

500 g/18 oz pears
250 ml/8 fl oz (1 cup)
  water
50 g/2 oz sugar
2–3 drops vanilla essence
  in 1 tablespoon sugar
1 cinnamon stick

1   Wash the pears, peel, halve, core and cut into pieces. Add the sugar, vanilla sugar, cinnamon stick and cloves to the water and bring to the boil.

2   Now add the pears, bring to the boil again, cover and cook over low heat for about 10 minutes until soft. Stir in the lemon juice. Leave the compote to cool down.

3   Add sugar to sweeten and remove the cloves and cinnamon.

Tip: Serve as a pudding with whipped cream or ice cream, or as a sweet meal with pancakes (page 252) or curd cheese pancakes (page 253).
The flavour of all fruit compotes can be further enhanced by the addition of the zest of ½ lemon (untreated). This is added to the pan at the beginning of the cooking and removed after cooking when the compote has cooled down.

Variation 1: Replace half the water with 125 ml/4 fl oz (½ cup) white wine.

Variation 2: **Plum compote.** Wash 500 g/18 oz plums, leave to drain, dry each plum with a cloth, remove the stalks, cut in half and remove the stones. Add 50 g/2 oz sugar to 125 ml/4 fl oz (½ cup) water or red wine in a pan and bring to the boil. Now add the plums, 1 cinnamon stick and 3 cloves, bring to the boil again, cover and braise over low heat for about 8 minutes. Remove the cinnamon stick and cloves, leave to cool down a little and add sugar to taste.

3 cloves
3-4 teaspoons lemon juice
some sugar (to taste)

Per serving:
P: 0 g, F: 0 g, C: 29 g,
kJ: 501, kcal: 119

Fruit salad
Fruity (6 servings)

1   Wash the apple, peel, cut into quarters and remove the core. Peel the mango, cut in half and remove the stone. Wash the nectarine and peach, wipe dry, cut in half and remove the stones. Cut all the fruit into pieces. Peel the orange so that the white pith is also removed using a sharp knife and "fillet" the segments, removing the membrane surrounding each segment.

2   Peel the kiwi fruit and bananas and slice. Wash the strawberries, drain, remove the stalks and cut into pieces.

3   Stir the lemon juice into the fruit and add sugar to taste. Put the fruit salad into a glass bowl and sprinkle with chopped walnuts, hazelnuts and almonds.

Tip: As a dessert, serve the fruit salad with cream, vanilla sauce (page 287) or ice cream. As a sweet meal, serve with hot semolina pudding (page 270) or rice pudding. The flavour of the fruit salad can be enhanced by adding a little orange liqueur. You can also stir 50 g/2 oz raisins or 1 tablespoon chopped peppermint leaves into the salad.

Variation: Fruit salad can be varied endlessly according to the season and taste. In winter some of the fruit can be replaced by grapefruit (prepared like the orange), persimmon (wash but do not peel, and cut into pieces, passion fruit or granadilla (remove the stone and whisk together briefly with 2 tablespoons orange juice, using a hand-held mixer with whisk attachment) or pomegranate (cut open and remove the seeds). You need about 1 kg/2¼ lb fruit in all.

Preparation time:
about 30 minutes

1 apple
1 small mango
1 nectarine
1 peach
1 orange
1 kiwi fruit
1 banana
100 g/3½ oz strawberries
2 tablespoons lemon juice
2 teaspoons sugar or honey (to taste)
30 g/1 oz chopped walnuts, hazelnut kernels or almonds

Per serving:
P: 2 g, F: 3 g, C: 22 g,
kJ: 548, kcal: 131

Welfenspeise (Vanilla sabayon)
With alcohol

Preparation time: about
30 minutes, excluding cooling time

For the custard:
whites of 2 medium eggs
35 g/1¼ oz cornflour
(cornstarch)
40 g/1½ oz sugar
2–3 drops vanilla essence
in 1 tablespoon sugar
500 ml/17 fl oz (2¼ cups)
milk

For the frothy sauce:
yolks of 3 medium eggs
80 g/3 oz sugar
10 g/⅓ oz cornflour
(cornstarch)
250 ml/8 fl oz (1 cup)
white wine

Per serving:
P: 9 g, F: 9 g, C: 48 g,
kJ: 1491, kcal: 356

1   To make the custard, whisk the egg whites until stiff enough to be cut with a knife (photograph 1). Mix together the cornflour, sugar and vanilla sugar and stir in 6 tablespoons of the milk.

2   Bring the rest of the milk to the boil in a saucepan, remove from the heat and stir in the mixture with the cornflour using a whisk and bring briefly to the boil.

3   Now stir the stiffly beaten egg whites into the hot mixture (photograph 2) and bring to the boil again. Pour into a glass bowl or individual glasses or bowls, filling them only half full, and put in the refrigerator.

4   For the frothy sauce, mix together the egg yolk, sugar, cornflour and white wine in a stainless steel saucepan or bowl. Place the bowl in a hot bain-marie, and whisk using a hand-held mixer with whisk attachment (photograph 3) until the mixture is thick and frothy; the volume should almost double. Do not let the water or sauce boil or it may curdle. Remove the bowl or saucepan from the bain-marie, loosen the mixture round the edges and stir again briefly.

5   Leave the sauce to cool down and pour on top of the custard in the bowls or glasses.

Note: Only use very fresh eggs; check the sell-by date!

Tip: Garnish with lemon balm leaves before serving.
To ensure that the egg white can be beaten stiffly enough, the bowl and whisk must be completely free of fat and there must be no trace of egg yolk in the white.

Variation: An alcohol-free variation of frothy sauce. Replace the white wine with 250 ml/8 fl oz (1 cup) apple juice and 3 tablespoons lemon juice.

Raspberry sorbet (photograph top)
Fruity

Preparation time:
about 30 minutes, excluding
freezing time

**150 ml/5 fl oz (⅝ cup)
water
160 g/5½ oz sugar
peel of ½ lemon
(untreated)
500 g/18 oz raspberries
2 teaspoons raspberry
spirit**

Per serving:
**P: 2 g, F: 0 g, C: 46 g,
kJ: 877, kcal: 209**

1 Add the sugar and lemon to the water in a small pan and bring to the boil and cook over high heat for about 5 minutes without a lid. This should produce about 100 ml/3½ fl oz (½ cup) syrup. Leave the syrup to cool down, then remove the lemon peel.

2 Sort out the raspberries but do not wash. Put the raspberries with half the syrup in a tall mixing glass and purée with a masher. Rub the mixture through a sieve if you like, add the rest of the syrup and flavour with raspberry spirit.

3 Put the mixture in a frost-resistant container and put in the freezer for 1 hour, stir and put back in the freezer for 3 hours, stirring several times to ensure a creamy texture.

4 Put the sorbet in a piping bag with a large star-shaped nozzle and squeeze into 4 individual bowls.

Tip: The sorbet can be made in an ice cream machine in 30–45 minutes, depending on the model.
200 ml/7 fl oz (⅞ cup) chilled whipped cream may be stirred into the fruit mixture before it is frozen.
Pour sparkling white wine over the sorbet in each bowl, 250 ml/8 fl oz (1 cup) in all.

Variation 1: **Red currant sorbet.** Use red currants instead of raspberries. Wash the red currants, drain thoroughly and remove from the stalks. Prepare the sorbet as described above, rub through a sieve and freeze.

Variation 2: **Strawberry sorbet.** Use strawberries instead of raspberries. Wash and drain the strawberries, remove the stalks and purée (do not rub through a sieve). Using only 100 g/3½ oz sugar for the syrup, prepare the sorbet as indicated above.

Variation 3: **Mango sorbet** (photograph bottom). For the syrup add 80 g/3 oz sugar, the peel of ½ lime (untreated) and 3 teaspoons lime juice to 125 ml/4 fl oz (½ cup) water and bring to the boil as indicated above (this will produce about 80 ml/3 fl oz syrup) and leave to cool. Remove the lime peel. Peel 2 mangoes, cut in half and remove the stones, cut the flesh into cubes and purée with a masher. Stir together the diced mangoes and the syrup and freeze for about 4 hours, stirring once or twice after the first hour. The sorbet may be crushed again with a masher just before serving or whisked with a hand-held mixer with whisk attachment.

Vanilla ice cream
Good for preparing in advance (8 servings)

Preparation time: about
30 minutes, excluding freezing
time

1 vanilla pod
yolks of 4 medium eggs
500 ml/17 fl oz (2¼ cups)
  whipping cream
100 g/3½ oz sugar

Per serving:

P: 3 g, F: 23 g, C: 15 g,
kJ: 1163, kcal: 278

1 Cut the vanilla pod lengthways and scoop out the flesh with the back of a knife. Mix together the egg yolk, sugar and the flesh scooped out of the vanilla pod with 3 tablespoons of cream in a stainless steel bowl or saucepan. Place in a hot bain-marie and whisk vigorously until the mixture thickens (the water in the bain-marie and the mixture should not be allowed to boil because this may cause the mixture to curdle).

2 Take the stainless steel bowl or pan out of the bain-marie, place in cold water and continue whisking the egg yolk mixture until it has cooled down.

3 Whip the cream until it is stiff and fold into the mixture. Put in a shallow freezer box holding 1 litre/1¾ pints (4½ cups) and freeze for at least 3 hours.

Tip: Serve the ice cream with fresh fruit, chocolate sauce (page 287), a little egg liqueur or whipped cream.
Using an ice cream maker, ice cream can be made in about 40 minutes, depending on the model; follow the manufacturer's instructions. In this case whisk only the egg yolk mixture in the bain-marie. Do not whip the cream but add in its liquid state.

Variation 1: **Vanilla and walnut praliné ice cream.** Chop up 100 g/3½ oz walnuts, fry over low heat in a pan without fat until golden brown and transfer to a plate. Caramelise 60 g/2 oz sugar in a pan until golden brown, stir in the chopped walnuts and spread the mixture evenly on a piece of greaseproof paper. Leave to cool down, crumble a little and stir into the egg mixture together with the whipped cream. If you are using an ice cream maker, only add the walnut and caramel mixture shortly before the end of the freezing process.

Variation 2: **Chocolate ice cream.** Coarsely chop 100 g/3½ oz plain chocolate and melt in a bowl placed in a bain-marie over low heat. Finely chop 50 g/2 oz milk chocolate. Prepare the egg yolk mixture in the bain-marie as described above but without the vanilla. Stir in the melted chocolate and leave the mixture to cool a little. First add the whipped cream in two stages, then add the chopped milk chocolate. When using an ice cream maker, stir the cream into the chocolate mixture without whipping it. Add the chopped chocolate just before the end of the freezing process.

Lemon pudding
Fruity

1 Soak the gelatine in cold water, following the instructions on the packet. Heat the lemon juice in a small pan but do not let it boil.

2 Squeeze the gelatine to remove some water, dissolve in the hot lemon juice, then stir in the sugar. Leave the gelatine and lemon mixture to cool down, then stir in the yogurt. Refrigerate the mixture until it begins to set, stirring occasionally.

3 When the mixture begins to set, whip the cream and fold in. Transfer this mixture into a glass bowl or individual bowls and refrigerate for at least 3 hours.

Tip: Serve the lemon pudding with whipped cream.

Variation 1: Serve the lemon pudding with **chocolate sauce.** To make the chocolate sauce, coarsely chop 100 g/3½ oz plain chocolate and melt with 3 tablespoons water in bowl placed in a bain-marie over low heat while stirring.

Variation 2: **Orange pudding.** Use freshly squeezed orange juice instead of lemon juice and use only 100 g/3½ oz sugar.

Preparation time: about 30 minutes, excluding cooling time

4 leaves white gelatine
150 ml/5 fl oz (⅝ cup) lemon juice, from about 3 lemons
125 g/4½ oz sugar
150 g/5 oz natural yogurt, 3.5% fat,
300 ml/10 fl oz (1¼ cups) chilled whipping cream

Per serving:
P: 5 g, F: 25 g, C: 36 g, kJ: 1669, kcal: 399

Vanilla sauce
Classic

1 Slit open the vanilla pod lengthways and scoop out the flesh with the back of a knife. Stir together the cornflour with 3 tablespoons of the milk, using a whisk. Then add the egg yolk, sugar and salt and stir well.

2 Bring the rest of the milk with the vanilla flesh to the boil. Remove the saucepan from the heat and stir in the mixture with the cornflour, using a whisk. Bring the sauce briefly to the boil.

3 Remove the sauce from the boil and leave to cool, stirring occasionally.

Tip: Vanilla sauce is delicious served with stewed fruit (pages 280, 281), red fruit pudding (page 278), baked apples (page 276) or apple pie. 100 ml/3½ fl oz (½ cup) of the milk may be replaced by whipping cream.

Preparation time: about 10 minutes, excluding cooling time

1 vanilla pod
10 g/⅓ oz cornflour (cornstarch)
500 ml/17 fl oz (2¼ cups) milk
yolks of 3 large eggs
40 g/1½ oz sugar
1 pinch salt

Per serving:
P: 7 g, F: 9 g, C: 18 g, kJ: 768, kcal: 183

Glossary and information

Herbs in cooking

Herbs and spices complete
and enhance the flavour of a
dish while also adding variation to the menu. Herbs can be
used on their own or together,
and they can also reduce the
need for salt. They are also
very good for the health.

Storing and preparing

- If the herbs are in bunches,
  cut the ends off the stems
  and place them in water, or
  wrap loosely in clingfilm and
  store in the fridge.
- Fresh herbs should be
  rinsed carefully under cold
  running water and thor-
  oughly patted or shaken dry.
- Strip off the leaves of small-
  leaved herbs such as thyme
  and marjoram. Hold the top
  of the stem with one hand
  and strip the leaves off the
  stems with the other, moving it from top to bottom.
- Chop up the herbs with a
  sharp paring or chopping
  knife just before using them
  so that they do not lose
  their aroma. Chives can be
  also cut with clean, sharp
  kitchen scissors.

More about herbs

Basil
Green, sturdy, oval, ribbed
leaves with an aromatic,
slightly peppery taste.
Recommended with: lamb,
poultry, fish, eggs, salads
(especially tomato salad), raw
and cooked vegetables.

Borage
Oblong, slightly hairy, pale to
deep green leaves and blue
flowers. Slightly cucumber-like
taste.
Recommended with: salads,
sauces, vegetables, eggs, curd
cheese and yogurt-based
dishes and soups.

Chives
Thin, tubular stems with violet-
blue flowers. Spicy, sharp
taste.
Chives can be used in almost
all dishes: soups, sauces, herb
butter, salads, pasta, rice, vegetables, casseroles, egg, curd
cheese and yogurt-based
dishes.

Coriander
Coriander can be bought
fresh or as dried, round,
brown seeds that are whole
or ground. Fresh coriander is
used in Oriental, Indian,
Caribbean and Mexican cuisine. Coriander seeds are
used in marinades, pickled

vegetables, cabbage and in
baking (e.g., in Christmas pastries and bread).

Cress
Garden cress has small, delicate, light green leaves and a
strong spicy taste. It is sold in
containers.
Recommended with: soups,
sauces, salads, raw vegetables,
curd cheese, yogurt and egg-
based dishes, herb butter and
on bread.
Watercress has larger leaves
and a stronger taste. Neither
type can be frozen or dried.

Dill
Stems with feathery, light
green leaves and a pleasantly
spicy aroma.
Recommended with raw veg-
etables, salads, crustaceans,
white meat and poultry, fish,
egg and curd cheese-based
dishes, soups and sauces.

Lemon balm
Pale green, oval, slightly hairy
leaves with white to pale yellow flowers. Its taste is reminiscent of lemon. Used to
flavour: salads, sauces, egg,
curd cheese and yogurt-based
dishes, tea, refreshing soft
drinks and fruit salads.

Lovage
Tubular stems with large, ser-
rated leaves. It is very spicy

and therefore used sparingly. Recommended with: soups, casseroles, stuffing, stocks, pulses, vegetables and spicy salads.

Marjoram

Small oval leaves with white to pale violet flowers. Very spicy and slightly bitter, it makes fatty food more digestible. Recommended with: soups, sauces, minced meat, casseroles, spicy salads, vegetables, potatoes and sausages.

Mint, peppermint

There are several varieties. Light green to violet green, oval, ribbed leaves. Very spicy, strong aroma, it should be used sparingly. Recommended with: ragouts, stuffing, lamb, casseroles, pulses and fruit salads.

Oregano

Very popular in Italian cuisine, it only develops its full aroma during cooking or baking. It is used in pasta dishes, spicy sauces, pizzas and vegetable dishes.

Parsley

There are both flat-leaved and curly varieties. The flat-leaved variety has a particularly intense, spicy aroma. Parsley can be used in almost all dishes, especially vegetables, soups, sauces, pasta, casseroles and gratins.

Rosemary

Green to dark green needle-like leaves with violet-blue flowers. Strong, spicy, slightly bitter taste. Recommended with: roasts, poultry, fish, offal, game, potatoes, pulses, spicy sausages, mushrooms, courgettes, aubergines and lamb.

Sage

Oval, silver-grey to olive green leaves with violet-blue panicles. Spicy, slightly bitter taste. Use only sparingly. Recommended with: offal, lamb, poultry, eel, pasta, rice, stuffing and tomatoes.

Salad burnet

Small pale green, lightly feathery leaves with reddish-blue flower heads. Slightly spicy with a faintly nutty taste. Recommended with: soups, sauces, raw vegetables, egg, curd cheese and yogurt-based dishes.

Samphire

Grows mainly in the wild. Oval, arrow-shaped, succulent leaves. Slightly sour taste. Recommended with: soups, sauces, fish, white meat and poultry dishes, egg, curd cheese and yogurt-based dishes, potato salad and herb butter.

Savory

Small, pointed, deep leaves with lilac to white flowers. Recommended with: green beans, spicy salads, casseroles, pulses and potatoes.

Tarragon

Bushy perennial with branching stems and narrow, oblong, deep green, smooth leaves and whitish flowers, grouped in umbels. Recommended with: soups, sauces, salads, fish, white meat and poultry, vegetables, curd cheese and egg-based dishes.

Thyme

Small grey-green leaves with violet-pink flowers. Used to flavour: meat, poultry, game, minced meat, spicy salads, pulses, vegetables, rice and herb vinegar.

Spices

Tips

- If possible always buy spices that have not been ground and only grind them just before using (using a peppermill, nutmeg grater, pestle and mortar, etc.).

This will help them maintain their full aroma.

- Only buy ground spices in small amounts and store them separately in well-sealed containers, protected from the light.
- Avoid storing in damp conditions, in which spices will become lumpy and go bad.
- Do not add to hot fat because many spices, such as paprika, become bitter and burn.

More about spices

Allspice
Round, red to dark-brown berries picked before they have ripened. Used dried, whole or ground, to flavour game and marinades.

Bay leaves
The dried leaves of the bay tree, used to flavour marinades, game, cabbage and pulses.

Caraway
Used in the form of seeds, whole or ground, to flavour cabbage, potatoes, minced meat, bread and curd cheese dishes.

Cinnamon
The dried inner bark of the cinnamon tree. The most important varieties are Ceylon

cinnamon (delicately spicy) and Cassia cinnamon (more pungently spicy).

Cloves
Dried flower buds that are used whole or ground to flavour sauerbraten (braised beef marinated in herbs and vinegar), rice, millet, game, stewed fruit, confectionery and mulled wine.

Cumin
Crescent-shaped seeds that are used whole or ground. Sharper than caraway with an oriental touch. Used to flavour aubergines and curries.

Curry powder
This is a combination of some 12–15 spices used to flavour rice-based dishes, poultry, fish and sauces.

Ginger
Bulbous rootstock that can be used fresh or dried (ground) to flavour poultry, roast lamb, sweet-and-sour preserved fruit, desserts and confectionery.

Juniper berries
Violet-coloured berries of the juniper bush, used to flavour marinades, game, meat, fish, cabbage.

Mace
The dried and ground seed

case of nutmeg, used like nutmeg.

Nutmeg
The fruit of the evergreen nutmeg tree, used to flavour stewed apples, creamed potatoes, vegetables and egg-based dishes.

Paprika
The dried, ground pods from special varieties of pepper which may be either sweet or hot.

Pepper
The round fruits of the pepper bush. The colour ranges from green, to red, black and yellowish-white. Black pepper is spicy and less ripe than mild white pepper. Green peppercorns are also available in brine.

Pink pepper berries
Used in the same way as pepper but whole. They have a sweetish-sharp juniper-like taste and are used to flavour fish and meat-based dishes.

Saffron
The dried stigmas of a variety of crocus, sold whole or ground. Because of the labour-intensive process of harvesting, it is very expensive. It is sold in sachets containing 0.02 g. It is a mild, slightly bitter-sweet spice that colours food a strong yellow.

Vanilla

The part mainly used is the pulp scooped out of the pod, but the opened, hollowed out pod itself can also be added and removed before serving. Vanilla is used in sweet dishes.

Size of servings

Here are a few guidelines of the sizes of one serving.

Starter:
150-250 ml/5-8 fl oz (⅝-1 cup) (finished dish)

Main course:
Soup: 375 500 ml/12-16 fl oz (1½-2 cups) (finished dish)
Thick soups: 500-600ml/ 16-20 fl oz (2-2½ cups) (finished dish)
Baked dishes: 500-600 g/ 18 oz-1¼ lb (finished dish)
Meat without bones: about 150 g/5 oz (uncooked)
Meat with bones: about 200 g/7 oz (uncooked)
Fish fillet: 150-200 g/5-7oz (uncooked)
Fish, whole: 200-300 g/ 7-10 oz (uncooked)
Pasta: 100-125 g/3½-4½ oz (uncooked)

Side dishes:
Sauce: about 100 ml/3½ fl oz (½ cup) (finished dish)
Vegetables: about 200 g/7 oz (washed)

Salad: 40-50 g/1½-2 oz (prepared)
Potatoes: about 200 g/7 oz (prepared)
Rice, millet, pearl barley etc.: 50-75 g/2-3 oz (uncooked)
Pasta: 60-80 g/2-3 oz (uncooked).

Dessert:
Fruit salad: 150-200 g/5-7 oz (prepared dish)
Stewed fruit: 100-150 g/ 3½-5 oz (prepared dish)
Pudding: 125-175 g/4½-6 oz (prepared dish)

Buying and storing food

All food should be as fresh as possible when it is prepared. However, it is advisable to have emergency supplies for about 2 weeks. Perishable fresh food can be stored for a longer period when kept in a refrigerator at a temperature between 2 °C/36 °F and 8 °C/ 46 °F. Food should be appropriately wrapped up or placed in suitable containers immediately after purchase and stored in the refrigerator in the place designated for it (for instance, vegetables in the vegetable compartment).

Tips for storing food in the refrigerator

- Fruit and vegetables should be stored in the drawers

intended for them. This will help them remain fresh longer.
- Store mushrooms in paper bags.
- Cover food to prevent it from drying out and to prevent odours from spreading.
- The contents of open tin cans and condensed milk (which comes in tinplate cans) should be transferred to other containers.
- Cooked food should be left to cool down first before being put in the refrigerator.

Deep freezing

Deep freezing makes it possible to store food for a longer period. However, it is important that the food and prepared dishes should be "shock-frozen". This means that most of the cell sap in the frozen food must be frozen at a temperature of at least -30 °C/ -22 °F as quickly as possible so as to prevent the formation of ice crystals. If the temperature is not low enough, large ice crystals will form that will alter and damage the cell tissue and affect the appearance of the food when it is defrosted. The storage temperature should be at least -18 °C/-0.4 °F.

Tips for freezing
- Some time before putting the food to be frozen in the freezer, turn the freezer lower to the boost setting.

- Only freeze fresh food or freshly prepared dishes.
- Cooked food should be allowed to cool down first before being put in the freezer.
- The wrapping material or container should be acid-proof, cold-resistant, airtight and non-tear (such as freezer bags, freezer boxes, extra-strong aluminium foil and foil boxes). Use resealable containers that can be stacked.
- Most vegetables should be blanched (this is especially important in the case of green beans; however, asparagus should not be blanched before freezing). Put the vegetables in a sieve in boiling water for 2–4 minutes, then place in ice-cold water to cool them down.

- Shock-freeze prepared berries on a tray or baking sheet, then put in freezer bags or boxes.
- Containers without any liquid (e.g. vegetables) can be filled to the brim but containers with liquid (such as soup) should only be filled 2 cm/¾ in below the

brim because the liquid expands when frozen.
- Mark the contents and date of freezing on the frozen food.
- Put the frozen food next to each other and not on top of each other in the freezer so that the cold can penetrate the food more easily. When the food has frozen through, it can be stacked.
- Arrange the freezer so that there is a clear view of the contents. This makes it easier and quicker to locate particular foods so that the freezer does not remain open too long (thus preventing the formation of ice).
- Only season food after it has been defrosted. Salt and sugar draw out the food's juices while spices lose some of their flavour.
- Low-fat foods can be stored longer in the freezer than fatty foods.
- Some foods are not suited for freezing: thickened sauces, puddings, yogurt, gelatine-based dishes without eggs and whipping cream, cheese (loses its aroma), salads, radishes and potatoes.

Tips for defrosting
- Frozen vegetables must be prepared or used immediately.

- Small amounts of meat and fish can be cooked from frozen.
- Meat that is not completely defrosted is easy to slice (e.g., when the meat must be sliced thinly or cut into cubes).
- Frozen meat packed in a freezer bag can be defrosted in a bowl of water that is then warmed up.

Salmonella
The following rules should help avoid potential salmonella infection:
- Easily perishable foods of animal origin should always be stored in a refrigerator at temperature below 10 °C/ 50 °F.
- Foods that could be carriers of the salmonella bacterium, such as poultry, game, fish, crustaceans, shellfish and molluscs, should be stored and prepared separately from other food.
- When defrosting meat and poultry, make sure that the defrosting water does not come into contact with other foods. Always prepare these foods on a washable board or work surface.
- Poultry, meat and fish should always be cooked through. Minced meat should be used on the day it is prepared.
- When cooking food in the

microwave make sure that it is cooked evenly at a temperature of at least 80 °C/ 180 °F.

- Only use very fresh eggs that are not more than 5 days old (check the sell-by date!) for food which is prepared with raw eggs, for instance mayonnaise. Store in the refrigerator and eat within 24 hours.

- Meticulous cleanliness and hygiene is vital in the kitchen. Always wash the hands with soap and warm water before and as often as possible during the preparation of food.

Cooking methods

Various cooking methods can be used depending on the ingredients and type of dish. To ensure a healthy diet it is important to prepare food with great care and with as little fat as possible. This means using cooking methods that preserve the nutritional properties of each food (for instance, braising and steaming), keeping cooking times as short as possible, and not keeping foods warm for long periods.

Boiling
Boil foods in a large amount of liquid at a temperature of about 100 °C/212 °F (see Advice on meat, page 50, and Advice on vegetables, page 153).

Braising
A cooking method in which the meat is first browned in hot fat, at about 180 °C/360 °F; the cooking process is completed in a small amount of simmering liquid and steam in a closed container at a temperature of about 100 °C/212 °F (see Advice on meat, page 50).

Pan-frying
Cooking and browning food in a small amount of fat at a temperature of 100-150 °C/ 212-300 °F. (see Advice on meat, page 48).

Roasting in the oven
Cooking and browning with or without the addition of fat in a container at a temperature of 160-250 °C/320-480 °F. (see Advice on meat, page 49).

Steaming
This method consists in cooking food placed in a perforated container or basket in steam at a temperature of about 100 °C/ 212 °F (see Advice on vegetables, page 153). Add spices and herbs to the liquid in the pan in which the food is steamed. Their aroma and taste will be transferred to the food being cooked.

Stewing
Cooking food in its own juice or with the addition of a little fat, a small amount of water and steam at temperatures below 100 °C/212 °F (see Advice on vegetables, page 153).

Simmering
Cooking in a simmering liquid at temperatures of 80-90 °C/ 180-195 °F. The liquid must not boil but only move very gently.

Deep-frying
Cooking and browning in a large amount of hot oil at temperatures ranging between 170 and 200 °C/340 and 400 °F. Deep-fried food is plunged in very hot oil that enables it to be cooked and browned evenly on all sides (e.g., potato chips, croquettes, individual portions of fish and meat coated with breadcrumbs). Deep-frying is a very fatty cooking method that should be used as little as possible. Drain deep-fried food as thoroughly as possible on absorbent kitchen paper.

Grilling
Cooking by browning through radiant or contact heat at a high temperature (about 250 °C/480 °F) under an oven grill or on a charcoal or electric grill. Place on a shelf under the grill in the oven following

the manufacturer's instructions. This is a very low-fat cooking method. Season the food after cooking. When cooking on a charcoal grill it is advisable to use aluminium foil or special grilling containers.

Bain-marie
Slow heating in an open container placed in hot but not boiling water or in a steamer (80–100 °C/180–212 °F). A cooking method used for sauces and custards which contain butter, eggs or cream (hollandaise sauce, Bavarian custard) and all dishes that would curdle or burn easily (e.g. cooked egg garnish).

Cooking in foil
With this method the food is wrapped in heat-resistant foil and cooked in its own juices in the oven at a temperature of about 200 °C/400 °F. This a very healthy way of cooking food whereby the food retains all its aroma. Food cooked in foil does not brown. It is important to seal the foil in such a way that the juices do not escape, but it is also important not to wrap it too tightly to enable steam to develop. Place the food wrapped in foil straight on a shelf in the oven, or in a heat-resistant dish. Food cooked in foil takes about one-third

longer to cook than otherwise.

Unlike food cooked in foil, food cooked in a roasting bag turns brown through the effect of radiant heat. Roasting bags impart no flavour, they can be heated up to 230 °C/450 °F and they are only used for cooking in the oven. It is important to choose bags that are large enough so that the steam can develop properly. Always follow the manufacturer's instructions when using roasting bags.

Römertopf (chicken brick)
Food cooked in a Römertopf or chicken brick cooks in its own juices, with or without browning. This method is low in fat and very healthy.

The clay container is made of porous clay and should be soaked in cold water for some time before using. The Römertopf is always put in a cold oven. The water which has been soaked up by the clay is converted into steam during the cooking process and the food remains juicy. Always follow the manufacturer's instructions when cooking in a Römertopf.

Pressure cooking
This method involves cooking under pressure in a hermetically sealed container (i.e. one that is both airtight and watertight) at a temperature ranging between 108 and 118 °C/ 226 and 244 °F. When the liquid inside the pressure cooker heats up it causes a rise in pressure which in turn enables the temperature to rise higher than the normal boiling point of water. Because of this high temperature, the cooking time is reduced by two-thirds. Foods that usually take a long time to cook, such as pulses, beef for making soup and boiling fowl, are ideally suited for pressure cooking. For dishes that are accompanied by a nourishing sauce, the ingredients are first browned before the liquid is added, then cooked under pressure (e.g. casseroles, beef or pork olives and braised dishes). Always follow the

manufacturer's instructions when using a pressure cooker.

Types of cookers

a. Electric cooker

Electric cookers have either a hob with 4 hotplates or a ceramic cooking top. Most hotplates have a range either of 1-3 settings (plus ½ settings), or of 1-9, or a slightly more sensitive one with a range of 1-12 settings. High speed rings heat up more quickly and are therefore more suitable for parboiling, bringing to the boil and frying. They are usually indicated by a red dot.

b. Gas cooker

The rings of a gas cooker consist of a burner and cover plate. When a gas ring is turned on the gas emerges from the slits in the burner's cover plate on the burner and is lit by a spark. The heat is produced very quickly and directly and is adjusted without settings.

c. Induction cooker

With induction cookers the heat is produced directly in the pan through alternating electro-magnetic fields. Thus the heat is produced immediately where it is needed, and the ceramic hob remains cool during the process. Cooking pots with a special base must be used.

Oven

Ovens are available with different heating systems. Many models also offer the possibility of switching to a different heating system depending on what is needed:

a. Top and bottom heat

The heating coils at the top and bottom of the oven emit radiant heat creating air currents that are then transmitted to the food and the dish in which the food is cooked. In order to achieve the maximum heat transmission, only one shelf should hold food at a time. The food should be on the middle shelf of the oven. Unless otherwise specified, the oven should always be preheated regardless of the cooking time.

b. Fan oven

A fan placed in the back panel of the oven circulates the hot air throughout the oven. This system makes it possible to cook food on several shelves at the same time. If the cooking time exceeds 30 minutes there is no need to preheat the oven.

c. Grill

Grills with large and small elements enable the grilling area to be adapted to the area of the food to be grilled. Flat items of food are cooked by radiant heat while becoming crisp on the surface. A hot-air grill is fitted with a fan that circulates radiant heat around the food. The food is browned without having to be turned.

Microwave

In a microwave oven the water molecules in the food are made to vibrate by electromagnetic waves, thus producing heat. Food can be defrosted, heated up and cooked in a microwave oven, thus considerably reducing cooking times. However, only special microwave containers should be used.

Cooking utensils

Among the most important utensils in a kitchen are knives which come in a vast range of shapes and sizes. Because they are used every day they should be of the best quality. It is essential that blade is made of high-quality steel so that the knife works as it should while also being hard-wearing. In addition, the handle of the knife should also feel comfortable in your hand.
A well-equipped kitchen should include the following basic equipment:

1 bread knife
1-2 kitchen knives

1 potato peeler
1 butcher's knife
1 garlic press
1 pair of kitchen scissors
1 chopping knife (for herbs)
1 large and 1 small cooking pot
1 roasting pan
1 saucepan with handle
1 set of bowls
1 gratin dish
1 small and 1 large frying-pan
  (could be non-stick)
1 kitchen timer
1 measuring jug
1 electric hand-held mixer with
  whisk, kneading hook and
  blender attachments
1-2 chopping boards
1 set of scales for weighing
  food
1 wire rack
1 potato or spätzle ricer
1 multi-purpose vegetable and
fruit grater
1 colander, 1 sieve and 1 tea
  strainer
1 set of salad servers
1 salad spin-drier
1 spatula for turning food in a
  frying pan
1 ladle
1 wooden spoon
1 sauce spoon
1 skimming ladle
1 whisk
1 baking brush
1 can opener
1 bottle opener
1 lemon squeezer
1 peppermill
1 salt shaker

Cooking terms

Adding liquid
Adding liquid to a roux, sauce
juices, fried meat or caramel
while stirring.

Barding
Wrapping lean meat or poultry
with slices of bacon or placing
them on top to prevent the
meat from drying out.

Beating, whisking
Working air into food (e.g.
whipping cream or egg white).

Blanching
Parboiling food briefly in boiling water. Then cool down
quickly in iced water.

Boning
Removing the bones from
game, meat and poultry.

Caramelising
Covering food with sugar that
is then cooked to turn it into
caramel (pale brown); used, for
instance, with carrots, potatoes and chestnuts.

Carving
Cutting raw or cooked food
into slices or pieces.

Clarifying
Removing particles that make a
liquid cloudy by adding beaten
egg white. This is cooked in the
liquid, then removed with a

skimming ladle. The egg white
traps the particles.

Coagulating
Thickening an egg-based mixture (e.g., royale) in a bain-marie,
in hot air (in the oven) or in a
frying-pan (scrambled eggs).

Coating in flour
Coating food that has been thoroughly dried (e.g. liver or
escalopes) in flour before frying.

Coating with beaten egg and flour
Coating seasoned food with
flour and beaten egg before
frying or deep-frying so that
the food becomes crispy on
the outside but remains juicy
on the inside.

Cutting out
Cutting out small balls from
dough or other mixture using
moistened spoons, in order to
shape them.

Deep-frying
Frying meat, fish, fruit and vegetables, usually coated in breadcrumbs or wrapped in pastry but
also on its own, in a large
amount of fat until cooked.

Degreasing
Skimming the fat off the surface of a sauce or stock using
a spoon.

Dressing
Giving the right shape to food

before cooking (e.g. poultry or rolled roasts), using kitchen string, skewers or cocktail sticks.

Evaporating
Removal of steam from cooked food (e.g. potatoes).

Filleting
Removing the skin, head and bones from raw meat and fish and cutting into pieces. Removing the membranes surrounding the segments of citrus fruit.

Flambéing
Pouring a small amount of alcohol, usually warmed, over food and lighting it.

Folding in
Mixing a whisked ingredient with other ingredients in order to distribute it evenly in a mixture by gently lifting one over the other with a spatula.

Hanging
Meat or game must be hung for a certain time in a cool place before being consumed so that the meat becomes tender.

Making a roux
Stirring a flour and liquid mixture over continuous heat until the mixture becomes detached from the pan.

Marinating
Soaking meat in a marinade that (unlike pickling or preserv-

ing) is used as a base for the sauce. Meat is often marinated in an oil mixture before grilling.

Peeling
Removing the skin of vegetables and fruit (e.g. potatoes, cucumbers, bananas, onions).

Pickling
Preserving meat or game in a vinegar or wine mixture or in buttermilk with herbs and spices.

Plunging in cold water
Placing hot food (e.g. eggs or rice) briefly in cold water. The eggs will be easier to peel and the rice will not be sticky.

Poaching
Cooking food slowly by simmering without ever allowing the liquid to boil (e.g. eggs in vinegar water).

Preserving in brine
Preserving in salted water (e.g. herrings).

Reducing
Reducing stock, soups and sauces in a wide saucepan without the lid until the desired amount of liquid has evaporated and the liquid has become concentrated and creamy.

Rendering/sweating
Heating up small pieces of fatty food so that the fat emerges (e.g., bacon).

Sautéing
Frying pieces of meat, poultry or fish in a frying-pan or saucepan in plenty of fat.

Skimming
Removing the foam after a liquid has come to the boil using a skimming ladle (for instance, with stock and fruit)

Straining
Rubbing or pressing soft raw or cooked food through a sieve.

Thickening over bain-marie
Slowly whisking the ingredients for sauces and custards in a bowl placed in a bain-marie to thicken the mixture.

Thickening with butter
Stirring butter into liquid that is no longer boiling.

Thickening with cream or egg yolk
Adding cream and/or egg yolk to thicken liquids such as milk, sauces, meat stock and spicy soups. Do not boil afterwards.

Thickening with flour etc.
Thickening liquids by adding a thickening agent such as flour, cornflour (cornstarch), arrowroot or gravy thickener.

Trimming
Removing the skin, fat and sinews from fish or meat and trimming as required.

Environmental information:	This book and its cover were printed on chlorine-free bleached paper. The shrinkwrapping to protect it from getting dirty is made from environmentally-friendly, recyclable polyethylene material.
Note:	If you have any suggestions, proposals or questions concerning our books, please call us on the following number: +49 521 520651 or write to us: Dr. Oetker Verlag KG, Am Bach 11, 33602 Bielefeld, Germany.
Copyright:	© 2006 by Dr. Oetker Verlag KG, Bielefeld
Editing:	Sabine Puppe, Carola Reich
Translation:	Rosetta Translations, London
Recipe development and consultancy:	Dr. Oetker Versuchsküche, Bielefeld Annette Elges, Bielefeld Anke Rabeler, Berlin
Nutritional calculator:	NutriService GbR, Hennef
Cover photograph:	Thomas Diercks, Hamburg
Photographs in the book:	Ulli Hartmann, Bielefeld Brigitte Wegner, Bielefeld Thomas Diercks, Hamburg Norbert Toelle, Bielefeld Bernd Lippert, Bielefeld Ulrich Kopp, Füssen Hans-Joachim Schmidt, Hamburg Christiane Pries, Borgholzhausen
Graphic concept:	Björn Carstensen, Hamburg
Design:	kontur: design, Bielefeld
Cover design:	kontur: design, Bielefeld
Reproduction:	Repro Schmidt, Dornbirn, Austria
Printing and binding:	Appl, Wemding

ISBN 978-3-7670-0505-1